Environmental impact assessment handbook

Second edition

A practical guide for planners, developers and communities

Barbara Carroll, *Enfusion*
and Trevor Turpin, *Nicholas Pearson Associates*

with

Adam Boyden, *Nicholas Pearson Associates*,
Alison Carroll, *Nicholas Pearson Associates*
and Ruth Thomas, *Enfusion*

Published by Thomas Telford Limited, 40 Marsh Wall, London E14 9TP, UK.
www.thomastelford.com

Distributors for Thomas Telford Limited are
USA: ASCE Press, 1801 Alexander Bell Drive, Reston, VA 20191-4400, USA
Australia: DA Books and Journals, 648 Whitehorse Road, Mitcham 3132, Victoria

First edition published 2002

Also available from Thomas Telford Limited
Planning and environmental protection. An introductory guide. RTPI, 2002.
ISBN 978-0-7277-3102-9
Environmental impact assessment. A guide to procedures. DETR, 2000.
ISBN 978-0-7277-2960-6
Better places to work. CABE and Llewelyn Davies Yeang. ISBN 978-0-7277-3398-2
ICE design and practice guides: Contaminated land – investigation, assessment and remediation, 2nd ed. J. Strange. ISBN 978-0-7277-3482-2
Energy and environmental issues for the practising architect. J. Ward. ISBN 978-0-7277-3216-3

A catalogue record for this book is available from the British Library

ISBN 978-0-7277-3509-6

© Thomas Telford Limited 2009

Typeset by Academic + Technical, Bristol
Index created by Indexing Specialists (UK) Limited, Hove
Printed and bound in Great Britain by CPI Antony Rowe, Chippenham

Contents

Foreword to the First Edition

Since its birth in the United States just over 30 years ago, a huge literature on environmental impact assessment (EIA), both within the UK and the rest of the world, has been spawned. As one who has contributed his fair share to this, I can confidently say that this practical handbook is unique. It is not academic, as so much of the literature tends to be (*mea culpa*), yet it is likely to prove very useful not only to students but also to academics seeking to familiarise themselves with a new field. It is not procedural, yet it explains how the EIA process works and refers the reader gently to the appropriate chapter and verse. It is not theoretical, but it describes many of the approaches and methods used in EIA. It is not an activist's charter, yet it provides the ammunition to challenge an environmental statement. Rather, it is an approachable and practical handbook, with numerous illustrated explanations and examples, written from the practitioner's perspective.

Over the dozen or so years we have had EIA in the UK, it has become part of our everyday life. It is increasingly common to hear on the news that the results of an EIA have revealed that some impact or other is likely to be problematic or that protesters have demanded an EIA before a development is allowed to proceed. The concept of environmental assessment is expanding from the evaluation of projects to the environmental appraisal of plans and policies. We all need an accessible, practical explanation of EIA, whether we are developers, consultants, central or local authority officers, environmental regulators, environmental activists, local residents, students or academics. This practical handbook is it!

Christopher Wood
EIA Centre
School of Planning and Landscape
University of Manchester, 2002

Foreword to the Second Edition

Since this book was first published in 2002, the world of environmental impact assessment (EIA) has continued to move forward and adapt to meet the current needs of decision-makers. Changing demands have brought forward new demands for the incorporation of climate change, health impact assessment, social deprivation, sustainable development, technology assessment and the greater demonstration of how consideration of environmental aspects has influenced final designs and development structures. This process has not been made any easier for the practitioner by increasing legal and public challenge and the negative stance to EIA adopted by the Barker Review amongst others. Finally, EIA practitioners now have to ride two horses, with the statutory introduction of strategic environmental assessment (SEA) demanding the application of new skill sets and mental gymnastics by those who attempt to operate in both fields of specialism. All this plus corporate governance, liability insurance and public participation!

The original book quickly earned its place in the bookcase of non-specialist and students alike, and was soon reprinted to meet demand. It was especially well received by engineers and planners as well as EIA practitioners. From experience, in my work as the manager of the Environment Agency's National Environmental Assessment Service we have found it useful for training purposes and for the insight many of its sections bring to key areas of practice.

However, with more experience, legislation and the sheer complexity of some EIA demands, it became apparent that an update was necessary. This new edition builds on the format and information of the first, updating broad legislative principles and including a new section on SEA, of which the authors have considerable practical experience.

It is this translation of practical experience into an easy to read and follow style that made the first edition so well received, and I welcome its successor!

Ross Marshall
President, International Association for Impact Assessment, 2006–2007
Manager, National Environmental Assessment Service
UK Environment Agency

Biographies

Barbara Carroll
Director, Enfusion & Visiting Professor, University of Glasgow

Barbara is a chartered environmentalist and planner with extensive practical and research experience in environmental assessment and sustainable development studies. She has developed and applied methods of strategic environmental assessment (SEA), cumulative effects assessment (CEA), and sustainability appraisal (SA) since the mid 1990s. This includes research on carrying capacities and development of sustainability threshold assessment (STA), a staged and pragmatic method that is used for comparative assessments and contributes to integrated appraisals. Barbara is the managing director of Enfusion who have undertaken over 150 SNSEAs at all levels and in many sectors. She is the Visiting Professor of Sustainability at the University of Glasgow.

Trevor Turpin
Director, Nicholas Pearson Associate & Visiting Lecturer, University of Bath

An environmentalist and social scientist, Trevor has over 35 years practical experience in central and local government, industry and is a director at Nicholas Pearson Associates. He has directed and undertaken EIAs in the UK and overseas since the mid-1980s for all development types. His research interests include the control of pollution through legal and administrative processes and the mitigation of environmental impacts. He has lectured on EIA at the University of Bath MSc in integrated environmental management since its inception and has lectured on other courses at Bath, Bristol, Plymouth and Manchester Universities. He was elected to the council of the Institute of Environmental Assessment to represent corporate members in 1997 and now serves on the technical committee of its successor, the Institute of Environmental Management and Assessment which sets standards and reviews the quality of environmental statements.

Preface

About this Practical Handbook

The aim of this handbook is to provide practical guidance to the practice of Environmental Impact Assessment (EIA). EIA is a systematic procedure for ensuring that the likely effects of new development on the environment are taken into account in deciding whether the proposed project should go ahead or not. EIA is explained here in accordance with the requirements and format of the UK EIA Regulations (1999, as amended). The process of assessing effects on the environment is EIA, and the document produced as a result of the assessment is an Environmental Statement (ES). This second edition includes a new separate chapter on Strategic Environmental Assessment (SEA), following the transposition of the SEA Directive into UK and Scottish Law in 2004 and 2005.

This guidance is written for planners, designers and developers who need sufficient introduction to EIA to know what needs to be prepared by whom and by when. It will be useful for development project managers as well as students and community groups. The handbook approach has been designed with cross-referencing and checklists, which also makes the guide readily useful for easy reference to the EIA practitioner and environmental specialist.

The Objectives of this EIA Handbook

- To present the requirements of EIA according to the UK EIA Regulations in a readily usable and practical way.

> **Legislation and guidance is generally given for England. The relevant legislation and guidance for Wales, Scotland, Northern Ireland or other countries should always be consulted.**

- To inspire and share experience towards good EIA practice by a practical handbook format illustrated with case studies.
- To inform and guide the use of EIA early and effectively in the development design and land use planning processes.
- To demonstrate the advantages of improvements in EIA practice to facilitate better-informed planning decisions.
- To outline the procedures associated with SEA and to demonstrate its benefits.

Who this EIA Handbook is Written For

- Planners of local authorities who need to advise on the requirements for EIA and receive planning applications accompanied by ESs. It will also be useful for other officers dealing with conservation, transport and environmental health issues who will be consulted on such planning applications.
- Planners and others who need to undertake SEA of plans and programmes.
- Professionals regulating projects subject to legislation other than spatial and development control planning.
- Developers who need to understand EIA prior to early discussions with local authorities and appointment of specialist consultants.
- Designers, architects, engineers, surveyors, planners and other professionals working as project managers on development proposals who need to understand why, when and how to include EIA in their projects. The handbook is also useful to specialists as an easy reference and to understand the requirements of other specialisms and the context within the planning process.
- The statutory consultees in the EIA and spatial and development control planning processes who need to understand their role.
- The community sector that could make use of this guide to assist its understanding of, and participation in, EIA, SEA and the development planning process.
- Students of specialist environmental planning courses as well as those students on, for example, engineering, architecture, planning and related courses who are required to study EIA as a core or subsidiary subject.
- Primarily for users in the UK; however, the principles and practice have world-wide applications.

How this EIA Handbook is Structured

The handbook is structured as six chapters. Each chapter is organised in a similar way such that elements, including case studies, key facts, checklists and sources of further information have the same layout for easy reference. It is designed to be dipped into but also follows a systematic approach which takes the reader through the EIA process step by step. There is extensive cross-referencing and signposting, since EIA is an iterative and multidisciplinary team process and environmental effects are often interrelated.

Chapter 1 Introduction

An overview of the EIA process, explaining why and when it is necessary to carry out an EIA. The role of EIA within the planning and development processes is introduced, together with standards and the role of environmental management. EIA is placed within the context of sustainable development and links are shown with other mechanisms and consenting procedures in the planning and environmental protection systems.

Chapter 2 Procedures

The roles of an EIA team, consenting authorities and consultees, together with the legislative and policy context, are introduced. The procedures of screening, scoping and consultation are explained. The assessment procedure is outlined with baseline studies, impact assessment and significance, mitigation options, alternatives and monitoring. The process of preparing the Environmental Statement (ES) is summarised, and a format for the document is suggested. Post-ES submission procedures are outlined.

Chapter 3 Environmental Topics

Each element of the environment likely to be affected by development is considered in a similar way: responsibilities, standards and legislation, the methodology including baseline studies, potential effects, assessment and significance of impacts, mitigation, further guidance and information. Each section is designed to be self-contained. The environmental topics are listed as presented in the Regulations. Interactions between topics and sustainability are drawn together in the final section.

Chapter 4 Development Types

EIA is site-specific, and the extent of potential impacts is dependent on the quality and characteristics of the receiving environment. However, development types tend to have characteristics also, and these may suggest typical environmental impacts. This chapter is presented in checklist format for easy reference, and lists key potential impacts, mitigation, monitoring, environmental management and further guidance for a range of development types. It also draws attention to the opportunities for environmental enhancement from development proposals.

Chapter 5 *Environmental Management*

Environmental management reduces the risk of pollution to the environment and improves the sustainable management of environmental resources. This chapter introduces the role of environmental management in EIA and explains how commitments to mitigation and environmental protection can be made in a systematic and transparent way.

Chapter 6 *Strategic Environmental Assessment (SEA)*

SEA is used during the preparation of policies, plans and programmes, and aims to provide a high level of environmental protection and to promote sustainable development. This chapter introduces SEA and discusses its role, procedures and methods. We conclude with a discussion of the links between EIA and SEA.

How to Use this Practical Handbook

Inspiration and insight
quotes and facts

Case example —
to illustrate good
(or bad) practice

Section

Screening

"
In each case, it will be necessary to judge whether the likely effects on the environment of that particular development will be significant in that particular location

– DETR Circular 02/99
"

'*Sensitive areas*' may be designated areas (or others) that may be affected **by projects having regard to:**

- existing land use
- relative abundance, quality and regenerative capacity of natural resources
- the absorption capacity of the natural environment.

It is impossible to be prescriptive about any particular development and all should be judged on a case-by-case basis. This screening process will need to be **applied – as** will the views of consultees. Just because a Schedule 2 **development project falls within** a '*sensitive area*' **does not automatically** mean that EIA will be required. However, **sensitive areas** do not have to be '**designated**' – a congested urban area can be just as sensitive to additional development as an Area of Outstanding Natural Beauty (AONB).

Regulators should also consider cumulative effects of other proposed development and indirect effects of projects.

case example

Bath Spa Project
A new Spa facility was proposed to provide treatment in the Georgian heart of the World Heritage City of Bath. It was considered that EIA was not required, since, although clearly a sensitive area, the project would not have a significant effect on the environment. (An environmental report was prepared to accompany the planning application.)

Screening Opinion

Developers can undertake the screening process themselves or can seek the views and help of the **planning** authority on whether EIA is needed in a particular case.

To obtain a formal '*screening opinion*' from the planning authority in accordance with the Regulations, the developer needs to submit:

- location plan
- brief description of the nature and purpose of the project
- possible scale of environmental effects
- **other representations**.

Checklists
basic information
presented in
bullet point form

It has to be **remembered that** the planning authority **may** (although not **under an obligation to) seek advice** from the **statutory or non-statutory consultees** at this stage – **and** the planning authority **may be influenced** by public **response** in **reaching** its decision, even though any opposition **should not affect such an opinion. The planning authority has to provide** its screening opinion within 3 weeks of receiving a request (or longer if agreed with the developer).

The screening opinion should include aspects of the **development's environmental effects** which the **planning authority considers significant** and it has to be made available for public inspection (together with the developer's request).

The Secretary of State may also be asked for a '*screening direction*' if the

- developer disagrees with the planning authority's opinion
- planning authority fails to provide an opinion within 3 weeks.

The Secretary of State has to give a screening direction within 3 weeks or such longer period as may be required. This direction will also be made available for public inspection.

Key fact
Both the planning authority's screening opinion and the developer's request have to be made available for public inspection

---

Since such opinions are not confidential, details of the project will appear in the public domain at this stage and developers are advised to manage **the release of project details prior to this.**

There are other circumstances where an EIA is deemed to have been required, where:

- the planning authority (or authorizing body) has given an opinion without a formal screening request that the project is to be subject to EIA and an ES prepared, and this view is not challenged or a ruling is not requested from the Secretary of State
- **the promoter volunteers an ES which states that it is an** "ES in accordance with the Regulations" and the planning authority accepts the ES
- the promoter and the planning authority (or authorizing body) informally agree that an ES should be prepared.

2.4 Scoping

Definition

Scoping is the way in which key issues are identified from a broad range of **potential** concerns for **inclusion** in EIA studies, the areas affected, and the level to **which they should be studied. The importance** of effective and **accurate scoping cannot be over-emphasized.**

Legislation

Schedule 4 of the EIA Regulations requires a description of those aspects of the **environment** likely to be **significantly affected** *including* **population,** fauna, flora, soil, **water, air, climatic** factors, **material assets (including the** architectural and **archaeological** heritage), landscape and the inter-relationship between them.

Discussion

The EIA guide to the procedures (DETR 2000) includes the above checklist of **matters to be considered;** it is **unlikely** that all **will be relevant** to any one **project. Being** at the **beginning** of the EIA **process it is fundamental** to get scoping right: studies of the quality of ESs have frequently blamed inadequacies on poor or inadequate scoping. Government advice is that the relevant **authorities** and the statutory consultees **should** be involved **from an early stage before the preparation of the ES.**

Many consultees, faced with an EIA development for the first time, and asked which issues should be addressed will reproduce the EC Directive, the Regulations, or both.

EIAs are carried out usually under time, budget and resource constraints. **Spending time on a non-issue will result in less for the important matters** and potentially non-determination for lack of information. This is frustrating

case example

Britannia Ironworks
Despite being allocated in the local plan for housing, the Secretary of State directed that, due to contamination from previous industrial uses, an application for redevelopment of the site, even in outline, required an Environmental Statement.

Further information

Further information

Guidance on Scoping 2001 Europa.Eu.int
Environment Agency 1996 Scoping Handbook

Key fact
Schedule 4 of the Regulations lists elements of the environment which might be affected – it does not require them all to be addressed

guiding principle

Early and effective scoping results in effective use of resources and time

Guiding principles

Acknowledgements

As we acknowledged in the first edition of this handbook, in a book of this nature, based as it is on practical experience, gratitude is owed to a wide range of people whose approach and decisions have guided environmental impact assessments in particular directions. These include clients, developers, planning authority officers, regulators – especially the Environment Agency and Natural England – and colleagues. To all of them we would like to express our thanks for contributing to what continues to be a rapidly developing field . . . we are all still learning.

For this second edition of the handbook, specific support and contributions have been made by:

- **Adam Boyden** at Nicholas Pearson Associates and chairman (2006–2009) of the Ireland and UK branch of the International Association for Impact Assessment
- **Alison Carroll** at Nicholas Pearson Associates and formerly at the Institute of Environmental Management and Assessment
- **Ruth Thomas** at Enfusion and formerly at the Ministry of Defence.

To all of them we express our sincere thanks for their interest, expertise and support.

The following have also reviewed or drafted particular sections:

- Andrew Brookes (water), Andrew Bullmore (noise), John Hawkes and Peter Cox (heritage), Duncan Laxen (air), Andrew Cooper and Mark Cartwright (landscape), Roger Prescott (planning and procedures), Chris Stapleton (soils), Mike Wells (biodiversity) – for which we are grateful.

Thanks to those who helped in the preparation of the first edition of the handbook and to those book reviewers in journals who provided useful constructive comments. In all cases, however, errors and omissions remain the responsibility of the authors.

Thanks are also due to Amanda Starr and Alastair Peattie for their help.

Finally, we must thank our development editor, Jennifer Barratt of Thomas Telford Limited, for her patience and persistence.

The cover image is printed with permission from Peter N. Sills and BP Exploration (copyright Peter N. Sills, www.sillson.com).

All other photographs and illustrations are either those of the authors or from the libraries of Nicholas Pearson Associates and Enfusion, for which permission to publish is gratefully acknowledged. Exceptions are where otherwise noted and those on pages 36 (case example, Wytch Farm Oilfield) and 125 (Energy), which have been kindly provided by BP Exploration.

Abbreviations

AGHV	Area of Great Historical Value
ALC	Agricultural Land Classification
AONB	Area of Outstanding Natural Beauty
AST	Appraisal Summary Table
BAP	Biodiversity Action Plan
BAT	Best available techniques
BERR	Department for Business, Enterprise and Regulatory Reform
BGS	British Geological Survey
BMA	British Medical Association
BMWP	Biological Monitoring Working Party
BOD	Biochemical Oxygen Demand
BREEAM	The Building Research Establishment Environmental Assessment Method
BS	British Standard
CABE	Commission for Architecture and the Built Environment
CAMS	Catchment Abstraction Management Strategies
CCW	Countryside Council for Wales
CEA	Cumulative Effects Assessment
CEH	Centre for Ecology and Hydrology
CEMP	Construction (or Contract) Environmental Management Plan
CFMP	Catchment Flood Management Plan
CHaMP	Coastal Habitat Management Plan
CIEH	Chartered Institute of Environmental Health
CIRIA	Construction Industry Research and Information Association
CITES	Convention on International Trade in Endangered Species
CIWEM	Chartered Institution of Water and Environmental Management
CInstWM	Chartered Institute of Wastes Management
CLEA	Contaminated Land Exposure Level
COMAH	Control of Major Accident Hazards
COSHH	Control of Substances Hazardous to Health
CPRE	Campaign to Protect Rural England
CRTN	Calculation of Road Traffic Noise
CZM	Coastal Zone Management
dB_A	decibel (A-weighted)
DCLG	Department for Communities and Local Government
DETR	Department of Environment, Transport and the Regions
Defra	Department for Environment, Food and Rural Affairs
DfT	Department for Transport
DMRB	*Design Manual for Roads and Bridges*
DoE	Department of Environment
DoE NI	Department of the Environment, Northern Ireland
DOH	Department of Health
DPD	Development Plan Document
DTI	Department of Trade and Industry
DTLR	Department of Transport, Local Government and the Regions
EAP	Environmental Action Plan
EC	European Commission

EcIA	Ecological Impact Assessment
EHIA	Environmental Health Impact Assessment
EHO	Environmental health officer
EIA	Environmental Impact Assessment
EMAS	Eco-Management and Audit Scheme
EMP	Environmental Management Plan
EMS	Environmental Management System
EQS	Environmental Quality Standard
ES	Environmental Statement
ESA	Environmentally Sensitive Area
ETSU	Energy Technology Support Unit
EU	European Union
FRA	Flood Risk Assessment
FRCA	Farming and Rural Conservation Agency
GDPO	General Development Procedure Order
GOMMMS	*Guidance on the Methodology for Multi-modal Studies*
GPDO	General Permitted Development Order
HAP	Habitat Action Plan
HBF	House Builders Federation
HDV	Heavy Duty Vehicle
HEMP	Handover Environmental Management Plan
HER	Heritage Environment Record
HGV	Heavy Goods Vehicle
HIA	Health Impact Assessment
HSE	Health and Safety Executive
Hz	Hertz
IAIA	International Association for Impact Assessment
ICRCL	Inter-Departmental Committee on the Redevelopment of Contaminated Land
IDB	Internal Drainage Board
IEEM	Institute of Ecology and Environmental Management
IEMA	Institute of Environmental Management and Assessment
IFA	Institute of Field Archaeologists
IHT	Institution of Highways and Transportation
IPPC	Integrated Pollution Prevention and Control
ISO	International Organization for Standardization
IUCN	International Union for the Conservation of Nature
JNCC	Joint Nature Conservancy Council
LAPPC	Local Air Pollution Prevention and Control
LAQM	Local Air Quality Management
LDF	Local Development Framework
LEAP	Local Environment Agency Plan
LPA	Local Planning Authority
LTP	Local Transport Plan
LVIA	Landscape and Visual Impact Assessment
MAFF	Ministry of Agriculture, Fisheries and Food
MAGIC	Multi-Agency Geographic Information for the Countryside
NATA	New Approach to Appraisal
NSCA	National Society for Clean Air
NTS	non-technical summary
NVC	National Vegetation Classification
ODPM	Office of the Deputy Prime Minister
OS	Ordnance Survey
pe	population equivalent
PDR	Permitted Development Rights
PM_{10}	Particulates
PP	plan or programme

PPC	Pollution Prevention and Control
PPG	Planning Policy Guidance
PPS	Planning Policy Statement
RBD	River Basin District
RBMP	River Basin Management Plan
RCEP	Royal Commission on Environmental Pollution
RCS	River Corridor Survey
RHS	River Habitat Survey
RIGS	Regionally Important Geological and Geomorphological Site
RIVPACS	River Invertebrate Prediction and Classification System
ROMP	Review of Old Mineral Permissions
RSPB	Royal Society for the Protection of Birds
RSS	Regional Spatial Strategy
RTPI	Royal Town Planning Institute
SA	Sustainability Appraisal
SAC	Special Area of Conservation
SAP	Species Action Plan
SD	sustainable development
SEA	Strategic Environmental Assessment
SEMP	Site Environmental Management Plan
SEPA	Scottish Environmental Protection Agency
SFRA	Strategic Flood Risk Assessment
SGV	Soil Guideline Value
SI	Système International d'Unites
SIA	Social Impact Assessment
SINC	Site of Importance for Nature Conservation
SM	Scheduled Monument
SMP	Shoreline Management Plan
SMR	Sites and Monuments Record
SNH	Scottish Natural Heritage
SPA	Special Protection Area
SPAB	Society for the Protection of Ancient Buildings
SPZ	Source Protection Zone
SSLRC	Soil Survey and Land Research Centre
SSSI	Site of Special Scientific Interest
SuDS	Sustainable Drainage System
TA	Transport Assessment
TCPA	Town and Country Planning Association
TIA	Traffic Impact Assessment
TPO	Tree Preservation Order
TRICS	Trip Rate Information Computer System
TRL	Transport Research Laboratory
UK	United Kingdom
UKBAP	United Kingdom Biodiversity Action Plan
UN	United Nations
UNECE	United Nations Economic Commission for Europe
UNESCO	United Nations Educations, Scientific and Cultural Organisation
VEC	Valued Ecosystem Component
WFD	Water Framework Directive
WHO	World Health Organization
WIA	Water Industry Act
WLMP	Water Level Management Plan
WRA	Water Resources Act
ZVI	Zone of Visual Influence

Chapter 1

Introduction

'Consult the Genius of the Place in all...'

Alexander Pope 1731

An overview of the Environmental Impact Assessment (EIA) process, explaining why and when it is necessary to carry out an EIA. The role of EIA within the planning and development processes is introduced, together with standards and the role of environmental management. EIA is placed within the context of sustainable development, and links are shown with other mechanisms and consenting procedures in the planning and environmental protection systems.

1.1 What is EIA?

Environment Impact Assessment (EIA) is a procedure which serves to provide information to local authority planners, other regulators and authorising bodies, other interested parties and the general public about certain proposed developments and their likely effects on the environment. It also enables developers, on whose behalf the EIA is generally undertaken, to meet their own environmental standards, to minimise environmental impacts and facilitate the approval process. It is a technique which has developed since the introduction of EIA by the National Environmental Protection Act 1969 in the USA. It is now applied by governments and international institutions throughout the world.

It must be emphasised that EIA is *part* of the wider process of deciding whether certain types of development projects should be approved. Other dimensions – political, local feelings and cultures, overriding need, competing proposals – also have to be considered. However, by including environmental factors *alongside* social and economic considerations, a more sustainable approach to development is ensured.

EIA is an ongoing process: the collection and assessment of environmental information (usually undertaken by, or on behalf of, a developer or promoter/investor), the preparation of an Environmental Statement (ES), consultation with a wide range of parties *and* the consideration of the environmental information. This is then taken into account in the determination of the application for development approval (undertaken by the authorising body). Early and continued positive dialogue is encouraged between the promoter, the authorising body, other consultees and the public. The process identifies the potential significant effects on the environment and develops appropriate options for their mitigation.

Contents

EIA is an important procedure for ensuring that the likely effects of new development on the environment are fully understood and taken into account before the development is allowed to go ahead

– Department of Environment, Transport and the Regions (DETR) 2000. *EIA: A Guide to Procedures*

Key fact

Environmental issues are not necessarily a constraint on development: environmental enhancement can facilitate sustainable development

1.2   Some Definitions

> - *Environmental Impact Assessment* (EIA): the process assessing the environmental impacts of development projects.
> - *Environmental Statement* (ES): the document reporting the EIA.
> - *Mitigation*: avoiding, reducing or remedying potential significant adverse impacts.
> - *Compensation*: replacing an adverse impact either in kind or by something of a different nature to that which may be lost.
> - *Enhancement*: improving elements of the environment.
> - *Screening*: the process to decide if EIA is required.
> - *Scoping*: the process to identify the key environmental issues.
> - *Consultees*: statutory and non-statutory interested parties who are consulted during the EIA process.
> - *Strategic Environmental Assessment* (SEA): environmental assessment of plans and programmes.

1.3   The Need for EIA

The need for EIA is derived from the EU Directive on the assessment of certain public and private projects on the environment, first introduced in 1985 and subsequently amended in 1997 and 2003. It was incorporated into UK legislation in 1988, and the current Regulations date from 1999 with subsequent amendments.

EIA applies to major developments for which planning approval is required from local authorities under the Town and Country Planning Act 1990. EIA also applies to many projects which are outside the planning system and require authorisation from other bodies:

- trunk roads and motorways
- power stations, overhead power lines and long-distance oil and gas pipelines
- afforestation
- land drainage improvements (including flood and coastal defence)
- ports and harbours
- marine fish farming
- marine dredging for minerals
- projects under the Transport and Works Act 1992 (e.g. railways, inland waterways).

Each of these different types of development requires EIA under separate pieces of legislation, e.g. the Environmental Impact Assessment (Land Drainage Improvement Works) (Amendment) Regulations 2006.

Major projects for which EIA may be required are listed in the Directive and the Regulations. They are divided into Annex I and Annex II developments in the Directive, and into Schedules 1 and 2 in the EIA Regulations. Schedule 1 projects, e.g. nuclear power stations, always require EIA. Schedule 2 projects are those listed in the Regulations and where EIA will only be required if significant environmental effects are likely to arise. Criteria and thresholds for significance are set out in the DETR Circular 02/99 and are reproduced in Appendix 2 of this handbook.

Key legislation and guidance

EU Directive 85/337/EEC as amended by 97/11/EC and 2003/35/EC: The assessment of effects of certain public and private projects on the environment. (The 'EIA Directive')

Planning and Compulsory Purchase Act 2004

Town & Country (EIA) (England and Wales) Regulations 1999 (as amended). (The 'EIA Regulations')

DETR 1999. Circular 02/99: *Environmental Impact Assessment*

DETR 2000. *EIA: A Guide to Procedures.* www.communities.gov.uk, www.opsi.gov.uk

Department for Communities and Local Government 2006 (Consultation draft). *Circular and Guide to Good Practice*

EU EIA studies, reports and guidance. www.europa.eu.int

EU Directive 2001/42/EC: The assessment of the effects of certain plans and programmes on the environment. (The 'SEA Directive')

The Environmental Assessment of Plans and Programmes Regulations 2004

UN Environment Programme studies, reports and guidance. www.unep.org

www.worldbank.org

www.iaia.org

Key fact

The planning system should:

- deliver key objectives such as housing, economic development, transport infrastructure and rural regeneration sustainably while protecting the environment
- create and sustain mixed and inclusive communities
- be transparent
- enable local communities to be involved positively
- deliver a higher quality and better respected public service

– Office of the Deputy Prime Minister 2002

The key word is *significant*, and the Circular suggests three main criteria of significance:

- major developments
- environmentally sensitive locations
- complex developments with hazardous effects.

N.B. the Consultation Draft of the revised Circular removes these criteria

The legislation allows developers to apply to the local authority for guidance, a '*screening opinion*', on whether an EIA is necessary for Schedule 2 projects, and to the Secretary of State (SoS) for a final '*screening direction*' if the developer disagrees with the *screening opinion*.

Permitted Development Rights (PDRs): Schedule 1 projects are not permitted development, and always require submission of a planning application and an ES. PDRs for Schedule 2 projects are also withdrawn unless the planning authority has given a screening opinion (or the Secretary of State has given a screening direction) that EIA is not required.

Major Infrastructure Proposals may be decided by an Infrastructure Planning Commission under new planning legislation and guided by National Policy Statements for nationally significant infrastructure. The IPC will consider, independently of local authorities, proposals for major developments such as airports, power stations and reservoirs. *Whilst the consenting regime may change, the need for EIA in accordance with the EU Directive will not change.*

1.4   The Purpose of EIA

Environmental protection: The EC directive on EIA was promoted by the Trade Department of the European Commission, and the underlying reason was to ensure that a level playing field prevailed in the competitive conditions of a common market. However, the stated aim, and the one which is often overlooked, is in the preamble to the 1985 Directive:

'*... the best environmental policy consists in preventing the creation of pollution or nuisances at source, rather than subsequently trying to counteract their effects; ... [and] to take effects on the environment into account at the earliest possible stage in all the technical planning and decision-making processes; ...*'

So, EIA is actually about the reduction or minimisation of pollution in its widest sense. While EIA is part of the planning system in the UK, separate approvals may also be required for certain developments, e.g. Pollution Prevention and Control (PPC), land drainage and discharge consents. Planning authorities look to other agencies to confirm compliance or satisfactory standards; Planning Policy Statement (PPS) 23, *Planning and Pollution Control*, encourages approval procedures to run simultaneously and to avoid duplication of controls.

Design and planning: The integration of the emerging design of a development into the EIA process can ensure that a proposal with the least damaging environmental effects is arrived at. This can facilitate consideration of alternative approaches to development and lead to a more robust planning application. By taking account of such issues as the design of the development, the process, the location and the site at the earliest possible stage, the design can be influenced such that major changes or onerous planning conditions are not required too late in the project programme.

Further information

Town and Country Planning (General Permitted Development) Order 1995

Planning Act, 2008

Key legislation and guidance

PPC Regulations 2000

PPS23: *Planning and Pollution Control*

Key facts

The EIA Regulations require consideration of '*the regenerative capacity of natural resources* [and] *the absorptive capacity of the natural environment*'

The government's commitment to good design is presented in PPS1, and confirmed in PPS3, which requires local authorities and housebuilders to design for quality

EIA regulations were amended in 2006 to require increased public consultation on the ES as a minimum, in line with the Aarhus Convention and the EU Public Participation Directive

The Process of EIA

" An ES provides a useful framework within which environmental considerations and design development can interact "

– DETR 2000

" Community involvement is vitally important to planning and the achievement of sustainable development "

– PPS1 (DCLG, 2005)

Further information

PPS1: *Delivering Sustainable Development*

PPS3: *Housing*

DETR 2000. *Urban Design in the Planning System: Towards Better Practice*

Urban Design Alliance

Commission for Architecture and the Built Environment (CABE)

UNECE Convention on Access to Information, Public Participation in Decision-making and Access to Justice in Environmental Matters. (The 'Aarhus Convention')

Public Participation Directive 2003/35/EC

Key fact

Sufficient information to assess the environmental effects must be provided for both outline and detailed planning applications

Key fact

In the UK planning system, consideration of a major planning application is subject to a 13-week determination period (with 8 weeks for minor applications) until an appeal can be made against non-determination – for applications with an ES, 16 weeks is allowed for decision-making

The presentation of the environmental information in a transparent and systematic way assists the competent authorities when determining the application for approval. This can also allay the general public's concerns, which are often based on the fear of unknown effects.

Management: EIA can also be used as a management tool by contributing to environmental risk assessment, identifying hazards at the design stage, and presenting the opportunity to design them out and ensuring that risks are managed throughout the project.

The commitment to environmental management which is made in the ES can be conditioned by regulators and incorporated into contract documents, thus ensuring continued protection of the environment from construction through to final restoration.

Consultation and participation: Government policy increasingly emphasises the need to involve local communities and stakeholders in the planning of development to allow those affected to be properly informed and consulted and to participate in decisions affecting their environment. EIA is an important way of helping to ensure that those likely to be affected by a proposed development are better informed and involved in the development planning process.

1.5   The Process of EIA

Those environmental issues which may be significant in the context of the proposed development and are the reasons why EIA is being undertaken are identified by '*scoping*'. Provision is made in the Regulations for formal scoping by consultation with interested parties. For each significant environmental issue, baseline conditions are identified through a review of existing information (desk study) and by site surveys. The likely effects of the development are then predicted. The magnitude and significance of the effects – including indirect and cumulative effects – are assessed. Mitigation measures are incorporated throughout the iterative process of design and EIA in order to minimise any likely significant adverse effects and to maximise likely beneficial effects. This requires team effort and interactions both within the development team itself and with the external contributors.

Consultation is inherent in the EIA process, and is continuous throughout, involving statutory and non-statutory consultees as well as the public: it feeds into the evolving design in an interactive way. Early and thorough consultation will identify those interested parties who might be concerned about the proposed development (see Section 1.4).

The Regulations and the Directive indicate what should be included within an ES:

- description of the site and development
- outline of the main alternatives studied
- significant direct and indirect effects
- measures to prevent, reduce or offset significant adverse effects
- a non-technical summary (NTS).

An important requirement is an NTS, and this confirms that the approach of EIA has to be understandable by planning professionals, elected members and the general public. The ES itself should, therefore, reflect this.

The EIA process continues through to determination: the ES, and the responses of consultation bodies and the public to the ES and the environmental implications of the planning application comprise the 'environmental information' that must be formally considered and taken into account by the decision-makers before determination of the planning application. A planning application can be refused or approved. Planning permission for an EIA development will be subject to a number of planning conditions; it may also be accompanied by a legal agreement negotiated with the local planning authority (including under Section 106 of the Town and Country Planning Act 1990).

Conditions and legal agreements can require detailed specification of mitigation commitments established as necessary in the ES (or otherwise in the EIA), together with monitoring and management of the development. They are in effect used to carry forward the commitments made in the ES through to the reality of the construction and occupation/operation (and, where relevant, decommissioning and restoration) stages. The ES should therefore preferably include a section on environmental management and 'follow-up' post-decision practices. This will provide a framework for identifying mitigation measures and the specification of the means of their implementation, including any monitoring, community involvement and feedback to future planning and management decisions.

1.6 Professional Standards and Review

As stated above, under the EIA Regulations the ES will be considered by the planning authority as part of the overall planning application documentation, in order for officers to prepare comments and recommendations to elected members making the decision on the application. It is likely at this stage that the authority will compare the ES with the information that it requested in any Scoping Opinion. The ES will also be reviewed and commented on by consultation bodies and members of the public. To supplement this local feedback, the ES may also be subject to a formal review for its quality and adequacy of its information. There are review systems available which systematically check the adequacy of the ES against the legislative requirements and good practice guidance. The Institute of Environmental Management and Assessment (IEMA) was established to improve the standard of ESs (Wood and Jones reported on the inadequacy of the majority of ESs in the 1980s) and, more recently, the adequacy of ESs has been challenged in the courts through judicial review. IEMA has established criteria based on the work of Lee and Colley at the EIA Centre at the University of Manchester. Many planning authorities will seek a quality review of the ES from IEMA or external consultants because of their own inexperience of such major developments, issues raised by consultees or lack of resources.

Key fact
The modernisation of the UK planning system has placed more emphasis on public participation

Further information
Department of Environment (DoE) 1995. *Preparation of Environmental Statements: A Good Practice Guide* (to be revised)

Department of Transport, Local Government and the Regions 2001. *Planning: Delivering a Fundamental Change*

Office of the Deputy Prime Minister (ODPM) 2005. *Sustainable Communities: Homes for all*

DoE Circular 11/95: *Planning Conditions*

ODPM Circular 05/2005: *Planning Obligations*

Jones, C., Lee, N. and Wood, C. (1991) *UK Environmental Statements 1988–90*

Links

IEMA

- Professional standards
- Research and opinions
- ES reviews
- Specialist interest groups

The Institute undertakes research in the field of EIA, produces guidelines on particular topics and delivers services to IEMA corporate members

www.iema.net

IAIA

- International fora, networks and conferences
- Principles of EIA best practice
- Guidelines for lead impact assessment practitioners
- Ireland–UK branch

www.iaia.org

Guiding principles of sustainable development

- Living within environmental limits
- Ensuring a strong, healthy and just society
- Achieving a sustainable economy
- Promoting good governance
- Using sound science responsibly

– ODPM 2005. *Securing the Future: The UK Government Sustainable Development Strategy*

we are all environmental managers now

– Environment Agency 2000. *An Environmental Vision*

Further information

ODPM 2005. *Securing the Future: The UK Government Sustainable Development Strategy*

PPS12: *Local Development Frameworks*

DETR 2000. *A Strategy for more Sustainable Construction*

ODPM 2005. *Sustainability Appraisal of Regional Spatial Strategies and Local Development Documents*. Guidance for RPBs and LPAs

IEMA is the professional institute for EIA in the UK and Ireland, and other institutions maintain professional standards for other disciplines which contribute to EIA. The International Association for Impact Assessment (IAIA), based in the USA (with an Ireland–UK branch), is the main international membership organisation for EIA and other forms of impact assessment, and also prepares good practice advice on EIA.

1.7   Links

Strategic Environmental Assessment (SEA) considers the environmental effects of plans and programmes, and is the process that the EC originally proposed prior to EIA. The long-overdue Directive on SEA was published in 2001, and is implemented into legislation through the Environmental Assessment of Plans and Programmes Regulations 2004 and separate Regulations in Scotland. Methodologies for Sustainability Appraisal (SA) have been developed to appraise the sustainability of development plans (and as required by PPS12, *Local Development Frameworks*). These have tended to evolve from SEA methods, and include the social and economic elements of the agenda as well as the environmental ones. In England and Wales, government guidance and practice is for SEA to be included within SA; in Scotland, SEA remains separate from other procedures.

Sustainable development (SD) is now enshrined in the UK planning system, and EIA is a technique that can assist in progressing the objectives and principles of SD by protecting natural resources and the environment. The relationships between the wider environment and health/social well-being are increasingly being understood. The practice of Health Impact Assessment for policies, plans and projects is being increasingly pursued by government health departments and agencies, either as part of or in parallel to EIA and SEA. Similarly, the opportunities to facilitate development and regeneration through improved environmental conditions are becoming recognised. The PPS1 supplement on climate change proposes an assessment of energy and climate implications for planning applications and plans, within the Design & Access Statement and/or ES for a development. Sustainability of resource usage in design and construction, including energy and materials, should, therefore, be reported in the ES.

The requirement for Appropriate Assessment of the implications of projects, plans and programmes on sites of designated international nature conservation importance (under the Habitats Directive 92/43/EEC, implemented by the Conservation (Natural Habitats &c.) Regulations 1994 (as amended)) is, although a separate legal requirement to EIA and SEA, often carried out either in conjunction with or in parallel to these procedures.

Cumulative Effects Assessment (CEA) is the practice that considers the cumulative effects of a number of development proposals or plans and programmes together, within the framework of EIA and SEA, while focusing on the receptors and issues affected.

The commitment to mitigation reported in an ES through a draft Environmental Management Plan (EMP) can provide the framework for the regulators and the contractors. If the developer and/or the contractor have an Environmental Management System (EMS), additional reassurance will be given to regulators and the public. The new international standard ISO/DIS 19011 will help organisations integrate quality and environmental management, allowing a single audit of both systems.

In the beginning we built cities to overcome our environment. In the future we must build cities to nurture it

– Sir Richard Rogers 1995. Reith Lectures

Greenwich Millennium Village and Ecology Park

1.8   The Future

This handbook aims to be a pragmatic guide for everyone involved in the EIA process and to ensure that legal requirements are met. However, legislation and practice continually change and, therefore, we guide the reader in the direction of good practice, where appropriate, and with an awareness of emerging issues and requirements. For example, the Human Rights Act 1998 has been shown to test claims made in ESs, and planning authorities will have to consider whether their decisions have an impact on the rights of the individual.

The European Commission has been considering whether consolidation of the EIA and SEA Directives might achieve greater consistency and efficiency in environmental assessment across Member States and also achieve harmonisation between the Directives. An example of the practical application of such an approach is being developed in the UK: the Radioactive Waste Management Directorate is preparing a plan for the geological disposal of the UK's radioactive wastes. Tiered Environmental and Sustainability Assessments are proposed from the strategic to the project level with a proactive approach to stakeholder engagement, including working in partnership with potential host communities, representing best practice. (See www.nda.gov.uk.)

This second edition of the handbook is published at the same time as international studies are beginning for an update on the effectiveness study of environmental assessment undertaken by IAIA. It is expected that these studies will signpost further improvements in the practice of environmental assessment.

Chapter 2

Procedures

The roles of an Environmental Impact Assessment (EIA) team, consenting authorities and consultees, together with the legislative and policy context, are introduced. The procedures of screening, scoping and consultation are explained. The assessment procedure is outlined with baseline studies, impact assessment and significance, mitigation and enhancement options, alternatives and monitoring. The process of preparing the Environmental Statement (ES) is summarised, and a format for the document is suggested. Post-ES submission procedures are outlined.

2.1 Introduction

This chapter focuses on what is required and expected of a team under-taking an EIA of a development proposal. In this sense, it is very much concerned with *development* and how that will need to fit in with:

- concepts and principles of sustainability
- plans, policies and programmes of local authorities, central and regional government, and guidance notes
- policies of other organisations, e.g. the Environment Agency.

The word 'team' is deliberate: the 1999 EIA Regulations encourage active dialogue between the developer and the authority who will ultimately receive the ES, far more than the previous Regulations. It is no longer necessarily left entirely to the developer to decide – however skilfully, professionally and impartially – which topics to address and to what level of detail. Such an active role by planning authorities will be welcomed by many who have encountered difficulties with indecision, prevarication or inexperience in the past.

It is recognised that inexperience will remain: there are some 480 planning authorities in the UK and, given that, in 2005, 590 ESs were submitted in the UK through the town and country planning regimes – inevitably usually focused on areas where development is encouraged or profitable – then there will be some authorities who are rarely involved in EIA. However, this is no excuse or reason for inaction or indecision. Planning authorities are required, *if asked,* to give both Screening and Scoping Opinions, and if they do not feel competent to give such opinions, they can readily enlist the support of other bodies or consultancies: many authorities use the services of the Institute of Environmental Management and Assessment (IEMA), who have produced EIA process guidelines (2004).

There has been provision since the implementation of the EC Directive into the UK EIA Regulations in 1988 for obtaining a Screening Opinion from the local authority, or a Screening Direction from the Secretary of State as to whether EIA is required. Some commentators have noted that Screening Opinions are rarely sought or challenged by requesting a Screening Direction from the Secretary of State. In practical terms,

Contents

"

EIA provides a basis for better decision making

– Department for Environment, Transport and the Regions (DETR) 2000. *EIA: A Guide to Procedures* "

case example

Even in 2000, one local planning authority asked for an extension of time to provide a Scoping Opinion and eventually sent a photocopy of a section of the Regulations. The legislation expects a more sophisticated response!

Further information

www.communities.gov.uk

www.iema.net

www.europa.eu.int

www.iaia.org

however, this is perhaps not surprising, since the primary objective of a developer is almost invariably to secure consent for development, not to avoid an EIA and ES.

The main steps in the EIA process are outlined in the following diagram, which makes it clear that consultation is an integral part of the process. On receipt of the ES, the determining authority will review it for content and completeness, and (in the case of a planning authority) the officer's report on the application, based on considerations of planning policy and taking account of the responses from consultees and members of the public, will be considered by committee usually within 16 weeks of receipt of the ES.

Outline of the EIA process

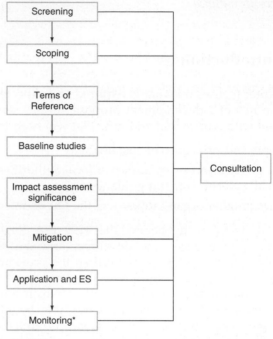

*Assumes approval is granted.

2.2   Getting Started

The Development Project and EIA Inception

The need for EIA will be decided, although frequently not immediately recognised, at the stage when a development requiring planning consent (or other authorisations) is proposed. For example, such development may be part of an energy company's programme in exploitation of new resources, a government department's road-building programme, the Environment Agency's flood protection programme, or landowners seeking to create a new settlement. For a continuing development programme, contact will already have been made with the relevant planning authority or equivalent. For a new development, early consultation with that body will be required. The authority should be mindful of the potential need for EIA and should advise the applicants as early as possible.

guiding principle

Seek specialist EIA advice early

Following legal rulings in the European Court of Justice and House of Lords in 2006, amendments to the EIA Regulations (in England and Wales in 2008, and in Scotland in 2007) now allow EIA to be required at the reserved matters stage of an outline planning application, when matters are approved under planning conditions, and for the approval of conditions under Reviews of Old Mineral Permissions (collectively termed 'subsequent applications' and 'subsequent ROMP applications'), where significant effects are considered likely and no EIA has previously been carried out. The amendments also allow for the updating, at the subsequent application stage, of any ES previously submitted at the outline/ROMP stage. Thus, the need for EIA needs to be kept under review throughout the development planning process.

Where alternatives to the proposed development are likely to be discussed in the EIA, i.e. location, process or construction methodology, their relative merits should be considered and recorded at this early stage – in a systematic and thorough manner using criteria to gauge the relative environmental impact of alternatives considered. Scheme promoters will have a development team, including a project manager, legal representation, surveyors, planners, architects and engineers. At this stage, it must be established whether the need for EIA falls within the planning system or other regulatory controls. At the point where the potential need for EIA is required, an EIA specialist should be appointed.

Key fact

EIA practitioners registered with IEMA have to satisfy necessary skills and experience criteria

Guidelines for registration: www.iema.net

The Project Team

The EIA element of a proposed development requires a project manager. Various professions have claimed that they are best suited to lead EIA studies, including planners, because EIA is usually part of the planning process, and architects, because EIA runs parallel to and should be integrated with the design process. There is also an increasing number of environmental planning professionals who specialise in managing EIAs.

In order to lead a successful approach to EIA, negotiation at all stages of the process will be required, combined with skills to co-ordinate with the development team and specialists. There are several approaches, any of which may work dependent on the circumstances, including:

- client appoints EIA team leader from within own organisation
- consultancy appointed to undertake design or planning, and EIA
- EIA specialist appointed to co-ordinate EIA and administer tendering process for specialist tasks.

Project Terms of Reference

Prior to '*going public*' on any development proposal, the following should be determined:

- development mix and objectives
- budget for planning and development costs
- programme for approval
- timescale for development
- options for alternatives (locations/processes)
- budget for construction, operation and restoration (if appropriate).

Getting Started

These will often require initial feasibility studies to help define. Ranges for these parameters should be decided by the development team, together with any options for flexibility, before consultation starts. If members of the team are not aware of flexibility or potential cost limitations, the consultation process will not be as beneficial as it could be. These issues have to be decided by the project team.

Communication and Initial Consultation

What is often neglected is the provision of advice on how the project is likely to be perceived by the receiving public. Therefore, public relations advice may be helpful. The role of such specialists is not to put a spin or gloss on the professional EIA process but to ensure that information is provided in a way that is least likely to alarm the general public. Advice of local planning officers is invaluable in this respect – they know the councillors and they should know what is likely to be required to inform local residents: advice can be provided about the need and timing of local exhibitions to explain the proposals.

If the proposer of the scheme is a multinational, then the advice of a local team member who can effect local introductions can be invaluable – both for the developer and for the planning authority: the last thing they need is a protest group disrupting the planning process. Confrontation between developers and the public – with the determining authority in the middle – is to be avoided and public participation is to be encouraged.

This process has to be managed carefully, yet it is frequently constrained by the urgency to submit a planning application and by commercial confidentiality.

While preparatory discussions can be held '*in confidence*', inevitably news will leak out – news which in the absence of hard facts will frequently be conjecture. The outline of the proposal should, therefore, be presented at an early stage in as much detail as possible and to a rigorous defined programme:

- local authority planners and statutory consultees – in confidence (include adjacent administrative areas)
- local authority members – these are the decision-makers
- local press
- parish council presentation
- public exhibition and a draft ES where appropriate
- full consultation with statutory and non-statutory groups.

The EIA Regulations require publicity of planning applications accompanied by an ES. However, these legislative requirements should be regarded as the minimum.

EIA good practice has always included early consultation, which then needs to continue as an iterative part of the whole EIA process. The government has made it clear that increased public participation is important in the ongoing modernisation of the UK planning system.

Key fact

Lack of information leads to fear of the unknown, which can result in opposition

case example

Combe Down Stone Mines

Combe Down Stone Mines are 18th- and 19th-century shallow mines under the World Heritage City of Bath. Several collapses led to a feasibility study with experimental stabilization techniques including the mobilization of plant on a village green – without advising residents or local councillors. This fear of the unknown provoked the rapid formation of a residents' opposition group and an atmosphere of mistrust which plagued attempts to find a solution. Five years later in 2000, a joint community and council team embarked on a new feasibility study – incorporating EIA.

Combe Down Stone Mines: poor condition of underground pillar

Further information

IEMA 2002. *Guidelines on Participation in Environmental Decision-making*

EU Directive 2003/35/EC: Providing for public participation in drawing up plans and programmes relating to the environment

> **Public consultation** has the following aims:
>
> - to explain the nature of the proposal and its potential effects
> - to understand the strength and nature of public views of the proposal and to input these into the assessment
> - to gather support for the scheme or to reduce opposition by eliminating the fear of the unknown.

Details of preliminary consultation for EIA are given in Section 2.4, and of full consultation in Section 2.5.

2.3   Screening

Key fact

Schedule 1 projects always require EIA

Schedule 2 projects may require EIA depending on size, nature and location

(See Appendix 2)

Definition

Screening is the process by which it is decided if an EIA will be required for a proposed development. For this purpose, it has to be determined if a development is described in Schedule 1 or 2 to the Regulations.

Legislation and Discussion

Further information

Guidance on screening 2001. http://ec.europa.eu/environment/eia/eia-support.htm

Guidance on the interpretation of project categories in the EIA Directive. http://ec.europa.eu/environment/eia/eia-support.htm

Schedule 1 projects are the major and potentially most polluting developments, and always require EIA. Many of these development types have thresholds, e.g. pipelines having a diameter of more than 800 mm and a length of more than 40 km (below which they are Schedule 2).

Schedule 1 projects: development types requiring EIA (some have thresholds below which they are Schedule 2)

- Crude oil refineries
- Power stations
- Nuclear fuel reprocessing
- Iron, steel and other metal works
- Asbestos works
- Chemical and other industrial works
- Railways, airports, motorways and new roads
- Waterways and ports
- Waste disposal plants and landfill
- Groundwater abstraction
- Transfer of water resources
- Wastewater treatment plant
- Extraction of petroleum and natural gas
- Dams
- Pipelines
- Intensive pig and poultry rearing
- Industrial pulp, paper and board production
- Quarries and open cast mining
- Storage of petroleum or chemical products

From DETR 2000. EIA: A Guide to Procedures, Appendix 2. Crown copyright: reproduced with permission of the Controller of Her Majesty's Stationery Office

Identifying **Schedule 2 projects** is less straightforward than Schedule 1. Appendix 3 to the EIA guide to the procedures (DETR 2000) sets out the descriptions of development and applicable (and indicative) thresholds and criteria for the purpose of classifying development as Schedule 2; the table is reproduced in Appendix 2 of this handbook, for ease of reference. For example, a proposed wastewater treatment plant treating effluent from more than 150,000 population equivalent (pe) is

Screening

Selection criteria on the need for EIA

- Characteristics of the development
- Location of the development
- Characteristics of the potential impact

"

In each case, it will be necessary to judge whether the likely effects on the environment of that particular development will be significant in that particular location

– Department for Communities and Local
  Government (DCLG) Circular Consultation
  Draft 2006   *"*

Schedule 1 and requires an EIA. A smaller plant with more than 100,000 pe but less than 150,000 pe is Schedule 2, and an EIA will be required to be formally considered if the area of the development exceeds $1000\,m^2$ (but not necessarily required).

Schedule 2 projects have to be listed in Schedule 2 and either be in whole or in part in a *'sensitive area'* or meet criteria or exceed certain thresholds.

The scope and definition of the 'Infrastructure: urban development' category within Schedule 2 has been at times open to question, and has been interpreted in the courts as being particularly wide and inclusive to cover residential development and other infrastructure that supports urban areas. The EU's guidance on the interpretation of Annexes I and II of the EIA Directive aims to reduce the uncertainty surrounding the scope of the EIA Directive and to assist in the definition of projects covered by the Directive, and this is reflected in the draft revised UK Circular on EIA (2006).

'Sensitive areas' in the context of EIA screening are specifically defined in the Regulations as designated National Parks, Areas of Outstanding Natural Beauty, Sites of Special Scientific Interest (including sites of European importance), Scheduled Ancient Monuments, and World Heritage Sites. However, the environmental sensitivity of other designated areas, wildlife habitats or urban areas (with heavier concentrations of population) may also be relevant in determining the need for EIA.

The basic test is the likelihood of significant effects on the environment arising from development, and will be assessed (by planning authorities) for projects generally as set out in Schedule 3 of the Regulations.

Provision in Regulations for screening for projects outside of the planning system is varied.

The environmental sensitivity of an area that may be affected by projects must be considered, having regard, in particular, to:

- existing land use
- relative abundance, quality and regenerative capacity of natural resources
- the absorption capacity of the natural environment.

It is impossible to be prescriptive about any particular development, and all should be judged on a case-by-case basis. This screening process will need to be applied. Just because a Schedule 2 development project falls within a *'sensitive area'* does not automatically mean that EIA will be required, and vice versa. Regulators should also consider the cumulative effects of other proposed development and the indirect effects of projects.

Screening Opinion

Developers can undertake the screening process themselves and volunteer an ES, or they can seek the views and help of the planning authority on whether EIA is needed in a particular case. When a planning application (or subsequent application (see Section 2.2)) is submitted without an ES for a project within the scope of the EIA Regulations, local planning authorities are required to provide a Screening Opinion if one has not already been requested.

To obtain a formal '*Screening Opinion*' from the planning authority in accordance with the Regulations, the developer needs to submit:

- a location plan
- a brief description of the nature and purpose of the project
- the possible scale of environmental effects
- other representations.

It has to be remembered that the planning authority may (although not under an obligation to) seek advice from the statutory or non-statutory consultees at this stage – and the planning authority may be influenced by the potential public response in reaching its decision, even though any opposition should not affect such an opinion. The planning authority has to provide its screening opinion within 3 weeks of receiving a request (or longer if agreed with the developer).

The Screening Opinion should include aspects of the development's environmental effects which the planning authority considers significant, and it has to be made available for public inspection (together with the developer's request). The Screening Opinion should state the reasons why EIA is or is not required. A number of legal challenges have been successfully made to EIA Screening Opinions, and local planning authorities need to ensure that they have followed the correct procedures.

The Secretary of State may also be asked for a '*Screening Direction*' if:

- the developer disagrees with the planning authority's opinion
- the planning authority fails to provide a Screening Opinion within 3 weeks.

The Secretary of State has to give a Screening Direction within 3 weeks or such longer period as may be required. This direction will also be made available for public inspection.

Since such opinions are not confidential, details of the project will appear in the public domain at this stage, and developers are advised to manage the release of project details prior to this.

There are other circumstances where an EIA is deemed to have been required, where:

- the planning authority (or authorising body) has given an opinion without a formal screening request that the project is to be subject to EIA and an ES prepared, and this view is not challenged or a ruling is not requested from the Secretary of State
- the promoter volunteers an ES which states that it is an 'ES in accordance with the Regulations', and the planning authority accepts the ES
- the promoter and the planning authority (or authorising body) informally agree that an ES should be prepared.

case example

The Bath Spa Project

A new Spa facility was proposed to provide treatment in the Georgian heart of the World Heritage City of Bath. It was considered that EIA was not required, since, although clearly a sensitive area, the project would not have a significant effect on the environment. (An environmental report was prepared to accompany the planning application.)

Key fact

Both the planning authority's Screening Opinion and the developer's request have to be made available for public inspection

Crystal Palace EIA

A local planning authority failed to require EIA before granting outline planning permission for a multiplex cinema in 1998, and in line with government guidance and legal advice did not require EIA (although some councillors had requested it) before granting permission for the reserved matters. After a lengthy legal challenge through the UK and European courts, the European Court of Justice and House of Lords found in 2006 that EIA should have been required at the later reserved matters stage when it became apparent that significant environmental effects were likely. As such, the way the EIA Regulations had been implemented in the UK was seen to be flawed. This has led to amendments to the EIA Regulations.

R. *v*. London Borough of Bromley, *ex parte* Barker

Harford Street Gasworks

In the case of a proposed residential development on a former gasworks in Stepney, the Court of Appeal determined in 2003 that it is permissible to have regard to proposed mitigation measures (which may render significant effects unlikely) when determining the need for EIA, if such measures are modest in scope, plainly and easily achievable, or where their nature, availability and effectiveness are plainly established and uncontroversial. However, because the remediation measures envisaged were instead 'special and elaborate', it ruled that EIA should have been required in order to assess their effectiveness and the likely significant environmental effects, and the planning permission was quashed.

Oldham Housing Renewal

Outline planning permission for a housing regeneration scheme in Oldham, which required the demolition of terraced housing, was quashed in the High Court in 2007 because, in concluding that EIA was not required, the local planning authority had failed to consider the likelihood of certain effects (cumulative effects, construction, land contamination and loss of architectural heritage), making its Screening Opinions invalid.

Further information

Guidance on Scoping 2001. http://ec.europa.eu/environment/eia/eia-support.htm

Environment Agency 2002. *Scoping Guidance*

DCLG 2006. *Evidence Review of Scoping in Environmental Impact Assessment*

Key fact

Schedule 4 of the Regulations lists elements of the environment which might be affected – it does not require them all to be addressed

2.4   Scoping

Definition

Scoping is the way in which key issues are identified from a broad range of potential concerns for inclusion in EIA studies, the areas affected, and the level to which they should be studied. The importance of effective and accurate scoping cannot be overemphasised.

Legislation

Schedule 4 of the EIA Regulations requires a description of those aspects of the environment likely to be significantly affected *including* population, fauna, flora, soil, water, air, climatic factors, material assets (including the architectural and archaeological heritage), landscape and the inter-relationship between them.

Discussion

The EIA Guide to the Procedures (DETR 2000) includes the above checklist of matters to be considered; it is unlikely that all will be relevant to any one project. Being at the beginning of the EIA process, it is fundamental to get scoping right: studies of the quality of ESs have frequently blamed inadequacies on poor or inadequate scoping. Government advice is that the relevant authorities and the statutory consultees should be involved from an early stage before the preparation of the ES.

Consultees, faced with an EIA development for the first time, and asked which issues should be addressed, will often reproduce the EC Directive, the Regulations, or both.

EIAs are carried out usually under time, budget and resource constraints. Spending time on a non-issue will result in less time for the important matters and potentially non-determination for lack of information. This is frustrating for the developer and time-consuming for the regulators and consultees. Focusing on issues focuses resources; issues can be scoped out as well as scoped in.

Impacts which are not addressed nevertheless should be referred to in the ES to show that they were properly considered. Agreement with a regulatory body not to study a particular issue should be recorded. Issues can include not only the topic itself but also consideration of alternative sites or processes where they exist.

Effective scoping allows the project promoter to assess:

- the appropriateness of the scheme
- the range of issues likely to be raised
- planning and development costs
- programme and timescale to secure determination.

Scoping Opinion

The Regulations make provision for obtaining formal '*Scoping Opinions*' from the local planning authority (provisions vary with 'non-planning' regulations) or directions from the Secretary of State similar to those for screening, as described above.

Formal Scoping Procedure

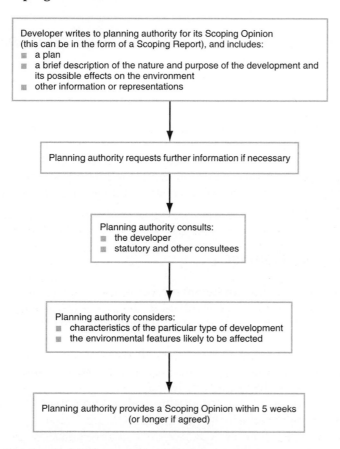

(The developer *can* request a Scoping Opinion at the same time as the Screening Opinion, although scoping is likely to require the development proposals to be more closely defined. The planning authority then still has 5 weeks after providing the Screening Opinion to provide the Scoping Opinion.)

If an authority fails to provide a Scoping Opinion within the agreed time, the developer may apply to the Secretary of State for a Scoping Direction; requests should be copied to the planning authority. The Secretary of State can ask for further information from both the developer and the planning authority, and will then consult with the developer and the consultation bodies. While the Secretary of State has 5 weeks '*or such longer period as he may reasonably require*', there is no provision to agree a time limit with the applicant.

Even though the planning authority and the Secretary of State may not have asked for additional information in giving their Scoping Opinion or Direction, they can ask for it if necessary after submission of the ES.

Early and effective scoping results in effective use of resources and time

Key fact

Scoping sets the terms of reference for the EIA

Statutory consultees for EIA

- Relevant local council(s)
- Natural England*
- The Environment Agency*
- The statutory consultees under Article 10 of the Town and Country Planning (General Development Procedure) Order 1995 for any planning application

* And equivalent bodies in Scotland, Wales and Northern Ireland

Key fact

The 2006 Draft Circular emphasises that an ES which does not fully comply with any Scoping Opinion or Direction would not necessarily be invalid but it '*will probably be subject to calls for further information*'

There is no requirement to seek a formal Scoping Opinion. However, the Regulations and Circular are very clear that the preparation of the ES should be a collaborative exercise involving discussions with the planning authority, statutory consultees and other parties. Seeking a Scoping Opinion can facilitate a useful mechanism for dialogue.

All parties in the EIA process should note that Scoping Opinions are available for inspection by the general public for up to 2 years at the planning authority's offices.

Requirement for assessment of environmental effects under other legislation

Any assessments of environmental effects required by other legislation should be identified at an early stage of the EIA process. Where more than one requirement applies, unnecessary time and effort is saved if links are identified and the different assessments co-ordinated. Planning Policy Statement (PPS)23 gives guidance on the links between the planning process and the pollution control regulatory system; similarly, PPS9 gives guidance on biodiversity and geological conservation regulatory links.

The Scoping Exercise

While EIA is essentially an iterative process, the scoping exercise begins to define who is likely to be involved in the proposals, what studies are necessary and to what level of detail the proposals are examined.

Like all activities in the EIA process, all requests and correspondence with consultees should be recorded for incorporation within a Scoping Report, which can form part of the ES. The Scoping Report is sent to the planning authority (or authorising body) with copies to consultees. The typical contents of a Scoping Report are:

- brief description of the development and the alternatives considered
- principal emissions
- sensitivity of the receiving environment
- results of initial desk studies and site surveys
- location plan/site plan/outline development plan
- consultations undertaken (e.g. record correspondence, meetings, exhibitions)
- principal opinions (e.g. reports from statutory consultees, analysis of questionnaires)
- principal issues to be addressed
- outline of the methodology for collating baseline information, assessing impact magnitude and significance, and identifying mitigation
- reasons for not addressing other issues.

The EIA Guide to Procedures (DETR 2000) provides a checklist of matters to be considered for inclusion when preparing an ES. These provide a useful guide to carrying out the scoping exercise.

Other EIA links

- Conservation (Natural Habitats etc) Regulations 1994, amended 2007
- Birds Directive 1979
- Water Resources Act 1991
- Pollution Prevention and Control Regulations 2000
- PPS9: *Biodiversity and Geological Conservation*
- PPG13: *Transport*
- PPS23: *Planning and Pollution Control*
- PPS25: *Development and Flood Risk*

Key fact

There are important links between the planning system and other regulatory arrangements. Negotiations for the range of required consents should take place in parallel

Assessment of effects should include:
- *direct*
- *indirect*
- *secondary*
- *cumulative*
- *short, medium and long term*
- *permanent*
- *temporary*
- *positive*
- *negative*

– DETR 2000

""

Checklist of EIA matters

Information describing the project:

- purpose and physical characteristics
- land-use requirements and physical features
- production processes and operational features: resource usage, residues and emissions
- alternative sites and processes, including a 'do nothing' scenario.

Information describing the site and its environment:

- physical features
- policy framework.

Assessment of effects on:

- humans, buildings and man-made features
- flora, fauna and geology
- land
- water
- air and climate
- other indirect and secondary effects.

Mitigating measures: description and likely effectiveness.

Risks of accidents and hazardous development.

From DETR 2000. EIA: A Guide to Procedures. Crown copyright: reproduced with permission of the Controller of Her Majesty's Stationery Office

The initial contact for scoping should be with the planning authority, who can also advise on other interested parties to be consulted, e.g. parish councils, local environmental groups and civic societies. It is helpful to provide the sort of information formally listed in the Regulations (see above) at this stage. Development team members should generally be able from experience and initial desk study and site survey to suggest most of the issues likely to arise in the locality concerned. Particular designations, e.g. Area of Outstanding Natural Beauty (AONB), Site of Special Scientific Interest (SSSI), Scheduled Monument, will influence the type of issue to be addressed. This will enable some initial thoughts to be presented in the Scoping Report to the consultation bodies.

The preparation of this can be facilitated through team discussion; checklists or matrices can be helpful to ensure nothing likely to be significant is missed.

Key facts

- Not all the environmental matters will be relevant to any one project
- Effects before and during construction should be considered separately from operation/occupation and decommissioning
- Pre-construction effects can include blight, off-site planting, ancillary developments, site preparation

Scoping

Matrix of Issues for Scoping

Environmental topic	Effects						
	Characteristic		Scale*	Significance			Project phase
	Adverse, beneficial, neutral	Direct, indirect, cumulative	I, N, R, D, L	Long-term, short-term	Irreversible, reversible	Major, minor	Pre-construction Construction Operation/occupation Decommissioning restoration
Population							
Transport							
Noise and vibration							
Biodiversity							
Soils, geology and agriculture							
Water							
Air, climate and odour							
Cultural heritage/ material assets							
Landscape							
Interactions							

* I: international, N: national, R: regional, D: district, L: local

Adapted from Department of Environment 1995. Preparing Environmental Statements for Planning Projects. Crown copyright: reproduced with permission of the Controller of Her Majesty's Stationery Office

guiding principle
Keep matrices and checklists simple

If matrices or checklists are used, it is essential to keep them simple, since at this stage we are only looking for the potential key issues: details of significance can be addressed later. A pragmatic approach is to use professional expertise and consultation to scope the EIA and then use such matrices as a checklist to ensure that no important issues have been overlooked. A useful guide as to whether an issue should be included or not is to ask the question 'will anyone be concerned about this – who does it affect?'

While it is important to focus on these key issues, for some types of development, e.g. outline applications for mixed-use development, it may be particularly difficult to eliminate any issues from consideration at this preliminary stage, and it is necessary to keep all issues under examination. This is of particular relevance when a preferred alternative emerges part of the way through the assessment process. If scoping has been done thoroughly from the beginning, no new issues should be raised.

If a Scoping Opinion is requested, then the proposals will enter the public domain via the consultation that a planning authority may undertake. Similarly, if the scheme proposals include a contentious licence required from the Environment Agency, then it is Agency policy to involve the public at an early stage via public meetings or exhibitions. Therefore, scoping cannot be guaranteed to remain confidential, and if commercial considerations are implicated, the preliminary scoping should be undertaken by the promoter's team alone.

The scoping exercise in summary

- Review relevant development plans.
- Review government and strategic policy guidance.
- Identify non-planning regulatory requirements.
- Determine an initial list of potential issues.
- Request a formal Scoping Opinion and/or consult with the planning authority.
- Consult with statutory and non-statutory consultees.
- Prepare a Scoping Report and agree it with the planning authority.

2.5 Consultation

Definition

Consultation is the process by which those organisations or individuals with an interest in the area proposed for development are identified, and their opinions or concerns recorded and incorporated into the EIA. These consultees may also hold environmental information relating to the locality.

Legislation

Developers are under no formal obligation to consult prior to the submission of an application or authorisation for development. There is a requirement for the authorising authority to undertake formal consultation after submission of the ES.

The government is promoting more *public participation* in planning and development decision-making, e.g. there is a requirement for local authorities to prepare Statements of Community Involvement as part of their local development schemes, community strategies and local strategic partnerships. An EU Directive has been published on public participation (Directive 2003/35/EC) which has been implemented through the Town and Country Planning (Environmental Impact Assessment) (Amendment) Regulations 2006 to align public participation in EIA more closely with the UNECE Convention on Access to Information, Public Participation in Decision-making and Access to Justice in Environmental Matters (the Aarhus Convention).

Discussion

Consultation is inherent in the iterative EIA process. This approach ensures that the design project team is informed, practicable alternatives are properly considered, and delay due to redesign requirements is avoided.

The stages of consultation may conveniently be summarised as follows:

- Preliminary consultation: screening, scoping.
- Consultation during the EIA process: information, opinions, public consultation.
- Formal consultation: after ES submission.

guiding principle

consult early; consult often

Further information

IEMA 2002. *Guidelines on Participation in Environmental Decision-making*

case example

Fulham Football Club

The club had applied for planning permission to build a new stadium, flats and a riverside walkway. An ES was not prepared. Consent was granted but then challenged on the grounds that the EIA Directive had not been followed. The House of Lords quashed the planning decision. Included in their reasoning was the fact that the Directive is rooted in rights of public consultation, which had not been followed. The judgement famously said 'EIA is not a paperchase'.

(Berkeley v. Secretary of State 2000)

Preliminary Consultation

This relates to the screening and scoping phases as discussed in the preceding sections.

Consultation during the EIA Process

When it has been established that an EIA is required and that an ES will be prepared, the authorising authority will notify the relevant statutory consultees (confirming this to the developer).

This formal notification obliges the consultees to provide the developer with such information as may be relevant to the preparation of the ES. (A reasonable charge for the information may be made.) It is then up to the developer to approach these consultees and indicate the type of information required.

Key facts

- Authorising authority duties are to advise consultees that an EIA is being undertaken
- Consultees have a duty to provide information in their possession
- The developer is required to approach the consultees for the information

---

Consultation bodies required to provide information for an EIA (other relevant bodies and departments in Scotland, Wales and Northern Ireland)

- The relevant planning authority(ies).
- Natural England.
- Environment Agency.

Other bodies who would be statutory consultees under the General Development Procedure Order 1995 – which could include (depending on the type of development or nature of the land):

- Health and Safety Executive
- Department for Transport
- Coal Authority
- English Heritage (Historic Buildings and Monuments Commission for England)
- Department for Communities and Local Government
- Sports Council
- British Waterways.

(Wider consultation with non-statutory consultees may also be advisable since these sources may have particular knowledge and information.)

Sources of preliminary information to determine environmental sensitivity

- Local authority: local development framework proposals, county wildlife sites, local nature reserves, archaeological sites and monuments records, historic maps, contaminated land, listed buildings, conservation areas.
- Multi-Agency Geographic Information for the Countryside (MAGIC) – statutory environmental designations and other map-based information (www.magic.gov.uk).

- Environment Agency: River Basin Management Plans (RBMPs), Source Protection Zones (SPZs), Nitrate Sensitive Areas, Flood Zones, Water Quality.
- Natural England: Sites of Special Scientific Interest (SSSIs), Natural Areas, Special Protection Areas (SPAs), Special Areas of Conservation (SACs). Ramsar Sites, National Nature Reserve: Areas of Outstanding Natural Beauty (AONB), National Character Areas.
- English Heritage: Scheduled Monuments, Historic Parks and Gardens

Information requests should include an indication of the proposals, a site location map, a specification of the information required, a date for reply and a request for an indication of any data retrieval costs. If information relates to a protected species that is subject to persecution, then a commitment should be made to keep this separate from that publicly available in the ES.

It is essential to allow sufficient time in the project development programme for responses to such requests since, for example, government departments and organisations may have different response times. Furthermore, the Environmental Information Regulations allow up to 2 months for the provision of information.

Non-statutory consultees can include:

- wildlife trusts and other nature conservation groups
- Royal Society for the Protection of Birds (RSPB)
- Campaign to Protect Rural England (CPRE)
- water companies and other utilities
- community and amenity groups
- local history and geological societies
- Society for the Protection of Ancient Buildings (SPAB)
- Environmental Protection UK (formerly the National Society for Clean Air)
- recreation groups.

Generally, it is advantageous for developers to also seek opinions once the proposals are clear enough to form the basis for discussion. Such opinions can be requested in the information request letters or at meetings. All such communication may be requested to be 'in confidence' at this early stage if no formal Scoping Opinion has been sought.

While under no obligation to publicise the proposals, there can be advantages to gauge general opinion and local concerns at this early stage: mitigation can be designed in if concerns are recognised early enough. It is important to manage this process carefully and, if opinions are to be sought, begin with local authority planners and members before going public. There are various techniques available for public consultation, but the most productive medium for public information and participation is via exhibitions and questionnaires. Public meetings allow the most vocal to create uneven representation, bias and conflict, and therefore need to be managed to ensure fairness (for communication and initial consultation see also Section 2.2).

Further information

Environmental Information Regulations 1992

guiding principle

Programme sufficient time for information retrieval

Key fact

Concerns expressed during early consultation can be incorporated in evolving design

guiding principle

Use exhibitions and questionnaires for the most-effective public consultation

Formal Consultation

Once the ES is submitted with the application for development, then the formal consultation can begin. The preceding informal discussions will help facilitate timely responses. If 'further information' of a substantive nature is required to be submitted to complete the ES, this too must be subject to formal consultation. Since amendments to the EIA Regulations in 2006, 'any other information' of a substantive nature relating to the ES that is provided by the applicant or appellant must also be subject to consultation.

The amendment Regulations also introduced the requirement for local planning authorities to notify any person (such as environmental groups) likely to be affected by, or having an interest in, the application, who is unlikely to become aware of it by means of a site notice or by local advertisement, that an ES has been submitted.

The Regulations make the following provisions:

Outline of formal provisions for consultation according to EIA Regulations

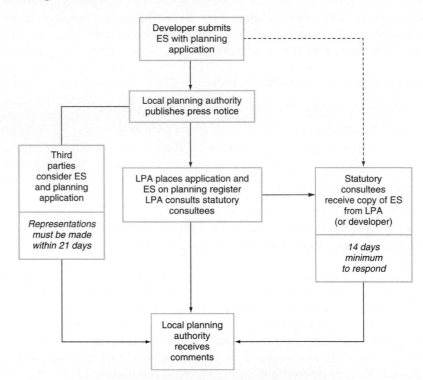

From DETR 2000. EIA: Guide to Procedures. Crown copyright: reproduced with permission of the Controller of Her Majesty's Stationery Office

---

Consultation in summary

- Consultation lies at the root of the EIA process: to gather information and to identify concerns.
- Early consultation allows concerns to be addressed and the scheme design adapted to incorporate mitigation.
- Time should be allowed in the EIA process for adequate consultation and responses.

2.6 Baseline Studies

Definition

Baseline studies describe the current (and predicted – see the section 'Discussion' below) condition of those elements of the environment which are likely to be significantly affected by the proposed development. The baseline environmental conditions should be evaluated according to their importance and sensitivity. This can be achieved by reference to relevant designations and standards. Baseline conditions can be described and evaluated using existing data but may require further surveys and studies to be undertaken.

Legislation

The Regulations do not specifically refer to 'baseline studies'; however, the need for such data to identify and assess the main environmental effects is a minimum requirement (Schedule 4, Part II). The Regulations require an indication of any difficulties (technical deficiencies or lack of know-how) encountered during compilation of the required information.

Discussion

An environmental impact is a change in an aspect of the environment which is predicted to occur over a particular time period and within a defined area as a result of the construction and operation of the proposed development. The question of what is the relevant baseline arises. It is recognised that neither the natural nor the human environment is static. For example, a woodland develops through growth and succession, a town grows as a result of population growth. The baseline studies should, therefore, be based on the predicted condition of the environment at the time of the proposed development, e.g. if a new harbour is to be built, the geomorphological studies for an EIA for a nearby coastal defence scheme should be based on the 'with harbour' situation. If there is any doubt about whether the harbour development will proceed, the 'without harbour' situation should also be considered.

The level of information also has to be appropriate for the development proposed. Recent case law indicates that there is a need now to provide far more information than was the original minimalist approach envisaged by the UK government in the 1980s. However, good practice in scoping is required to minimise 'unnecessary elaboration' in the ES.

It is, therefore, necessary for the developer, consultants and the regulators to carefully consider and agree the level of detail appropriate to a particular development (this applies to the description of the project as well as the environmental information: see Section 4.2). The test is that it should be sufficient to assess the significant impacts – planning consent cannot be granted without it – regardless of whether it is for an outline or detailed application.

The issues, their relative importance and their boundaries for which such information is to be provided should be detailed at the scoping stage and through consultation. They should be drawn widely enough to cover indirect effects, cumulative effects and, possibly, alternative sites that may be suggested during the consultation process.

Key fact

The information required should have regard to current knowledge and methods, and be such that the applicant could *reasonably* be required to compile

case example

The EIA for an inner-city regeneration project had to take into account the additional traffic and emissions generated by an adjacent, but not yet built, supermarket with planning permission granted.

guiding principle

Judicial review decisions have emphasized the need to provide sufficient information in order to assess the likely main or significant environmental effects

case examples

R. *v.* Cornwall County Council (*ex parte* Hardy) 2001

The ES for an extension to a landfill site recorded that while no bats had been found during survey, the habitat was suitable for bats, and further surveys were recommended. English Nature and the Cornwall Wildlife Trust were content that permission should be granted subject to a condition requiring such survey. Since the bats were specifically protected by European Directives, and if present would represent a main or significant effect, the ES was held to be defective since it did not contain sufficient information about the baseline environmental conditions or the significant adverse effects of the project.

R. (PPG11 Ltd) *v.* Dorset CC 2004

An ES for a landfill of a quarry site predicted minimal effects on reptiles. The court held that as effects on ecology were not likely to be significant, further reptile surveys were not required before granting planning permission, and could be undertaken afterwards as proposed.

Baseline Studies

Programme sufficient time for seasonal surveys

case example

Minehead Coastal Defences

The local authority archaeologist required full information on the nature and condition of medieval fish weirs before approval could be granted for new coastal defences. These could only be examined during daylight and at extreme low tide, and the project was delayed by several months as a result.

Methodology

Baseline studies may generally be initiated through desk studies of existing information generated as a result of the scoping exercise. This confirms the key issues and the level of detail required for particular issues. The need for further field surveys is then identified. At an early stage, consideration should be given to any seasonal constraints or requirements for survey: specialist fauna and flora surveys may only be valid at certain times of the year, and visual impact assessment may require photomontages during both summer and winter – sufficient time should be programmed into the project for such surveys.

It does have to be emphasised that baseline studies are not intended to fall into the category of 'original research'. Experts can predict how particular habitats will react or develop and surveys can be selected to provide accurate information, e.g. a chemical survey will do little more than provide a snapshot of the water quality of a river, whereas a biological survey (which may be more expensive and constrained by seasons) can provide a more accurate assessment of long-term conditions.

The field studies and their interpretation can be developed and refined as the iterative process of EIA unfolds. (Developers and regulators should also be aware of the need for assessment under other European Directives, e.g. the Habitats Directive and the necessary scope of the baseline studies.)

When designing the methodologies for baseline studies, it is necessary to consider the relevant environmental boundaries and the interactions of the environmental topics. For example, impacts on water resources may be best considered at the regional level, while surface water drainage and flood risk effects are likely to be local or at river catchment level. The interactions with traffic, noise and air quality are so interrelated that the traffic studies need to be designed to provide the necessary baseline for air quality and noise predictions as well as traffic numbers. Similarly, baseline drainage studies designed to assess flood risk effects may need to consider water quality and ecological parameters.

Baseline studies should be designed and undertaken in such a way that they can be replicated during any post-construction monitoring exercise.

Baseline studies in summary

- Key parties should, at the scoping stage, agree the scope and depth required of the baseline studies in order to properly assess the effects of development.
- The baseline should consider other foreseeable future and consented developments, natural processes, as well as the 'do nothing' scenario.
- Project management should programme time for seasonal surveys.
- Baseline studies are not research studies.
- Baseline studies should be broad enough to consider emerging alternative development sites/processes.
- Study methods progress from scoping to desk and field studies, and are designed to be readily replicable.

2.7 Impact Assessment and Significance

Definition

Impact assessment refers to the change that is predicted to take place to the existing condition of the environment as a result of the proposed development. Significance is commonly judged by comparing the extent of the change with particular standards and criteria relevant to each environmental topic. For example, if concentrations of a chemical emission will double (the change or impact), this will result in exceeding an air quality objective, leading to potential harm to health (the significance of the effect).

Legislation

The Regulations require a description of the likely significant effects of the proposed project on the environment resulting from the:

- existence of the project
- use of natural resources
- emission of pollutants, the creation of nuisances and the elimination of waste.

The potential significant effects of projects must be considered in relation to the characteristics and location of the project, with particular regard to the:

- extent of the impact (geographical area and size of affected population)
- transfrontier nature of the impact
- magnitude and complexity of the impact
- duration, frequency and reversibility of the impact.

Furthermore, the predictive methods used to assess the effects on the environment should be described.

The description of the effects should address:

- direct, indirect and secondary
- cumulative
- short, medium and long term
- permanent and temporary
- positive and negative.

Impact Assessment and Significance
Key fact

Significance is influenced by the values of individuals and how the project or the changes in the environment are perceived to affect them

Discussion

'Significance' in EIA is a judgement based on the:

- context in which the impact is likely to occur
- intensity or severity of the impact
- importance to decision-making, the community and consultees of the resulting effect.

This last point highlights the fact that significance is, as some authors maintain, essentially anthropocentric. While science can often describe an impact with reasonable accuracy, and EIA has developed as a process to present and communicate the findings of studies, development proposals have to take political acceptability and promotability into account.

Impacts and their significance should be clearly stated, avoiding the use of palliative phrases, of which the readers will be justifiably suspicious. Similarly, transparency of sources, judgements and any uncertainties will generate confidence in the conclusions reached. Predictions should be based on a reasonable worst-case scenario, to comply with the precautionary principle of sustainable development.

Significance is often subjective, and professionals may well disagree. The adoption of methodologies for defining significance in the EIA may ideally be defined in consultation (e.g. in the scoping stage) with decision-makers and other stakeholders, so as to be inclusive and take account of varying opinions as to what is important. It should also be noted that the significance of an impact is not necessarily the same as its acceptability. The community may be more prepared to accept and approve projects which will relieve unemployment or where inward investment is needed despite negative environmental impacts. This does not detract from the judgement of the significance of the effect with regard to the environment. It can be particularly relevant where component or cumulative effects are indicated.

The increasing requirement for improved community and neighbourhood participation in the UK spatial and development planning process has also driven the development of new techniques and approaches in assessing what is important to the public.

Methodology

There are two stages in the assessment of the significance of impacts. The first stage characterises the nature of the impact or the impact magnitude (e.g. $10\,dB_A$ increase over $100\,m$ for x receptors) and then the second stage determines the significance (e.g. this exceeds a set Environmental Quality Standard or it will affect a particularly sensitive receptor such as a hospital).

The determination of significance ultimately relies on professional judgement, although exceedence of standards, criteria and thresholds can help guide this judgement. Such standards are different for each environmental topic, and details of these and methodologies are given in Chapter 3.

However, a simple matrix is often used to give an early indication of the degree of significance of any impact.

Scale \\ Magnitude	Low	Medium	High
Local			
County			
Regional			
National			
International			

Impacts should be considered for each phase of a project:

- construction
- operation/occupation
- restoration
- decommissioning.

It is also worth bearing in mind that it is not only the effects of development on statutorily designated areas that give rise to significant impacts. The effects on features which are not on any register can be important to local neighbourhoods, and their identification at an early stage is essential. The success of this stage of the EIA, therefore, relies on thorough consultation.

> **Impact assessment and significance in summary**
>
> Good practice for impact assessment and significance requires:
>
> - a systematic approach, carefully organized, managed and recorded
> - an understandable method, clearly stated, reproducible and verifiable
> - a description of the basis on which judgements are made
> - where difficulties are encountered or the impact predictions rely on subjectivity or are unquantifiable, this should be stated
> - assumptions made and levels of confidence to be stated.

> *The intrusion of wider public concerns and social values is inescapable and contentions will remain even with well defined criteria and a structured approach*
>
> – Sadler, B. 1996
>
> *Environmental Assessment in a Changing World.* Canadian Environmental Assessment Agency, IAIA.

case example

Gas-powered Power Station

A gas-powered power station was proposed to replace a redundant coal-fired plant. Separate ESs were produced for the proposed 40 km gas pipeline, the power station itself and the electricity transmission lines to the national grid. While the local authority where the power station was proposed was very keen to grant approval, the Department of Transport (the authorizing body, now the Department for Business, Enterprise and Regulatory Reform (BERR)) had to take account of the overall development, which affected neighbouring communities and planning authorities.

guiding principle

- A systematic approach, clarity and transparency are vital
- Avoid confusing the characteristics and magnitude of the impact with its significance
- Acknowledge uncertainty and margins of error associated with impact prediction

case example

Inner-city Regeneration

An EIA for a mixed-use inner-city regeneration project identified at the first stage listed buildings and parks in the locality, but it took discussion with the local history society to realize that a fountain in the park had been erected by the founder of a disused factory. This had been an important local employer, and the community would have been most upset if plans had involved its removal.

2.8 Mitigation

Definition

Mitigation has been defined in UK government research as 'measures which are incorporated into the design or implementation of a development project for the purpose of avoiding, reducing, remedying or compensating for its adverse environmental impacts. It may also include measures to create environmental benefits' (DETR 1997). The distinction between compensation, remediation and enhancement is often not clearly defined or understood.

Legislation

The EC Directive and the Regulations require 'a description of the measures envisaged in order to avoid, to reduce and if possible remedy significant adverse effects'.

Discussion

The purpose of addressing mitigation is to develop a scheme which aims to progress towards a 'no net loss' effect on the environment.

The Regulations allow for a hierarchy of mitigation; however, sustainability principles require avoidance or compensation to achieve no net loss to the environment. Opportunities for environmental enhancement could also be identified.

Mitigation as part of the EIA process plays a key role in terms of sustainability, since it addresses issues such as resource usage, capacity and biodiversity within a project life cycle framework.

Mitigation is for negative impacts: other environmental measures might be enhancement, planning gain or compensation in kind. Mitigation is, by definition, focused on identified significant negative impacts.

Methodology

The descriptions of the mitigation proposed need to be precise and clearly stated if a planning authority is to rely upon them for setting planning conditions in any subsequent approval. If the descriptions are clearly related to the potential impacts of the scheme before mitigation, then the likely benefits can be predicted; the degree of confidence in the effectiveness of the mitigation proposed – and the means of implementation – should be stated. Monitoring proposals, to identify the actual effects and help correct any deficiencies in mitigation, should also be stated. Finally, the impacts remaining after mitigation and for which no mitigation is proposed or possible – the residual impacts – should be clearly identified, as these are the predicted impacts of the proposed development. Any uncertainty should be reported, and measures to correct unforeseen consequences stated.

It must be remembered that the mitigation process is an iterative one which is continuous throughout the project design development. Each stage should be reported to and recorded by the EIA co-ordinator for inclusion in the ES. The identification and incorporation of mitigation can only be effective if the EIA co-ordinator is engaged from the start.

Further reading

DETR 1997. *Mitigation Measures in Environmental Statements*

Key fact

Mitigation hierarchy:

- avoid
- reduce
- remedy

Key fact

Mitigation is the principal design tool in EIA

guiding principle

The ES should specify for each mitigation option:

- who is responsible
- what will be done
- when it will be done
- how it will be achieved
- how effective it will be

Key fact

Requirements under other legislation such as environmental protection are not considered to be mitigation, e.g. a bund to contain chemical or oil spillages is not mitigation

guiding principle

EIA is an iterative process, and mitigation should be designed in, not 'bolted on'

To identify whether mitigation is actually necessary, cross-reference to an environmental risk assessment exercise should be carried out. Risk assessment is a management tool that aids decision-making; it considers the likelihood, the consequences of an event and how best to manage any unacceptable risks. This will have identified impacts, their probability and their severity so that it can then be decided at what level of probability/impact, mitigation should be triggered. If this is implemented throughout the design process the impacts will be minimised – remembering to mitigate for cumulative and indirect impacts.

Risk assessment is a management tool that aids decision-making and is used by environmental regulators. It involves the consideration of the likelihood and the consequences of an event, and how best to manage any unacceptable risks. Environmental risk assessment requires an understanding of the:

- source of a hazard (e.g. a chemical that can cause harm) to, or from, the environment
- characteristics of an environmental receptor (e.g. human, ecosystem)
- means or pathway (e.g. the air, groundwater) by which the receptor may be affected by that hazard.

Adapted from DETR, Environment Agency and CIEH 2000.
Crown copyright: reproduced with permission of the Controller of Her Majesty's Stationery Office

Key fact

Environmental regulation is based on risk assessment and management

Further information

COMAH and COSHH Regulations

Health and Safety at Work Regulations

DETR, Environment Agency, and the Chartered Institute of Environmental Health (CIEH) 2000. *Guidelines for Environmental Risk Assessment and Management*

Environment Agency, Scottish Environmental Protection Agency and the Department of Environment (Northern Ireland) 2002. *Risk Assessment for Environmental Professionals*

Royal Commission on Environmental Pollution 1998. 21st Report: *Setting Environmental Standards*

Mitigation Strategy

Projects which comply with policy and have minimal impact on the environment are most likely to achieve planning consent. Mitigation should be considered at the commencement of the project design, and in this respect, choice of site and/or process can play an important part by avoiding or minimising the impact and thus reducing the need for mitigation. These considerations should be set out in the ES in a transparent and methodical way. There is a requirement to describe alternatives in the ES (see Section 2.9).

Options for mitigation:

- strategic
- design
- management.

Strategic mitigation will consider the alternative sites or processes available. The first step is to consider alternative ways of achieving the stated objective of the project. Using leakage control or public education to reduce water demand thus obviating the need for a new high-impact reservoir is an example of strategic mitigation cited by the government (DETR 1997).

The second step is to consider alternative sites which avoid or reduce the significance of a potential impact. Continuing with the example of the reservoir, a location outside of environmentally designated areas may be considered. This should be stated in the ES even if the location is rejected on other grounds, e.g. safety or economic.

Finally a different process may be considered – again the provision of water may be sourced by a desalination plant or by river regulation and abstraction.

Mitigation through design is implemented once the strategic decisions on the method, site and process have been determined.

In the case of a reservoir, the dam may be curved to reflect its surroundings, shallows may be provided for wildfowl, construction access roads may be built below the final top water level, or new woodland may be planted to replace that lost as a result of the development.

Mitigation by management is the final level of mitigation. This will include such measures as dust control during construction or operation, working hours, and reporting and control of pollution incidents. These can most usefully be listed as a schedule of all key mitigation measures in a separate chapter. The environmental management measures required to implement them can then be identified in a draft Environmental Management Plan (EMP) included in the ES, and can, therefore, act as a checklist for conditions to be imposed by planning authorities as well as a schedule for the developer and contractors to take into consideration when preparing and tendering for the construction contract. A contractor having a formal Environmental Management System (EMS) can assist the confidence levels of regulators in this respect – in the knowledge that auditing, monitoring and remedial action will take place (see Section 5.1).

Mitigation Hierarchy

The approach is to avoid impacts and if they cannot be avoided, to reduce them. If impacts still remain, then the next option is to remedy the damage or to compensate for it. It is often held that compensation is only true mitigation if it genuinely replaces what is lost. New planting in place of ancient woodland which will be destroyed as a result of the development will obviously not be a totally satisfactory substitute.

All options for mitigation should be considered at all stages of the potential project – construction, operation/occupation, decommissioning and restoration.

Mitigation hierarchy	
Option	*Example*
Avoid at source	Avoid machinery
Minimize impacts at source	Use quiet machinery
Abate impacts on site	Use acoustic barriers
Abate impacts at receptor	Provide double glazing
Repair impacts	Monitor and remedy
Compensate in kind	Move residents for duration of construction
Other compensation and enhancement	Liaise with residents

Adapted from DETR 1997. Crown copyright: reproduced with permission of the Controller of Her Majesty's Stationery Office

Choosing an option as high up the hierarchy as possible is in accordance with the EU Directive, which states that community policy on the environment is based on the following principles:

- precautionary principle
- preventative action should be taken
- environmental damage should be rectified at source
- the polluter should pay.

Commitment to Mitigation

The authorising bodies and regulators must remember that mitigation measures are only enforceable if they are included in the planning permission or other authorisation via conditions: their inclusion in the ES alone is not enough to guarantee their implementation. Another option is to use planning obligations – Section 106 Agreements under the Town & Country Planning Act 1990 – under which the developer and the planning authority enter into a contract to restrict use of land, undertake specific operations on the land or make payments to the authority to provide facilities which are needed to enable the development to proceed.

Mitigation which is suggested in the event that its requirement becomes apparent subsequently is termed 'deferred mitigation'. For example, a watching brief for archaeological remains will be provided and archaeological investigations undertaken if anything is found during the watching brief.

The developer can also demonstrate a commitment to mitigation through an EMP or an Environmental Action Plan (EAP) – a draft or 'brief' of which should be included in the ES. A schedule of environmental commitments offers a useful method of clarifying the mitigation measures that a developer is committed to and can be progressively updated as the project design evolves. The means of implementation and follow-up monitoring and management (see Section 2.10 below) should be described.

It is also clear that the environmental commitments, proposed in the ES and as may be subsequently amended during consultation and approval, will need to be included within contract documents for the construction and maintenance (and, where relevant, restoration and decommissioning) of the project. The extent to which mitigation measures can be defined reliably in an ES is likely to depend on how the project is managed and the type of contracts that are awarded – particularly how involved the actual site developer, construction contractors and other key parties are in the project at the time of preparing the ES.

> **Further information**
> DCLG 2006. *Planning Obligations: Practice Guide*
>
> **Key fact**
> A commitment in an ES is not enforceable unless conditioned or specified by the regulator

---

Mitigation in summary

- Consult early to identify mitigation opportunities.
- Consider mitigation from the earliest stage of project identification.
- Select mitigation as high up the hierarchy as possible.
- Review mitigation options at all stages of the design, construction and management process.
- Clearly state the mitigation considered, its likely effectiveness and the monitoring proposed.
- Commit to mitigation that will be implemented and monitored – via an EMP.
- State measures to correct unforeseen consequences.

2.9 Alternatives

Definition

There is a legal requirement to address alternatives, but there is no statutory EIA definition of 'alternatives', and so this is open to interpretation. It is usually taken to be the examination of alternative approaches to deliver the scheme objectives and alternative sites, processes or management:

- **alternative ways** of achieving the objective, e.g. leakage control rather than a new reservoir.
- **alternative means**, e.g. different locations for a reservoir or several reservoirs.

Legislation

Schedule 4 of the Regulations requires an outline of the main alternatives studied by the applicant or appellant and an indication of the main reasons for this choice, taking into account the environmental effects.

Discussion

The reasons for examination, recording and reporting of alternatives considered at all stages of the EIA process are closely linked, and such methodologies have been described in Section 2.8: alternative approaches may result in a viable, practicable scheme that is more acceptable in environmental terms. Methods of evaluating significance also indicate useful ways of comparing alternatives (Section 2.7).

Consideration of alternatives . . . results in a more robust application for planning permission

– DETR 2000

The EIA Circular states that the Directive and the Regulations 'do not expressly require the developer to study alternatives'. This may appear to be at variance with Schedule 4 of the Regulations, and the explanation is that alternatives must be outlined and reasons for the final choice given *where alternative approaches to development have been considered*. So, developers are encouraged to consider alternatives – if they do so they must report them, but if they are not considered, it does not nullify the ES. Notwithstanding this, good practice recognises that consideration of alternatives facilitates the decision-making process. It is recognised that options may be limited, e.g. mineral extraction schemes – but the Circular advises that the nature and location of some developments may make consideration of alternative sites a material consideration.

The government has always emphasised the benefits of starting the EIA process at the inception of projects, which allows for full consideration of alternatives – site, process or procedures – because it adds to the credibility and objectives of the ES. This can demonstrate that environmental factors have been taken into account throughout the project design process.

When deciding at what level of detail to study with respect to alternatives, the best guidance is to investigate only those which are 'practical', i.e. those fulfilling the criteria of 'need' and 'purpose', i.e. keep the development objectives clear.

The advice is to start the examination of alternatives early, but how early? If house builders are proposing a housing development, in accordance with a local authority allocation, they cannot be expected to examine alternative locations – these should be evaluated at an earlier stage using Strategic Environmental Assessment (SEA) at the development plan preparation stage. Policy evaluation is outside the scope of private developers.

However, what house builders *can* study is, for example, alternatives in housing density, mix, infrastructure provision and masterplan, layout and detail design.

Approach and Methodology

Stages in the analysis of broad alternatives are shown below.

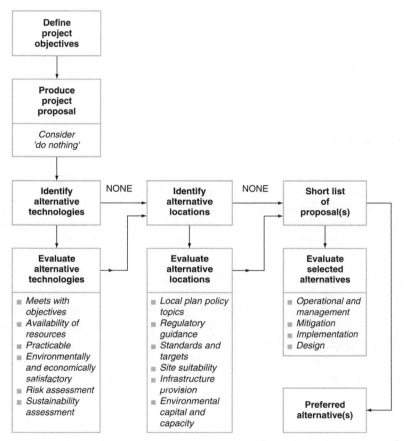

Data from World Bank 1996

Having selected this short list of practicable alternative proposals, they are then examined in terms of their respective design, construction and operational alternatives, taking mitigation into account. At this stage it is useful to hold an exhibition explaining the various identified options and inviting public comment – recorded by means of questionnaires – but note that the views of the majority may not necessarily reflect the best practicable environmental option. It is then for the planning authorities and regulators to explain their views. This systematic approach will identify the most robust development option – the process should be fully documented and reported in the ES. It is essential to be clear about the use of the criteria – which can be those presenting opportunities, e.g. near to a major transport route as well as constraints, e.g. near to an educational establishment.

case example

Alternatives: Technologies

The sewerage system of a major city was over 100 years old, and combined sewer overflows were subject to premature and frequent operation, causing pollution and affecting amenity and recreation. Updating of the system was required to meet the standards of the Urban Wastewater Treatment Directive. The responsible water undertaker commissioned feasibility studies which examined a range of alternative options for treatment, storage and transmission of sewage, including EIA of these options.

case example

Alternatives: Locations

A coastal conurbation had limited sewage treatment facilities, discharging screened sewage to the marine environment. An assessment was undertaken of alternative locations for a new sewage treatment works. Criteria for the suitability of such sites were set, which were based on availability, local plan policy issues, and regulatory constraints. The site which the water company and the planning authority agreed had the least environmental impact was strongly opposed by the local residents and the 'second best' site had to be promoted and eventually approved.

> **Alternatives in summary**
>
> ■ Description of alternatives studied is mandatory.
> ■ Alternatives can refer to locations, processes or procedures.
> ■ The criteria for assessing alternatives should be clear.

2.10   Monitoring and Follow-up

Definitions

■ **EIA follow-up** is the monitoring and evaluation of the actual impacts of a development project (subject to EIA) on the environment, together with the management of, and communication about, the environmental performance of that project.

■ **Monitoring** comprises the collection of data or information on a range of specific environmental variables. It is subject to a time-related programme of measurements or observations.

■ **Evaluation or auditing** is the objective comparison of monitoring results with pre-defined criteria or predictions. It may also relate to, and be a requirement of, an organisation's EMS (e.g. ISO 14001 EMS) or policy.

■ **Management** is making decisions and taking appropriate action in response to issues arising from monitoring and evaluation. It can include decisions and actions by both the developer (e.g. responding to unexpected impacts) or regulators (e.g. informing future decisions and enforcement of planning conditions and management requirements).

■ **Communication** is informing stakeholders about the results of EIA follow-up, by developers and regulators, which can include regular reporting and liaison to feed back information into future decisions, and the direct participation of stakeholders in monitoring, evaluation and management stages.

Legislation

There is no specific requirement in the EIA Directive or the Regulations to undertake monitoring or follow-up (although the SEA Directive does require monitoring), however there is a requirement to describe the mitigation measures that are envisaged. However, follow-up should be an integral part of EIA practice, in order that the many predictions made in the ES can be checked, and so that the provisions and findings of an EIA are implemented effectively during project implementation. A lack of any follow-up can allow some mitigation measures to be forgotten or implemented poorly, and impacts being greater than were predicted, which can bring the EIA into disrepute with those affected. Responsible developers are also likely to consider it useful to monitor and manage the actual effects and performance of their development in order to avoid misinformation and build acceptance within affected communities. The need for EIA follow-up measures should ideally be considered at the scoping stage, identified in the ES, and detailed in an EMP/EAP, which can be outlined in the ES (see Section 2.8 above).

Further information

Morrison-Saunders, A., Marshall, R. and Arts, J. 2007. *EIA Follow-Up International Best Practice Principles. Special Publication Series*, No. 6: International Association of Impact Assessment.

case example

Wytch Farm Oilfield

This development, the largest on-shore oilfield in western Europe at the time of its proposal by BP Exploration, was set in an area of considerable environmental sensitivity and tourism activity. The LPA was concerned that above-ground elements should either not be visible from publicly accessible viewpoints or should not be intrusive in the view. Planning approval was granted, and appropriate conditions were imposed. During construction and operation of the oilfield the planning officers regularly monitored the visibility of activities to confirm:

■ the predictions of the EIA
■ compliance with conditions.

Corrective actions were applied if necessary.

Photograph courtesy of BP, reproduced with permission. © BP

In order to secure a commitment to monitoring and follow-up, the planning authority may use planning conditions or obligations. Other regulators may require monitoring under other legislation, and planning authorities should not duplicate such requirements.

The EIA Circular refers to the fact that developers can apply or adopt EMSs to demonstrate implementation of mitigation measures and to monitor their effectiveness. Links between a developer's overall EMS and a site- or route-specific EMP should also be carefully planned and managed to be most effective. The follow-up arrangements will need to be reflected in the project management arrangements, and contracts prepared to construct and operate the development in order to be implemented.

Discussion

Monitoring can be undertaken at various stages of the EIA process. In the first instance, **baseline monitoring** may be required in order to assess or predict potential effects and to provide the basis for comparison with later, **post-construction monitoring**. This is essentially undertaken for two principal reasons:

- to ensure commitments to mitigation or predictions are met
- to correct unforeseen negative effects of development.

Compliance monitoring may also be undertaken in order to comply with other regulatory consents or licences: in this instance, it may be undertaken by other regulators.

It is clear that follow-up should be put in place when it is necessary, to ensure that mitigation is achieved as well as is assumed in the decision. Whether any follow-up should be undertaken (screening), and what it should cover (scoping), will first need to be decided. It is essential that the planning authorities or other regulators ensure that they have the arrangements and resources to monitor and enforce planning conditions and obligations. The resources required to do this could be reduced for local planning authorities (LPAs) and consultees if a developer can report the results of its monitoring and follow-up activities regularly to local authorities and other stakeholders.

The results of monitoring on a project by a developer can be fed into the design of future projects and also improve the quality of future ESs.

Again, although not a requirement, feedback from residents or affected communities will be useful to ensure that issues are identified and corrective action taken, and also to be able to demonstrate to other communities best practice and actual effects.

Methodology

The need and proposals for follow-up should be explained in the ES, and drawn together in the environmental management section of the ES (see Chapter 5). This would describe what is proposed to be undertaken, who would undertake it, why, how and when. This may involve

case example

Coopers Edge, Gloucestershire

The development of a new neighbourhood of 1900 new homes, at a former airfield on the edge of Gloucester, has required mitigation to minimize significant effects on the adjacent species-rich grassland SSSI and Cotswolds AONB, on veteran trees, and on other rare and protected wildlife on and off site, and to prevent pollution of the brook running through the site. These measures were implemented through environmental monitoring and management plans for the construction phase and longer term, secured through planning conditions and a Section 106 agreement. Reports and regular liaison provide feedback on progress and the actual effects of the development to the two local authorities, parish councils, Natural England and the Environment Agency, keeping promises made in the ES. Public information and community liaison efforts ensure feedback directly to local people.

guiding principle

Follow-up proposals need to be explicit and targeted

To be effective, the predictions in the ES need to be quantified a combination of site attendance by an environmental clerk of works during construction, specialist monitoring surveys, and liaison with the developer's project management team and contractors.

The purpose of the follow-up should be decided in advance. For any identified environmental issue the methodology should be clearly focused on the effects which will be attributable to the development rather than other external or natural pressures or changes. It should be clear from the follow-up proposals and reporting that the results of monitoring of the actual effects of the development are to be used in managing the actual effects by implementing effective mitigation measures, and communicating the results to local authorities and other stakeholders.

Monitoring and follow-up in summary

■ Monitoring (including follow-up) is used to ensure compliance with planning consents or conditions, regulatory requirements or to check the effectiveness of mitigation.

■ It provides a means of correcting any unforeseen impacts.

■ It should be clearly focused on its objectives.

■ It should be committed to in the ES, detailed in an EMP/EAP and linked to the developer's EMS.

2.11 Environmental Statement: Preparation, Content and Review

Introduction

The preceding sections in this chapter have outlined the various components of the EIA process. This section summarises the procedural process highlighting the various legislative requirements and possibilities. It suggests a format for the ES itself, and finally introduces various review methods for checking the quality of the ES. These review methods may be used by developers, their consultants, local authorities or local communities to ensure that the ES is a robust statement of the environmental effects of the proposal.

Legislation

The various procedures required during the EIA process are discussed in the EIA Circular Guide to Good Practice. The required contents of an ES are presented in the Schedule 4 of the Regulations, which is reproduced here in Appendix 4 for ease of reference. Schedule 4 is in two parts: Part I describes such information as may reasonably be required, and Part II indicates the minimum information which must be reported in an ES.

Summary of preparation procedures

■ **Screening:**
- Deciding if EIA is legally required.*
- Is it a Schedule 1 or 2 development?
- If Schedule 2, is it in a 'sensitive area' or likely to give rise to significant environmental effects?

■ **Planning authority** informs statutory consultees of the intended proposal.

■ **Scoping:**
- Identifying the topics to be addressed in the EIA and reported in the ES, and the methods proposed to assess them.

■ **Consultation:**
- Initial consideration of alternatives and mitigation.
- Provision of available environmental information to the developer by statutory consultees.
- Consultation with statutory and non-statutory consultees and the general public.
- Consideration of exhibitions and other publicity.

■ **ES with non-technical summary (NTS)** to planning or regulatory authority.

Note that any permitted development rights, e.g. in the case of a statutory undertaker, do not apply if an EIA is required. Screening can also be directed by the Secretary of State.

Format and Content of the ES

There are no statutory requirements for the format of an ES, but it must contain the minimum information in Schedule 4 of the Regulations (see Appendix 4).

A suggested format for an ES which includes all the items as may reasonably be required and which is compatible with the review criteria (see below) as used by IEMA is as follows:

1. Non-technical Summary	Included within the ES and available separately; the preparation of an NTS is a statutory requirement. Written in plain English. This should reflect the structure, contents and findings of the ES itself. It should not be a promotional leaflet – but can legitimately include information about the applicant. It should include contact details for the applicant and details of where to obtain copies of the full ES. It should be illustrated with at least a location map and a site plan of the development.
2. Introduction	This should give details of the EIA team, including the applicant. This should clearly state that the document is an ES for the purposes of the EIA Regulations and why the scheme is considered to be an EIA development. Structure of the ES. Contact details of the applicant.

Environmental Statement

3. Description of the Project	Size, scale, physical characteristics, proposed land uses and infrastructure. Discussion of need and alternatives considered, including environmental design considerations. Programme, phasing, materials, resources, emissions. Site preparation, construction, operation, decommissioning and restoration stages as appropriate. Consultation undertaken, including any public exhibitions.
4. Methodology	How the key issues discussed in the ES were identified. This could include a copy of Scoping Report, Scoping Opinion and consultee responses as appendices. Discussion of how the scope has changed since the Scoping Report was published.
5. Assessment of Environmental Effects	This should include an analysis for each topic (as identified in the scoping process): ■ methodology ■ baseline conditions ■ potential effects and significance ■ mitigation and enhancement proposals ■ residual effects and significance ■ follow-up This could also include a description of the plans and policies which are relevant to the development. This could include development plans (local and regional), government guidance, national or international policies, or advice given by statutory environmental agencies.
6. Environmental Management	This draws together the environmental commitments made in the ES in a schedule, and provides an overall description of how the project would be managed throughout construction, operation/occupation and decommissioning/ restoration, where appropriate. It includes an outline EMP which describes arrangements for follow-up monitoring, evaluation, management and communication. This can be used by planning authorities for identifying potential planning conditions/obligations and by contractors as an indication of environmental requirements.
7. Appendices	Bibliography or references used. Abbreviations used in the ES. Glossary – this should be relatively brief since the document should be understandable to the non-specialist. Scoping Report, Scoping Opinion and consultee responses. Technical appendices – details of technical data.
8. Figures	Plans, maps, illustrations.

The assessment of individual topics is described in Chapter 3, but the description of the project itself is important and discussed in Chapter 4. The following is a checklist of items to be included, focusing throughout on those elements of the development which could have an environmental effect.

1. **Nature, purpose, need**

   - Function and economic context.
   - Alternatives considered – strategic, process, locations and criteria for choice.

2. **Land-use context**

   - Broad description of the site and its environs.
   - Topography and location.
   - Other similar developments in the locality.

3. **Characteristics of the development**

   - Size and scale parameters, land uses, amount of development, layout, building and landscape design.
   - Access and movement links.
   - Environmental design and mitigation.
   - Utilities.
   - Employment – during construction and operation/occupation.
   - Operational hours and procedures.

4. **Programme and phasing (including alternative options)**

   - Construction:
     - frequency of operations that may cause nuisance
     - traffic
     - materials
     - environmental management and mitigation
   - Operation/occupation:
     - number of occupiers, employees
     - traffic
     - resource, energy used
     - materials
   - Decommissioning.
   - Restoration.

This section should be richly illustrated with photographs, maps, figures, plans, sketch impressions or photomontages of the proposals.

The ES itself can follow any format. Common formats are:

- single A4 document with appendices, including illustrations
- A4 document with accompanying A3 landscape appendix for illustrations.

Recent ESs have been produced as CDs, although this is unlikely to replace the need for paper copies entirely. It is worth discussing preferred formats with the planning authority.

Whatever format is selected, each volume should be clearly annotated to indicate the overall ES structure, e.g. Non-technical Summary Vol. 1 of 3 (Vol. 2, ES; Vol. 3, Appendices). Ideally, the ES itself should be a 'stand-alone' document without the need to refer to other documentation. It should be visually attractive and easy to read and understand.

Environmental Statement

Rochdale

Rochdale MBC gave outline planning consent for the development of a business park on a greenfield site outside Rochdale on the basis of being in accordance with local plan policy. The decision was challenged in the High Court by third parties on the grounds of insufficient information. It was held that EIA is carried out on development *proposed* not on development which *might* be carried out based on purely illustrative details. The result of this is that ESs for outline planning applications must be provided *with sufficient details and certainty of the proposals* to assess and have full knowledge of the main or significant environmental effects before planning permission is granted. The revised application with an extended ES, proposed masterplan layout and schedule of development quantum was submitted. It was challenged again, but the court held that the ES was now adequate as it had assessed the likely significant effects of the development, based on details which were tied to the planning permission by conditions.

Rochdale MBC ex parte Tew [1999], Milne [2000]

There are no limits to the length of ESs, but good practice experience indicates that they should be between 150 and 200 pages in length. This length ensures that the ES is readable without becoming cumbersome; technical detail can be reported in appendices. They can be longer for complex projects involving multiple issues. ESs of less than 50 pages are unlikely to have examined the issues in sufficient detail.

Level of detail: In all cases, whether for a detailed or an outline application, sufficient information must be provided in the ES for the determining authorities and regulators to reach a reasoned decision on the acceptability of the proposals.

Timescale: This should include the:

- construction period and phases
- time through to full occupation or operation
- time for mitigation to be effective, e.g. planting to mature
- restoration or decommissioning if appropriate.

Style: While the NTS has to be readable by the general public, the ES itself has to be understandable by the non-specialist. This can best be achieved by avoiding the use of jargon and by clearly explaining technical terms in a glossary.

The ES should be unbiased and objective, with any qualitative statements defined, e.g. a 'minimal' visual impact could be defined as affecting no public views. Remember, an ES 'accompanies' a planning application: it is not a 'supporting document'. At all times the audience should be borne in mind.

Reviewing the Quality of Environmental Statements

If the accompanying ES is considered inadequate, it will not necessarily invalidate the planning application: further information can be requested. If substantial further information is requested by the planning authority but not then provided by the applicant, the application can be refused on these grounds. The developer can also voluntarily supplement the ES with additional information. The EIA Regulations now require that further information of a substantive nature (either required by the LPA or volunteered by the developer) is subject to the same publicity requirements as the ES (see Section 2.12 below). The majority of local authorities have limited experience as to what to expect from an ES. For this reason, a number of review packages (which have been developed out of research into ES quality) are available. The most commonly cited is Lee and Colley (1990, 1992), *Reviewing the Quality of Environmental Statements*. The review may be carried out by the LPA, IEMA or by independent consultants. IEMA is frequently and regularly engaged to independently review the quality of ESs, and it uses its own package, initially based on Lee and Colley. Both packages have been updated and revised. Such an approach is useful for those LPAs with limited experience of ESs or those with limited resources to handle a number of applications. Where external reviews are undertaken, the LPA will need to consider these carefully and apply its own experience of the development and its locality to determine whether or not the ES is adequate.

The review criteria used in such packages are reproduced as Appendix 5.

ESs are generally reviewed independently by two reviewers, who then compare and collate results. Sometimes, additional experts are appointed to carry out certain aspects of the review for especially complex or technical ESs.

As well as being of assistance to planning and regulatory authorities, the review process often helps the applicant as an internal audit on the content and adequacy of the ES. It should be noted that such reviews are often judging the ES against 'best practice'. If an ES does not achieve top grades according to 'best practice' it could still be compliant with the EIA Regulations.

Also, such reviews do not usually involve site visits or review of consultee comments, unless these aspects are specifically included.

A major criticism of review packages is that, having been set up to review quality, they tend not to encourage innovation in EIA technique since ESs have become standardised in order to conform with the packages. However, since such packages were introduced the overall quality has improved – although whether this is due to the review process or to the greater experience of applicants and their advisors is a matter of conjecture.

Further information
www.iema.net
EIA Review Check List 2001.
www.europa.eu.int

ES preparation, content and review in summary

- Plain English and readable.
- Appropriate length with technical details in separate appendices.
- In sufficient detail to assess significant impacts – whether detailed or outline application.
- Consider internal or external audit review.

2.12   Environmental Statement: Submission

The EIA Regulations allow for an ES to be submitted with or after the planning application (or 'subsequent application', see Section 2.2). It is in the developer's interest to submit an ES at the same time as the application, since this will facilitate decision-making as soon as possible. The LPA will suspend consideration of the application until the ES is submitted. **If an ES is submitted after the application, the applicant rather than the LPA becomes responsible for publicity**. This section is concerned with planning regulations; the determining process varies with other regulations and determining bodies and authorities.

guiding principle

Programme a timescale for decision-making into the project schedule

When an ES is submitted at the same time as the planning application (or 'subsequent application'), the developer must also submit a number of other copies of the ES:

- sufficient to send one to each of the statutory consultees (or the developer can forward one copy each directly to the statutory consultees and advise the LPA who they have issued them to)
- two copies for the LPA to send to the Secretary of State
- copies for the general public (a reasonable charge may be made)
- copies of the NTS freely available.

Environmental Statement: Submission

Submission of ES with the planning application

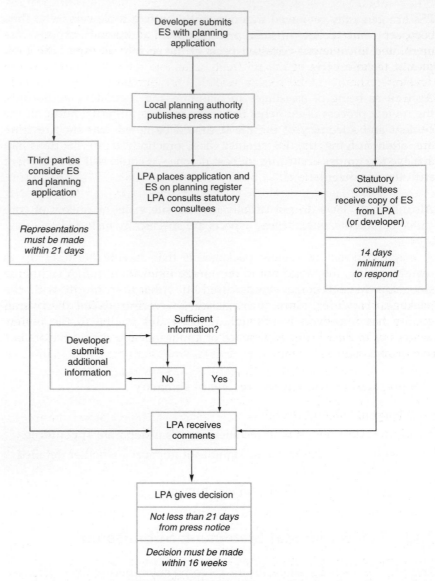

Adapted from DETR 2000. EIA: A Guide to Procedures. Crown copyright: reproduced with permission of the Controller of Her Majesty's Stationery Office

The LPA must publicise receipt of the ES and application as follows:

- notice in the local newspaper
- notice at or near the site of the proposed development
- specifically notify any particular persons affected by or with an interest in the application, who are unlikely to become aware via the site notice or the local newspaper, e.g. national bodies promoting environmental protection such as non-governmental organisations
- place the application and ES on the planning register and on its website (where it is used for such purposes)
- notify and send the ES to the statutory consultees
- place the ES in an accessible location, e.g. at the LPA's offices, public library or post office, for consideration by the general public.

Note: if the ES is submitted after the planning application (or 'subsequent application', see Section 2.2), the applicant becomes responsible for publicity.

Key fact

Notices should include:

- details of the ES
- where available
- timescale for receiving comments
- charge for ES
- address for comments

The developer may send copies of the ES directly to the consultees. When submitting the application, the developer must inform the LPA of all names (statutory and non-statutory) to which a copy of the ES has been sent. The public must be provided with an opportunity to comment, and any views expressed must be taken into account. The LPA should make a copy of the ES freely available for inspection, and the developer should make copies available for purchase at a reasonable charge.

The LPA must decide if the ES includes sufficient information to enable the impacts of the proposed project on the environment to be assessed: this is necessary for both outline and detailed planning applications, and also subsequent applications (see Section 2.2). The LPA can require further information to be provided, or evidence to substantiate that information in the ES. Clearly, this will delay decision-making; the principle has been confirmed through UK case law (R. *v.* Rochdale MBC).

The LPA must take account of the environmental information (which includes the ES, consultation and public comments on it, and any further and additional information to the ES) when reaching its decision and so must thoroughly read and understand the ES. A structured review process utilising review criteria can provide a systematic and transparent way of evaluating if the environmental information is sufficient to reach a decision (see Section 2.11 above).

Where external reviews are undertaken, the LPA will need to consider these carefully and apply its own experience of the development and its locality to determine whether or not the ES is adequate. The LPA must reach a decision within 16 weeks (not 13 weeks, as for other major planning applications) from the date of receipt of the ES, unless the developer agrees to a longer period. The LPA must consider the views of the general public and the statutory consultees. Planning conditions and/or obligations may be used to ensure implementation of mitigation and monitoring commitments. Many LPAs have limited resources to monitor or enforce implementation, so a commitment to monitoring and management of actual effects and to communicate the results of follow-up by the developer and/or contractor, e.g. through an EMP, indicates self-regulation and environmental responsibility.

Committee Report

Having received the planning application (or subsequent application), the ES and any review, together with representations from consultees and members of the public, the local authority planning case officer will make a report and recommendation to committee. It should be noted that councillors are not obliged to follow officer advice! The structure of such a report is facilitated and can be guided by a competently prepared ES. Typically, it might be as follows:

- summary
- background
- the site and its environs
- development proposals
- planning context – compliance with policy

Environmental Statement: Submission

- summary of environmental impacts
- views of consultees and public
- views of other authorities
- planning officer's comments
- recommendation, including draft conditions if approval is recommended.

Appeals and call-ins are the same for planning applications whether the EIA Regulations apply or not – the developer has the right of appeal to the Secretary of State against an adverse decision or against a failure to determine within the time period. The Secretary of State may call in the application or request a developer to provide further information. The LPA must publish its decision with the main reasons and considerations, a description of the main mitigation measures and information about the public participation process (and procedures for challenging the decision!) in the local press and on its website (where used).

Key fact

The LPA cannot rule that an application is invalid because it considers that the ES does not include sufficient information to assess the environmental impacts. It can, however, refuse the application if there is not enough information to assess the effects

Chapter 3

Environmental Topics

Each element of the environment likely to be affected by development is considered in a similar way – responsibilities, standards and legislation, the methodology including baseline studies, potential effects, assessment and significance of impacts, mitigation, further guidance and information. Each section is designed to be self-contained. The environmental topics are listed as presented in the Regulations. Interactions between topics and sustainability are drawn together in the final section.

3.1   Introduction

This chapter looks at each element of *'the environment'* recognised by the European Directive as likely to be affected by development, and provides guidance on the possible approaches to impact assessment on each in turn. Such work should only be carried out by experienced and qualified assessors in the relevant field and with membership of an appropriate professional body.

The chapter aims to introduce specialist environmental topics to:

- local authority planners and other regulators
- developers/investors and their advisors
- communities and special interest groups
- specialists within the Environmental Impact Assessment (EIA) and design team, to aid understanding of each others' approach
- students of specialist topics, to aid understanding of how their specialism fits into EIA
- EIA co-ordinator, to provide a quick and easy reference.

These introductions provide no more than an overview of the topics, and the reader is guided to more detailed information and guidance throughout; relevant organisations, sources of information and publications are also detailed in the appendices.

The environmental topics are presented separately, since there is specific legislation, guidance and standards applicable to each. Similarly, each topic has characteristic methods and timescales of study, including surveys, and assessment of impacts and significance. Nonetheless, the interactions between environmental issues are a requirement of the EIA Regulations, and this is discussed in Section 3.11.

The interrelationships between environmental factors are also recognised by other legislation which operates in parallel with EIA for the most complex and potentially polluting industries: the Pollution Prevention and Control (PPC) regime requires environmental assessment of best available techniques (BAT), including:

- consumption and nature of raw materials

Contents

Key fact

Pollution Prevention Control (PPC) is a regulatory regime for controlling pollution from certain industrial activities. Whilst recognising that the planning and pollution control systems are separate but complementary, PPS23, *Planning and Pollution Control*, advises that EIA and other regulatory requirements such as PPC should be carried out at the same time. PPC is incorporated into the framework of the Environmental Permitting Regulations (EPR) (Department for Environment, Food and Rural Affairs (Defra) 2008)

Links

Social Impact Assessment (SIA)

Health Impact Assessment (HIA)

Cumulative Effects Assessment (CEA)

Sustainability Appraisal (SA)

Integrated Assessment (IA)

Environmental Risk Assessment (ERA)

- energy efficiency
- waste issues
- accidents and risk
- site restoration.

Sustainable development (SD) has become enshrined within the UK planning and development management system. SD aims to integrate environmental, social and economic issues, thus recognising the inter-relationships between the environment and socio-economic factors. Accordingly, sustainability and EIA is discussed within considerations of interactions in Section 3.11.

3.2 Population

Introduction

The 1999 European Directive refers to '*population*' in terms of an aspect of the environment that may be affected by the development (the 1985 Directive had used the term '*human beings*'). However, Article 3 of the 1999 Directive still refers to the effects on human beings. Annex III of the Directive, which describes selection criteria for determining the need for EIA, refers to '*the environmental sensitivity of geographical areas ... in particular the absorption capacity of the natural environment ...* [including] *(g) densely populated areas*'.

> *EIA: A Guide to Procedures* (Department of Environment, Transport and the Regions (DETR) 2000) provides a checklist of matters to be considered for inclusion in an environmental statement, including the following:
>
> **Information describing the project**
> Numbers to be employed and where they will come from.
>
> **Information describing the site and its environment**
> Population – proximity and numbers.
>
> **Assessment of effects on human beings**
> Change in population arising from the development, and consequential environmental effects (this also refers to visual effects, effects of emissions, effects of noise, effects on transport).

Discussion

It may be understood from this that the 1999 Directive is mostly concerned with *demographic changes* rather than socio-economic or health effects: this is indicated by the change from the use of '*human beings*' to '*population*'. This section therefore focuses on population. However, major developments clearly have the capacity to affect or displace communities, the study of which is generally known as Social Impact Assessment (SIA). This area of expertise, which is often also linked with Health Impact Assessment (HIA) and Environmental Health Impact Assessment (EHIA), has grown in recent years in parallel with EIA.

Key fact

Planning authorities are increasingly requesting sustainability assessments with mitigation and/or enhancement commitments set out in a sustainability strategy, to accompany planning applications for major development proposals.

For the purposes of this guide, we regard SIA as a separate topic outside EIA. Nevertheless, it is clearly an issue which should be of principal concern to planning authorities and regulators, who may well wish to see such appropriate studies commissioned or reported separately with respect to a development proposal. It is then the role of these authorities – or the inspector at public inquiry – to make judgements addressing the relative effects of development on communities and the natural or heritage environment. Having said this, if a proposed development is likely to have an effect on the health of a community, then that is clearly an issue to be addressed in the EIA (see below).

The British Medical Association (BMA) recommended that an EIA should be judged inadequate unless it shows that the implications for occupational and public health have been addressed. There is no statutory requirement for developers to undertake an HIA. However, the Chartered Institution of Water and Environment Management suggests in a policy statement that ' ... *one of the benefits of HIA to developers is that it is able to demonstrate positive effects for the community... EIA tends to highlight the negative impact aspects. Thus, the major incentive for developers is the possibility that HIA can be used to promote the proposal*'.

Town and Country Planning Acts focused on and emphasised social issues before the concept of '*environment*' was introduced, and some may contend that to amalgamate the two areas would be a retrograde step. Planning legislation and guidance are now founded on sustainable development such that all impacts can be identified for proposed development and its cumulative effects assessed as a whole – assessing the overall sustainability of a proposal.

Regulators and Consultees

The Health and Safety Executive (HSE) notifies planning authorities of areas which contain toxic, highly reactive, explosive or inflammable substances. It will be consulted by the planning authority on any development proposal which is likely to result in a material increase in the number of persons living, working within or visiting such a notified area.

The key consultees, however, are the planners and environmental health officers (EHOs) in the local authority. Other consultees may include the emergency services and port health authorities.

Potential Effects

A new development in less populated areas may have beneficial as well as negative effects. The development may stem the outward migration of the population, providing new life to the local economy and community; alternatively, the influx of newcomers or those with special skills not available locally may lead to conflict of interest and potential community strains. Certain development types, e.g. reservoirs, may result in the involuntary displacement of communities or individuals on a temporary or permanent basis. On the other hand, they could also provide community benefits in the form of fishing and other forms of recreation or enterprise. It is therefore important to be able to identify the relationship between anticipated population levels and those existing, the timescale over which the changes will take place and the

case example

Kings Cross Redevelopment

The London Borough of Camden requires HIA of major policy or infrastructure developments. HIAs were carried out for the redevelopment of Kings Cross.

– www.camden.gov.uk

"

HIAs and their materiality to planning decisions have become ' ... an extremely important and contentious area of EIA and planning regulation. For major developments, local planning authorities have required health impact studies to be prepared'

– Friends of the Earth 2005. *EIA: A Campaigner's Guide* "

Further information

Vanclay, F. and the International Association for Impact Assessment 2003. *International Principles for Social Impact Assessment*

BMA 1998 *Health and Environmental Impact Assessment*

Health Impact Assessment. www.dh.gov.uk

Key legislation

- Control of Substances Hazardous to Health Regulations 2002
- Control of Major Accident Hazards (Amendment) Regulations 2005

case example

Port Health Authority

For a proposed new treated discharge to an estuary, the Port Health Authority took a particular interest in the effects of the discharge on shell fisheries and recreation

case example

Proposed Windfarm

A proposed windfarm in Wales was opposed by the community, citing a number of grounds, including the need to consider the flicker effect of the blades on a member of the community who suffered from epilepsy

ability of the existing infrastructure to absorb such changes. Other effects will include potential dominance, coalescence or severance of settlements and communities and effects on property values.

Elements of proposed developments that may have an effect on the health of members of the community – especially those sick or infirm, should be addressed in an EIA. However, they are notoriously difficult to predict, since health changes can be caused by a variety of (often pre-existing) conditions, and changes may be very small. Links between environmental change and health are also difficult to confirm or quantify. There is frequently a fear of the unknown and a perceived risk – which is difficult to disprove and which those opposed to a scheme may exploit to gather support for their opposition.

The most effective approach is to consider local environmental quality standards – which are designed to protect environmental health – and to estimate if changes will cause these levels to be exceeded.

It is important to recognise the interaction between effects when addressing population issues: issues such as air, noise and landscape, in particular, may have effects on the community – not always of a negative nature.

Methodology

Baseline Studies

Data will be required on the characteristics and trends of the local population in terms of age, sex, marital status, socio-economic status, skills, and vulnerable or sensitive members of the community.

Data will also be required on existing infrastructure (in the case of outward migration, this will be required for the relocation area): housing and property values; schools; hospitals; services (water, gas, electricity, sewerage, telecommunications); transport provision and parking; shops and other commercial needs, e.g. banks, garages; and entertainment.

The Highways Agency (2000) *Guidance on Methodology for Multi-modal Studies* (GOMMMS), for example, requires community facilities to be addressed. Footpaths, rights of way and other recreational facilities should be identified and considered. However, views from footpaths are strictly a landscape issue – see Section 3.9.

The environmental boundaries for these baseline studies are clearly going to vary. While they will best be agreed with the planning authority, individual catchments may include travel-to-work times, Primary Care Trust area, education areas, etc. Consultation by means of questionnaires or notices in local journals and websites may be most effective at estimating these boundaries.

Project Proposals

These must describe or estimate the potential for population immigration. This will be related to the various phases of the development, i.e. construction, operation/occupation and restoration (where applicable), and how much the needs of the development can be met from the indigenous population. Secondary effects of others being drawn to the area to provide support services also need to be considered. In most instances, local communities will be concerned to ensure that they are able to benefit from new employment opportunities, and the developer or local agencies may seek to provide training if the working population does not already possess the necessary skills. If this assessment predicts a population increase, its mix (see above) and relative requirements must be estimated.

Impact Prediction and Significance

From the above, the demand for services and infrastructure over and above those existing can be estimated. The scale of differences will indicate the significance of the effects in terms of percentage change over time. It is important to remember that some changes will potentially take many years to take effect, and it is also important to take into consideration variations in culture which may be implied by immigration into a locality. If new housing on a large scale is required, this indirect impact will clearly need detailed assessment in terms of land allocation and environmental impacts.

Mitigation

If significant change is predicted as a result of the proposals, it is essential that new provisions or changes are planned, managed and provided for. New employment opportunities should be offered to the local community in the first instance so as not to increase the strain or pressures on existing services, e.g. transport or housing. Mitigation can take the form of strategic alternatives, design or operation. For reasons referred to above, monitoring of effects and implementation of mitigation strategies is essential for social issues.

Sources of information	
Type	*Source*
Demographic data	Office for National Statistics, planning authorities
Housing stock	Housing department (local planning authority), estate agents
Infrastructure	Utility undertakers
Commercial facilities	Chambers of Commerce, Economic Development Department (planning authority),
Education	Education department (planning authority)
Health provision	Primary Care Trusts
Health and safety	Health and Safety Executive
Emergency services	Police, Fire Service, Maritime and Coastguard Agency, Mines Inspectorate
Environmental standards	Environmental Health Department (local planning authority), Environment Agency, Natural England

Key Features

■ Population is concerned with demographic changes and consequential environmental effects (visual, emissions, noise, transport, etc.).

■ SIA is a specialist study beyond the scope of EIA.

■ EHIA and Environmental Risk Assessment are closely related studies.

■ Early and continued consultation is needed to allay fear of the unknown from local communities and to promote proactive participation.

3.3 Noise and Vibration

Introduction

Our ability to hear sound is one of the means by which we gather information about our surroundings. From the earliest stages of development of the human species, sound has been used to warn of impending danger. However, evolution has seen our use of sound become much farther reaching. Sound still provides essential information about our surroundings, but now it also provides a means of communication through speech and a means of recreational enjoyment through music and the spoken word. Indeed, there are numerous sounds detectable by the human ear that bring pleasure: the sound of laughter, birds singing and music. However, there are also an ever-increasing number of sounds that can cause annoyance: the sound of industry, a pneumatic drill, heavy traffic, a car alarm or music breaking out at 2 a.m. Such unwanted sounds are generically termed 'noise'. The increased impact of noise on society may in part be due to a general increase in noise and in part due to a reduced tolerance of society towards noise. Whatever the root cause, it has become clear over the past few decades that noise is now a serious environmental issue that must be addressed.

Noise in the environment is tackled on two fronts:

■ Across all EU Member States, existing noise environments are being mapped to provide a baseline against which to judge future strategic noise mitigation schemes. It is written into EU legislation, now transposed into the legislation of all Member States, that the first round of strategic noise management action plans had to be submitted to the EU for approval by 2008. Some plans will be aimed at retaining existing areas of tranquility, whilst others will target reductions in existing high-noise environments. The legislation further requires that noise maps and their associated strategic noise management action plans be reviewed on a five-yearly basis.

Notwithstanding any long-term strategic approaches to environmental noise management that are necessarily retrospective in their application, the primary instrument for controlling any increases in noise remains the planning system. There are few new developments that do not give rise to noise impacts at some stage. As a result, the EIA Regulations require noise and vibration emissions from developments to be described, together with the resultant noise and vibration levels at potentially affected receptor locations and their effects.

Noise terms and concepts

- *Sound* consists of pressure variations in the air detectable by the human ear. The unit of measurement of sound pressure is the decibel (dB). Pressure variations have two characteristics, frequency and amplitude.

- Sound *amplitude* is heard as volume or loudness. It is the excess of pressure over the local atmospheric mean at any instance. It can be measured as a sound power, intensity or pressure.

- Sound *frequency* is heard as pitch or tone. It is the speed of pressure variation in the air measured in hertz (Hz, cycles per second). The range audible to humans is approximately 20–18,000 Hz. However, human hearing is not equally sensitive to sounds at all frequencies. Maximum sensitivity lies within the 500–5000 Hz range, important in speech communication.

- Sound *power* is an inherent property of a machine or process. A compressor or a jet engine at a certain throttle or load setting generates a certain amount of sound energy, irrespective of environmental factors. The sound power level is usually measured in decibels relative to a standard.

- Sound *intensity* is the amount of sound energy passing through a unit area. Measurement is technically difficult and is rarely used in environmental noise assessment.

- Sound *pressure* is the instantaneous excess of pressure over the mean atmospheric pressure caused by the passing of a wave of sound energy – in contrast to sound power, which is a function only of the source of sound, sound pressure is influenced by intervening environmental variables. The sound pressure level is usually measured in decibels relative to the lowest sound pressure audible to humans (i.e. the threshold of hearing). Thus, a sound pressure level of 0 dB equates to the threshold of hearing.

It is the **sound pressure** *level* that is almost exclusively referred to in EIA when assessing the potential impact of sound.

Summary of Terms Used in EIA

- In EIA it is important to determine the loudness experienced by people rather than the physical magnitude of the sound. The human ear is not equally sensitive to sound at all frequencies. In order to make sound measurement comparable to the sensitivity of the ear, the reduction in sensitivity to high and to low frequencies has to be introduced by weighting. The commonly applied weighting is A-weighting, and is internationally standardised.

- A-weighted sound pressure levels in the natural and built environment range between 0 and about 120 dB. Because the scale is logarithmic, decibels do not add and subtract arithmetically. A doubling or halving of sound pressure equates with a 3 dB increase or reduction in level.

- The sound level terms most commonly used in EIA are as follows:

  - $L_{A10,t}$ is the level exceeded for 10% of the measurement period. It is an indicator of the noisier events, and is most often used to characterise road traffic noise.

– $L_{A90,t}$ is the level exceeded for 90% of the measurement period. It is an indicator of the underlying tranquility behind event noise, and is used to characterise the background noise in an environment.
– L_{Amax} is the instantaneous maximum level, and has no time dimension.
– $L_{Aeq,t}$ is an all-encompassing measure describing all of the noise in an environment, both steadily in the background and occurring in transient events. It is a description of the ambient noise level.

This section has focused on noise. Vibration is less commonly a significant issue in EIA, though it is an important factor in some circumstances such as piling in construction, blasting, soil compaction, and rail and road traffic. Vibration may be a major issue with regard to protected buildings and assessment of cultural heritage effects. As is the case for environmental noise, the measurement and assessment of environmental vibration should be undertaken by experienced specialists.

Discussion

Noise assessment to date has generally been carried out at the planning stage on a project-by-project basis, with the impact of a proposed development being assessed and mitigation measures proposed. However, little attention has been paid to the cumulative effects of environmental noise generated by human activity from the multitude of possible sources encountered in our everyday lives. Such sources include road traffic, railways, air transport, industry and recreation. Noise is a growing problem, and needs to be dealt with in a more holistic manner.

In recognition of the need to tackle noise pollution, the EU has issued a Directive relating to the assessment and management of environmental noise. Member States now have responsibility for developing their own methods and approaches to assessing the current noise environment in their state and for setting in place noise management action plans for the long-term management of noise in the environment. This responsibility of Member States includes providing information on noise to the public and developing additional indicators of impact, such as the percentages of the population exposed to noise at different levels. Within the UK, Defra is engaged on a National Ambient Noise Strategy.

Clearly, all of these initiatives have implications for noise impact assessment within EIA, potentially affecting the way noise assessments are carried out and the standards that are worked to. The direct noise impacts of an individual project will continue to be the focus of attention at the EIA stage, but these direct impacts will need to be examined within the wider context of area-wide noise management measures considered as part of wider strategies.

Regulators and Consultees

For noise impact assessments, the local EHO should be the principal point of contact. EHOs should be able to provide advice about key concerns or issues within the local area. They can also advise on the approach to the assessment, such as monitoring locations and potentially sensitive receptors, the noise indices to consider (e.g. L_{Aeqt}, L_{AIO}) and the time periods over which baseline noise monitoring and impact predictions should be made.

Depending on the nature of the impacts, other consultees may also need to be consulted. For example, if noise is likely to affect bird populations within a designated area, such as a Site of Special Scientific Interest (SSSI) or Special Protection Area (SPA), then Natural England and others should be consulted. Similarly, if the development is likely to generate levels of vibration that can cause structural damage to historic buildings, then English Heritage should be consulted.

Potential Effects

Noise and vibration impacts can arise during all phases of a project. For many developments, the most significant noise impacts often arise in the phases leading up to operation. Demolition, site preparation and construction often involve the use of noisy plant and activities such as piling and the transportation of materials by large numbers of heavy goods vehicles. During operation, noisy activities may subside and traffic might become the principal concern. However, industrial, and increasingly commercial and retail developments, might generate noise. Significant sources include air-handling machinery providing ventilation, heating and cooling, and sound systems in shops, bars and other entertainment premises. Activities such as mineral extraction can be persistently or intermittently noisy throughout the lifespan of the project.

Key fact

A change of 3 dB in a steady noise is the smallest perceptible under normal conditions, and a change of 10 dB corresponds to a doubling or halving of perceived loudness. The level of an intermittent noise changes as the number of events in a certain time varies: a doubling or halving in the number of events produces a change of 3 dB in level. A change of 1 dB is perceptible in an intermittent noise level because the perception of noisiness is a compound both of the noise level of each event and of the frequency of the events

Between 5% and 15% of the EU population suffers serious noise induced sleep disturbance

Effects of Sound on People

The potential health effects of environmental noise are summarised by the WHO as:

- interference with speech communications
- sleep disturbance
- disturbance of concentration
- annoyance
- social and economic effects.

The WHO (1999) *Guidelines for Community Noise* presents guideline benchmark values for environmental noise levels in specific environments. The noise levels relevant to residential dwellings are listed in the following table:

Specific environment	Critical health effects	L_{Aeq} (dB)	Time base (hours)	L_{Amax} (dB)
Outdoor living area	Serious annoyance, daytime and evening	55	16	–
	Moderate annoyance, daytime and evening	50	16	–
Dwelling, indoors	Speech intelligibility and moderate annoyance, daytime and evening	35	16	–
	Sleep disturbance, night-time	30	8	45
Outside bedrooms	Sleep disturbance, window open (outdoors)	45	8	60
School class rooms (*included for potential effects on concentration*)	Speech intelligibility, disturbance of information extraction, message communication	35	–	–

The WHO guidelines explain that the levels given are set at the lowest levels at which the onset of any adverse health due to exposure to noise has been identified.

Effects of Noise on Wildlife

Just as noise impact assessment on humans is made difficult by the variability of responses between different people and between different situations, noise impact assessment on wildlife is even more problematical, not least due to the problem of monitoring the response of wildlife to noise.

The only truly robust determinant to the impact of noise on wildlife is the long-term desertion of traditionally inhabited areas, or a reduction in breeding numbers. The most sensitive time for animals is during the nesting or breeding seasons. Animals that take flight whilst sitting on their eggs or tending their young can leave them open to predators, even if they return fairly quickly. However, many species of animals have been shown to habituate to noise of all types, including road traffic noise, aircraft noise or even the decreasing effectiveness with time of impulsive-type bird scarers, such as those used around airports.

Summary of Effects

Noise can lead to annoyance and disturbance such as interference with speech communication and interruption of rest and sleep. At extreme levels, it can induce hearing impairment, and under some circumstances it has been shown to affect physiological and mental health, performance and social behaviour. Noise can disturb wildlife and domestic animals. Ground vibration can provoke annoyance, and in extreme cases can lead to damage to buildings.

Methodology

Baseline Studies

Key fact

Sound measurements have to be carried out over sufficient time to get statistically reliable results.

Baseline noise or vibration survey results may fulfill any of a number of purposes. The baseline conditions might affect the proposed development (e.g. the noise exposure of housing development sites, requiring assessment under PPG24), so survey data might feed back into the development design process. The proposed development might be a source of noise or vibration, and assessment of its impact will involve comparison with the baseline conditions. In the case of road and rail developments, the noise impact might trigger statutory compensation, and the baseline condition is one of the factors determining eligibility. Each of these purposes might demand a particular approach to the design of the survey.

It should not be automatically assumed that a noise measurement survey is always the best approach to be adopted for any particular assessment. Due to the inherent variability in environmental sound fields, the results of such measurement surveys cannot always inform the decision to the required degree of certainty. The development of advanced noise-modelling techniques means that, in some cases, software tools may now provide viable alternatives to field measurements, particularly where the background noise environment is dominated by quite predictable sources of noise, such as road, rail or air traffic.

The ultimate aim of any noise impact assessment is to formulate an objective rating of the noise field in question in a manner that is both consistent and reliable for decision-making purposes. These ratings can be produced in a wide variety of ways based on the results of measurements or predictions, or a combination of the two. Environmental sound fields are inherently variable both in time and space as a result of the continually changing nature of the sound source and propagation effects that influence the total noise occurring at a point of interest. Unidentified or misunderstood variability creates the risk that any objective rating derived from a measurement or prediction will provide an incomplete representation of the sound field, ultimately increasing the likelihood of incorrect assessment.

Thus, addressing the risk of incorrect assessment outcomes requires an understanding of the factors affecting the noise field, and how these factors may change and contribute to variability of the noise field in question. Recognising these factors at the outset of an investigation provides the best opportunity to design assessment strategies that will most effectively reduce the risk of a misrepresentation and thus an incorrect outcome. Acknowledging that practical and technical constraints will often be a limiting factor, understanding the nature of the noise environment will provide a basis for gauging the relative merits and limitations of alternative assessment methodologies, including both quantitative (i.e. measurement and prediction studies) and qualitative considerations.

Any baseline study should identify existing sources of noise in an area and characterise variations in noise over time, e.g. variations between day and night, between weekdays and weekends or at different times of year, as appropriate. The scope of the studies will depend on the characteristics of the proposed development.

Survey sample durations should take into account the temporal stability of the noise climate. Where the ambient noise is steady, interval samples over a typical day may be sufficient. Where the ambient noise is variable, automatic monitoring over several typical days may be needed. Some sites, such as those close to railways or under flight paths, might exhibit stable, predictable ambient noise levels because of the dominant intermittent source, but variable underlying background noise levels.

While the greatest volumes of traffic resulting from a development may not occur during the night, this may be the time of the greatest noise impact. The noise indices to be measured will also vary, e.g. for roads the $L_{A10,18hr}$ index is generally used. The locations selected for noise monitoring also need to reflect the position of sensitive receptors and the area of impact, e.g. the study area for a proposed airport will be considerably larger than that for a new residential development. Sensitive receptors include residential areas, schools and hospitals.

In addition to temporal stability, sample locations should also take into account the spatial stability of the noise climate. In particular, the effects of local screening, including existing/proposed buildings that may

Proposed Energy Recovery Facility

The Environmental Statement for this proposal included an assessment of the effects of noise and vibration on over-wintering and resident bird populations. Birds such as lapwing, redshank and black-tailed godwit can react to disturbance by avoiding the area from which noise was emitted.

The proposed facility is located in close proximity to an SSSI, SPA, Special Area of Conservation and Ramsar site. The increase in noise during construction was predicted to make the foreshore unattractive for use by the majority of wildfowl and waders for the duration of that activity. Impacts were, however, only considered to be localized and short-term.

Key legislation and guidance

Control of Pollution Act 1974

Environmental Protection Act 1990

Noise Act 1996

Noise Insulation Regulations 1975, 1988

BS 7445:1991: *Description and Measurement of Environmental Noise*

BS 6472:1992: *Guide to Evaluation of Human Exposure to Vibration in Buildings*

BS 4142:1997: *Method for Rating Noise Affecting Mixed Residential and Industrial Areas*

BS 5228:1997: *Noise and Vibration Control on Construction and Open Sites*

BS 8233:1999: *Sound Insulation and Noise Reduction for Buildings – Code of Practice*

WHO 1999. *Guidelines on Community Noise*

PPC Regulations 2000

PPG24: *Planning and Noise*

Building Regulations

Environmental Noise (England) Regulations 2006

Environmental Noise (Identification of Noise Sources) Regulations 2007

EU Environmental Noise Directive 2002

Proposed Airport

The scoping exercise for a proposed airport identified the following potential noise sources:

- aeroplanes taxiing, taking off, flying overhead and landing
- vehicle movements within the airport
- traffic on surrounding roads
- trains serving the airport
- other miscellaneous activities

significantly affect background and/or ambient noise levels, should be considered when deciding on spatial sampling for noise surveys, to ensure that the selected sample location(s), be these for measurements or predictions, adequately represent the noise environment requiring assessment.

As already stated, baseline noise levels can also be calculated rather than derived from direct measurement. Calculation is possible where the existing environment is dominated by a single noise source, such as traffic, and a recognised methodology, such as the Calculation of Road Traffic Noise (CRTN), is available.

While baseline surveys will establish the existing noise climate of the area, it may also be necessary to project the baseline forward to a future year, such as the proposed year of opening or design year. This may need to take into account anticipated changes in the volume of traffic on nearby roads and other factors that may affect noise levels in the area.

Project Proposals

The description of the project proposals should be sufficient to identify all significant noise and vibration sources and for the level of noise or vibration to be predicted. It should also include the time periods when impacts are likely to arise, e.g. working hours during construction and operation, and a description of the characteristics of the noise.

Noise sources can, for example, give rise to high-pitched noise, low-frequency hums, or intermittent or continuous noise. The characteristics of the noise are important in determining peoples' reaction to them, i.e. the degree of nuisance they cause. The sound of traffic may become part of the general background noise that a person hears, while reversing alarms on construction vehicles or the sound of a pneumatic drill may be highly irritating. Noise with any information content, such as music or speech communication, is potentially annoying at any audible level.

Impact Prediction and Significance

The noise or vibration impacts should be assessed at a number of representative sensitive receptors. Worst-case conditions should be described with a commentary, where appropriate, on the risk of their occurring.

A number of standard prediction procedures are defined in relevant legislation and guidelines. These include the methods for the calculation of road traffic and railway noise, and for the prediction of construction noise. Prediction methods for other noise sources such as industrial and commercial installations and processes are not standardised, and it is important that the Environmental Statement (ES) reports the method chosen. In all cases, the input assumptions should be reported, including **source variables** such as emission factors, traffic flows, times of occurrence and diurnal patterns; **geographical variables** such as ground cover, topography, meteorological conditions and the presence of permanent barriers; and **receptor variables** such as the heights above ground of the locations for which calculations have been undertaken and whether facade reflections have been included.

An EIA method for evaluating road traffic noise is specified in some detail in the Highway Agency's *Design Manual for Roads and Bridges,* and aspects of the process can be adopted for other types of project. BS 4142 offers a method for evaluating noise from industrial and commercial sources, while various industry-specific guidelines are available for projects such as wind farms.

In the case of residential developments, a noise assessment will not only need to examine the impact of the development on the environment but also the impact of the surrounding environment on the development.

PPG24, *Planning and Noise,* introduces the concept of Noise Exposure Categories, to help local planning authorities with their consideration of applications for residential development.

When considering the significance of the impact, many EIAs only consider the resultant noise levels in relation to standards or guidelines, e.g. BS 4142, as it provides a method for assessing the likelihood of complaints. However, '*the likelihood of complaints*' depends on a number of factors in addition to the increase in noise levels, and these are often overlooked. Additional factors include the sensitivity of the receptor(s), the number of people/area affected, and the time and duration of the impact. Noise is often considered more acceptable during the daytime; however, it is not acceptable in the vicinity of schools or hospitals. Noise impact assessments also tend to define night-time as being between 11 p.m. and 7 a.m. However, this overlooks the sleeping patterns of shift-workers and infants.

Predicting vibration impacts is a complex process but models to help do exist. BS 7385-2:1993, *Evaluation and Measurement for Vibration in Buildings,* gives guidance on the levels above which building structures could be damaged. Disturbance to people can be assessed in accordance with BS 6472:1992, *Evaluation of Human Exposure to Vibration in Buildings.*

Mitigation

Noise impacts can be avoided through careful consideration of the site location, layout and design, the selection of appropriate plant or technology, or controls on working hours. Noise reduction measures include fitting silencers to noisy plant, screening off areas where particularly noisy activities are taking place, and erecting acoustic bunds or barriers. Compensation measures may include the provision of specific glazing for properties adversely affected by noise from a development.

Establishing good relations with the affected community is an important part of managing noise impacts. Warning of any particularly noisy activities should be provided during both the construction and operation phases. A procedure should be in place to allow people to register their complaints when adverse noise impacts arise, and for these complaints to be responded to (see also Chapter 5).

Vibration infrequently occurs at levels which require mitigation measures to be introduced. However, vibration control measures would include altering construction techniques to avoid piling, or using alternative forms of piling that generate less vibration; where explosives are used, the energy within each explosion could be reduced.

Key fact

Traffic noise is likely to be a factor in most development proposals. It is, therefore, important for the noise and traffic consultants to ensure that appropriate data for noise modelling is available early on in the EIA process

Further information

Department of Transport 1988. *Calculation of Road Traffic Noise*

Department of Transport 1995, 2007. *Calculation of Railway Noise*

The Working Group on Wind Turbine Noise 1996. *The Assessment and Rating of Noise from Windfarms*, ETSU-R-1997

Highways Agency 2008. *Design Manual for Roads and Bridges*, Vol. 11. *Environmental Assessment*

The local planning authority can control noise and vibration using powers under the Control of Pollution Act 1974 or the Environmental Protection Act 1990. Developments may also be carried out under conditional prior consents in accordance with Section 61 of the Control of Pollution Act (Section 61 agreements).

Sources of information	
Type	*Source*
Existing noise survey data and advice on scope of assessment	Local authority (environmental health department)
Technical advice	Institute of Acoustics
Relevant standards	British Standards Institute
Tranquil Area Maps	Campaign to Protect Rural England (CPRE)
National Noise Maps	Defra
Briefing and fact sheets	Environmental Protection UK

Key Features

- Noise and vibration impact assessment is a specialist activity, involving the use of complex calculations and technical terminology. It is, therefore, important to ensure that data are presented as clearly and systematically as possible, and that the effects of any increase in noise are clearly explained.

- Noise and vibration impact assessments should not simply determine whether a given threshold is met but should explain the actual effects on people, wildlife and buildings.

- The assessment of noise and vibration is interrelated with other topics in the ES, and close liaison with other EIA and design team members is required. For example, traffic data may be required to predict noise impacts; noise may affect wildlife; and noise mitigation measures, such as bunds, can have landscape and visual impacts.

3.4 Biodiversity (Flora and Fauna)

Introduction

The EIA Directive and Regulations refer to the need to assess impacts in relation to *'flora and fauna'*. The study of flora and fauna in relation to their habitats and the physical, chemical and other processes affecting them is generically termed 'ecology', and chapters relating to this in ESs have been generally titled 'Ecology' or 'Nature Conservation'. This is still sometimes the case. In recent years, however, the emphasis has been on 'biodiversity', which is the variety of life forms, the ecological roles they perform and the genetic diversity they contain. The body of legal protection for biodiversity has developed in the UK over the past quarter of a century or so, and recent changes to the law have significantly raised the strength of biodiversity protection, and hence its importance in EIA. A key reason for this has been the recent significant increase in general awareness of the critical state of much of global biodiversity.

"

For the purposes of this Convention: 'Biological diversity' means the variability among living organisms from all sources including, inter alia, terrestrial, marine and other aquatic ecosystems and the ecological complexes of which they are part; this includes diversity within species, between species and of ecosystems

– The Convention on Biological Diversity 1992 "

"

We are now in the midst of a man-induced mass extinction of biodiversity at a scale in keeping with the largest extinctions of prehistory

– The Millennium Ecosystem Assessment 2005 "

Ecological Impact Assessment (EcIA), whether or not part of formal EIA, should cover habitats, species, varieties and ecological processes within the site and its surroundings. Depending on the location of the development, the assessment should address both the *terrestrial (including the air space above the development) and freshwater aquatic environment*. For developments involving offshore changes to the environment, e.g. oil and gas projects and pipelines, marine fish farming, harbour works and such terrestrial activities that may involve discharges or potential spillages to the marine environment, assessment of likely effects on *marine or estuarine* ecosystems will also be required.

Assessment of potential impacts on biodiversity under the EIA Regulations should not be confused with legally required 'Appropriate Assessments' of potential effects on SPAs and Special Areas of Conservation (so called Natura 2000 sites) as required by the Habitats Regulations 1994 (as amended).

Key legislation and guidance

Habitats Directive 1992 (mandates the designation of Special Areas of Conservation)

Wild Birds Directive 1979 (mandates the designation of Special Protection Areas)

Habitats Regulations 1994 (as amended which implements the above Directives in England)

Wildlife and Countryside Act 1981 (as amended)

Protection of Badgers Act 1992

Hedgerow Regulations 1997

Countryside and Rights of Way Act 2000 (the CROW Act)

Natural Environment and Rural Communities Act 2006

UK Biodiversity Action Plan

PPS9: *Biodiversity and Geological Conservation*

Institute of Ecology and Environmental Management 2006. *Guidelines for Ecological Impact Assessment in the United Kingdom*

Appropriate Assessment

The Habitats Regulations prescribe that an 'Appropriate Assessment' be undertaken where it is considered that there would be 'likely significant effects' in relation to a Natura 2000 Site should a plan or project be implemented, whether alone or in combination with other relevant plans or projects. English Nature (now Natural England) provides guidance (see English Nature 1999, *Habitats Regulations Guidance Note 3*) on what may constitute 'significant effects' in this context, namely any action that could affect the conservation objectives of the features for which the site was designated. The guidance really sets this test of 'likely significant effects' as a 'broad filter' of projects excluding only those where any chance of such an effect would appear extremely remote. This definition of a significant effect differs from that used in general EcIA in the Institute of Ecology and Environmental Management (IEEM) Guidelines (see below). Adverse effects on conservation objectives caused by a plan or project could, but would not necessarily, result in an adverse effect on *site integrity* (see below) – a judgement that is made through the detailed study. The legal process and assessment is separate from that of the EIA. The duty of undertaking an Appropriate Assessment falls to the so-called 'competent authority', which in the case of applications made under the Town and Country Planning Act is the local planning authority (but varies greatly for EIA undertaken under other legislation). The competent authority usually makes this assessment largely based on information provided by the proponents of a development in the form of a 'Statement to Inform' the Appropriate Assessment. The information required for assessing potential effects on such important sites would need to be gathered by the proponents for the EIA in any case, but the presentation of the information may be different, and is often set out in more technical detail in an Appropriate Assessment with focus on the qualifying interests for which the Natura 2000 site was designated and the specific and stated conservation objectives for these interests.

Biodiversity (Flora and Fauna)

EIA Screening and Biodiversity

The selection criteria for screening Schedule 2 development draws special attention to the environmental sensitivity of geographical areas likely to be affected by development, having regard to the **absorption capacity of the natural environment**, including:

- wetlands
- coastal zones
- mountain and forest areas
- nature reserves and parks
- areas classified or protected under Member States' legislation, as well as by the Habitats and Wild Birds Directives.

The screening process uses the overused and ill-defined term 'significant', requiring that EIA be undertaken to assess '*likely significant effects on the environment*'. Effects that are considered sufficiently significant to trigger EIA are not by any means the only effects considered once an EIA is being undertaken. It is common practice for the EIA of features of ecological value to address potentially significant effects on features of much less than those at the 'EIA trigger level', to ensure a full reflection of planning policy at all administrative levels.

EIA and Development for Net Biodiversity Gain

The EIA Regulations have not as yet caught up with UK planning policy with respect to biodiversity. They set requirements only to assess potential adverse effects on valued biodiversity, requiring a description of the baseline conditions or state, the likely significant effects and measures envisaged to prevent, reduce or offset such adverse effects. It is more widely realised now, however, that biodiversity in the UK has been dramatically reduced with industrial and agricultural development, and the capacity of the remaining semi-natural environment to absorb adverse intervention without loss of ecological integrity in much of the UK has already been exceeded. In parallel, there has been a significant increase in the understanding of the value of biodiversity to man in terms of ecosystem goods and services, including (for example) effects on promoting human health and well-being.

Reflecting these changes in awareness, there have been recent major changes in law and policy towards reparation for the past losses and positive interventions for biodiversity, including through development schemes. The first key step in this regard was the bringing of the biodiversity action planning process into legal obligation for government.

Under Section 74(2) of the CROW Act the Secretary of State prepared a list of habitats and species important to biological diversity in England in accordance with the 1992 UN Convention on Biological Diversity. The Act placed a duty on the Secretary of State to be pro-active and *further the conservation of these species* directly or promote the taking of steps by others to do so. The list was compiled from the list of Priority Species under the National Biodiversity Action Plan (UKBAP).

> "
> *A body of research over the past two decades has firmly established that 'greenery and nature' are good for the health and well-being of modern man. Recent research in the UK has shown not only that untrained people can accurately detect varying levels of biodiversity in the landscapes and habitats that they experience, but that people benefit more in terms of well-being and reduced stress levels the more biodiverse the habitat*
>
> – Fuller, R. *et al.* 2007. *Psychological Benefits of Greenspace Increase with Biodiversity* "

> **Biodiversity Action Plans (BAPs)** prioritize species and habitats for conservation action over the next 20 years. BAPs are prepared by the statutory advisors on nature conservation (Natural England in England) in partnership with the other environmental regulators, local authorities and interested parties. They are prepared at national, regional, county and local levels; Habitat Action Plans (HAPs) and Species Action Plans (SAPs) are subsumed within BAPs. BAPs set targets which are used by local authorities and others to guide policy and strategy, the implementation of which in respect of biodiversity now also has a legal mandate. Recently, the UKBAP priority list was augmented to include 1149 priority species and 65 habitats (including, for example, familiar but much beleaguered features such as ponds and orchards), thereby creating a much more extensive list of key considerations in EcIA.

HAPs and SAPs under the UKBAP are in place or under preparation for all the listed habitats and species. This stipulation of the CROW Act has now been superceded by Section 41 of the Natural Environment and Rural Communities Act 2006 (although the associated lists have yet to be published). Interpretation of this recent law as national planning policy on biological and geological conservation is set out in PPS9 and the associated Government Circular (ODPM Circular 06/2005, Defra Circular 01/2005). As in the case of previous planning guidance, strong emphasis is placed by PPS9 and associated documents on avoidance of any net harm to designated sites and legally protected species remain material considerations. PPS9, however, extends this requirement for strong protection to a wider goal of *biodiversity* protection, and states:

> *'where significant harm to biodiversity cannot be prevented, adequately mitigated against, or compensated for – planning permission should be refused.'*

It is stated in Para 84 of the Circular that:

> *'The potential effects of a development, on habitats or species listed as priorities in the UK Biodiversity Action Plan, and by Local Biodiversity Partnerships are capable of being a material consideration in the preparation of regional spatial strategies and local development documents and the making of planning decisions.'*

Moreover, much more is also expected in PPS9 from development projects than mere avoidance or mitigation of harm:

> *'Development proposals provide many opportunities for building-in beneficial biodiversity or geological features as part of good design. When considering proposals, local authorities should maximise such opportunities in and around developments, using planning obligations where appropriate.'*

Of specific relevance to planning submissions and hence EIA, the associated circular states:

> *'In PPS9, the Government has indicated that local authorities should take steps to further the conservation of habitats and species of principal importance through their planning function (see PPS9 paragraphs 11 and 14). The lists of the habitat types and species subject to this duty were published by Defra in 2000 and comprise the list of species and habitats identified as priorities under the UK Biodiversity Action Plan.'*

Biodiversity (Flora and Fauna)

Taking these parts of PPS9 and the Circular together, planning authorities are clearly now required to actively seek in development proposals measures that aim to *promote* appropriate priority habitats and species listed in the UKBAP and, in accordance with the CROW Act, treat these as 'material considerations' as they have in the past treated species protected under the Wildlife and Countryside Act and Habitats Regulations.

In summary, national BAP species are both protected from adverse effects and encouraged through the expectation of positive measures towards their conservation achieved through development. These considerations have major implications for biodiversity appraisals within EIA, where the emphasis on significant positive effects/impacts is clearly increased.

In brief, in terms of biodiversity, EcIA should now show that developments, wherever possible, are 'too beneficial to refuse' rather than 'not quite bad enough to refuse'.

Regulators and Consultees

Key regulators and consultees

Natural England

Environment Agency

Local authority – nature conservation and biodiversity officers

Wildlife Trusts

Biodiversity records centres

Expert groups and individuals

The key statutory consultees on biodiversity-related issues on planning applications made under the Town and Country Planning Act in England are Natural England and the Environment Agency. The local authority will be consulted *de facto*. There are also other bodies and individuals that it is good practice and frequently invaluable to consult.

Natural England will be particularly concerned with the effects of development in or within 2 km of or likely to affect an SSSI or Local Nature Reserve. Natural England also holds information on and will be consulted on projects likely to affect Ramsar sites, National Nature Reserves, Local Nature Reserves and, in some cases, Ancient Woodlands. The Environment Agency will be consulted on most wetland sites, and is the main contact for certain BAP habitats and species. More and more local authorities now employ ecologists, and early consultation with these individuals about any development proposals is essential, not only in relation to what to protect but, now ever more importantly, what *biodiversity gain to secure*. Some authorities indeed are developing supplementary planning guidance that sets out schedules of financial penalties where biodiversity enhancements are not adequately in keeping with the scale of the development project in question.

The Wildlife Trusts (local branches of the Royal Society for Nature Conservation) should also be consulted as a matter of course, since they often hold local ecological information, especially about sites that are not SSSIs, candidate SACs or SPAs, e.g. County Wildlife Sites or Sites of Importance for Nature Conservation (SINC). The Wildlife Trusts are also key players in the development and implementation of subnational BAPs, and are frequently direct advisors to local authorities.

It is also always best practice to contact expert bodies and expert local natural historians about any potential impacts, positive or negative, relating to biodiversity, as they may often hold information not held by central Biodiversity Records Centres or possess local understanding of ecosystem functionality that it would otherwise take years to accumulate.

Relevant Biophysical Changes

To understand the potential effects of a development on biodiversity it is necessary to understand the biophysical changes that the development could cause, the nature and behaviour of any biodiversity that could be affected by these biophysical changes, and any inter-actions between all of the above. Moreover, these biophysical changes should be considered at all phases of development, including construction, operation and, where appropriate, decommissioning and restoration.

Habitat Loss and Fragmentation

The most obvious direct effect of development is the removal or change (e.g. through draining) of a habitat. This can be caused not only by changes within the final development footprint itself but also by changes along access routes or by contractors' compounds, working or lay down areas which may lie outside and sometimes at quite a distance from the final space required by the development. Typical direct losses may include individuals of species using the site, their feeding grounds, breeding areas or refuges.

While some direct losses may appear to be of a relatively minor nature, developments, especially linear ones such as roads, railways or pipe-lines, may sub-divide habitats or damage and remove links between them (wildlife corridors) such as hedgerows. Such effects can threaten the viability of species dependent on critical habitat features and characteristics for foraging or movement. Small or fragmented areas may be difficult to manage in traditional ways, e.g. heathland management by burning.

Pollution

Pollution of soils, water or air by direct discharge or spillage can alter a habitat (in some cases irrevocably) which is dependent on particular conditions. Effects may be chemical change, e.g. in pH of a watercourse altered by a new discharge, or physical, e.g. blanketing of a river bed or sensitive flora/invertebrate populations by particulates.

Microclimate

Developments, especially those which emit heat or light, can affect the local climate on which some species depend. For example, a new reservoir in an upland region can have a warming effect on surrounding habitats or species which may only thrive in cool conditions. Built form can completely alter the local microclimate.

Groundwater

Pollution or alteration in the level of groundwater on which habitats are dependent can indirectly affect them and the associated species.

River Regimes

Changes in rates of flow or flooding associated with new hardstanding or flood prevention schemes can affect surrounding habitats.

Disturbance

New developments bringing people in close contact with previously undeveloped areas can have particular detrimental effects via disturbance, accidents (such as fire) or trampling. Of concern in connection with new residential developments is the effect of pets (especially cats), vandalism, fly-tipping, recreational pressures and increased traffic.

Distant Effects

Habitats at some distance and apparently not affected by a development may be at risk. For example, emissions from a power station or industrial installation can affect pollution-sensitive lichens for tens or even hundreds of miles downwind.

Methods of EcIA

National Guidelines

The IEEM EcIA Guidelines for terrestrial and freshwater habitats have been endorsed by all the relevant government agencies/statutory advisers; further guidelines in relation to estuarine and marine habitats are being prepared. The following sections summarise the approach recommended in these guidelines. The guidelines refer to the assessment of potential impacts on ecological features, which may include any definable unit of biodiversity, most typically populations of species, particular habitats and, occasionally, ecosystems.

Scoping

The iterative scoping process involves both consultation with statutory and non-statutory consultees and progressive compilation of the results of baseline studies. The geographical extent of the studies and any subsequent surveys is particularly important to consider carefully and agree in advance, e.g. for wetland SSSIs, Natural England will generally require assessment within at least 2 km. The distance around a site appropriate for obtaining existing information will vary with context: in most EIAs, distances of between 500 m (for some urban sites) and 10 km (e.g. where Greater Horseshoe Bats may be affected) will apply.

The decision as to what ecological features to include within the scope of the assessment and the level of detail to collect in relation to each is a very important one, not only for the overall validity of the EcIA but also because of the constant limitations placed on the assessment by available resources of time and money. Scoping involves making several 'iterative' impact assessments at different stages throughout the whole EcIA process and hence developing an ever-improving understanding of potential biophysical changes that the development will cause, the values of different ecological resources and the likely responses of these resources to the biophysical changes. At the outset there also needs to be a decision, based on consultation and consideration of nature conservation policy at all geographical levels, as to the 'cut-off level of value' below which no, or only very fleeting, reference to potential impacts is to be made.

In many ESs, much time is spent in discussion of species with direct legal protection generally referred to as 'Protected Species'. Protected Species include species of fungi, lichens, bryophytes, higher plants, invertebrates, fish, amphibians, reptiles, birds and mammals listed (in England) in the Schedules of the Wildlife and Countryside Act 1981. The protection afforded to different species varies. Some are only protected against sale, others are fully protected against any injury, or any damage to their habitat. A number of species are also protected through listing on Schedules of the Habitats Regulations. These 'European protected species' are particularly strongly protected against adverse effects resulting from development, and are subject to stringent licensing procedures. Badgers and their setts are also protected under the Protection of Badgers Act 1992.

As with all topics in EIA, the utility of formally agreeing the scope of the EcIA with the assessing authority prior to completion and submission of the ES *cannot be overestimated.*

Baseline Studies

Data on biodiversity required for EcIA are now frequently well collated and available via local and regional Biodiversity Records Centres, with standard pro-formas and charging systems for data supply. Nevertheless, wide consultation and desk studies are still also required to meet best practice standards, as national and local expert societies, recorders and naturalists will often have more intimate knowledge of a locality or particular species in that locality than the statutory consultees and possess records not yet (or ever) submitted to Records Centres. (It is up to the statutory consultees and the assessor to assess the reliability of such information and place it in context.) County and national atlases, published registers and inventories and the now widely available aerial photographic databases should all also be consulted, although they will not necessarily be currently accurate, depending on the date of publication and recorder effort. It is important to remember that the sources of all information should be stated in the assessment, since data quality or timing may be questioned at a later date.

Desk studies, often in association with a preliminary site visit and inspection of aerial photographs and current and historic maps, are the key tools used to identify the necessity for field surveys. Whilst it may often be the case that existing data on Natura 2000 Sites, SSSIs or Nature Reserves may be abundant and thorough, this is by no means always the case. The level of detail of data required to properly assess the likely effect of a particular biophysical change is frequently not available.

The initial field survey undertaken in terrestrial habitats is frequently a Phase I Habitat Survey (Handbook for Phase 1 Habit Survey, Nature

Key fact

Whilst species with direct legal protection referred to as 'Protected Species' are material considerations in planning, legal protection is often an imperfect guide to biodiversity value. Many other ecological features may be as or more ecologically valuable as Protected Species and merit as great or greater attention in the EcIA, and greater emphasis should be placed, for example, on priority species listed in the national BAP

Biodiversity (Flora and Fauna)

Conservancy Council 1990). This identifies all the habitats within the area of search. Initial survey should result in lists of dominant species of plant (and sometimes animal), measuring areas of each habitat type and commenting on any features likely to be of particular local interest for wildlife or which do not fit one of the standard habitat classifications by use of target notes.

Phase I Habitat Survey is really designed, however, for large-scale habitat mapping rather than impact assessment. It makes allowance, for example, for areas to be surveyed 'remotely'. For this reason, the Institute of Environmental Assessment developed the concept of an Extended Phase I Habitat Survey, which, while using exactly the same mapping symbols, entails close investigation in the field to check for the presence or absence of valued fauna. Extended Phase I Habitat Survey is, therefore, the most common preliminary field survey method in most proposed development contexts, certainly for the proposed development footprint.

Phase 1 Habitat Survey should also generally be undertaken around project sites to provide at least an understanding of surrounding habitats and features that may be of value to mobile fauna which also utilise the site.

Key fact

Legal protection status of directly protected species often imperfectly reflects ecological value in the UK. Nevertheless, it is necessary to document the location of such species in any development proposals to ensure that proposals will be in compliance with the law.

The degree of statutory protection varies with different species

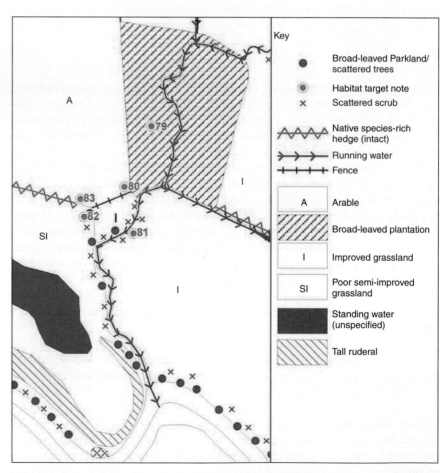

Example of map produced following Extended Phase 1 Habitat Survey with target notes (original in colour)

For developments including watercourses, River Corridor Surveys (RCSs) or River Habitat Surveys (RHSs) are often undertaken. The RCS maps habitats, vegetation and physical features of the bank and adjacent land in 500 m linear sections. Again, target notes are useful since the RCS tends to focus on dominant plant species. The RHS focuses on physical features, and by comparison of results with those in the national database may be used to put the value of a watercourse in its wider context. In the most sensitive sites, e.g. river SACs, exact locational mapping (using geographical positioning systems) of river habitats and features may be required. (Water quality evaluations using biological indicators or measurements are referred to in Section 3.6.)

Specific habitat guides should be used for sub-tidal habitats, and the Marine Nature Conservation Review categorises habitats in marine and estuarine environments. Further details of assessment methods will be addressed in the forthcoming IEEM Guidance on EcIA in such habitats.

If the desk and initial habitat studies identify particular valued features as being sensitive or vulnerable to development impacts, further detailed surveys will be required. At this stage the developer should be advised of the potential problem so that alternative approaches can be agreed or additional funding for survey be resourced. For example, there may be a need for a more detailed survey of plants to permit categorisation of communities according to the National Vegetation Classification (NVC) or of particular species of conservation value or with legal protection status, e.g. bats. Detailed criteria and outline survey evaluation methods for Phase 2 and other surveys are provided by IEEM (see http://www.ieem.net/survey-sources/). It should be noted that such guidance is constantly updated on different types of animal, plant and habitat. Expert advice is necessary in order to follow current best practice.

> **guiding principle**
>
> Ecological surveys have to be planned well in advance due to access and seasonal constraints

If data are collected regarding protected species, it is often advisable that such information is kept confidential to reduce the risk of subsequent illicit disturbance or damage. When contacting local recorders in this respect, it is important to reassure them that such information will only be made available to Natural England and will not enter the public domain without their prior consent.

Species vary in both number and in the ease with which they can be detected, both within and between years. It is very important, therefore, to carefully estimate the number of seasons or years of data that it will be necessary to collect to develop a baseline suitable for determining as clearly as possible (sometimes to a given level of statistical significance) whether any changes were caused by the proposals. It is also, therefore, important to plan surveys well in advance. For example, absence of breeding amphibians from a pond in one year does not prove that the pond is not important to amphibians, as various factors may lead them to choose to breed in different ponds in different years.

A hedgerow survey may be required for a hedgerow in excess of 20 years old and which meets one or more of the detailed criteria as set out in the Hedgerow Regulations 1997 and associated guidance notes (though these regulations do not apply in the case of development subject to planning applications). Consultation with early edition Ordnance Survey maps may be required for this survey to assist in the assessment.

> **guiding principle**
>
> Some surveys and assessments may require interaction between specialists, e.g. ecologists, hydrologists, archaeologists, and landscape architects

Biodiversity (Flora and Fauna)

Marine or estuarine conditions are subject to the continuous changes brought about by coastal processes, sedimentation, water quality and tidal flows. The Environment Agency, Defra or the water company may be able to provide background data. It may be necessary to undertake an underwater survey using vessels for sampling and divers for observation of topography and habitats.

It is important to record and discuss the implications of the date and time of surveys. If it is not the optimum time of year for a particular survey, the reasons should be stated, providing all necessary caveats regarding the level of comprehensiveness and reliability of the results. Field surveyors may need to be licensed when conducting surveys for protected species.

Valuation

Various values can be placed on biodiversity and many systems of ecological valuation have been used in the past. The EcIA Guidelines identify the following 'currencies' of value of ecological features:

- biodiversity value – intrinsic value of the conservation of genetic diversity
- direct human amenity, benefits in terms of mental and physical well-being, and value for education
- direct economic value (e.g. through a fishery).

EcIA requires identification of selected features above a certain level of value and the characterisation of the likely interaction between the features and changes brought about by the proposed development.

The EcIA should concentrate on biodiversity value, but also comment upon the value of features in relation to both amenity and, if appropriate, direct economic worth.

The EcIA Guidelines provide a recommended geographic frame of reference for defining biodiversity value as follows:

- international
- UK
- national (e.g. England/Northern Ireland/Scotland/Wales)
- regional
- county or metropolitan
- district (or unitary authority, city or borough)
- local or parish and
- within the zone of influence only, which might be the project site or a larger area.

There are many criteria which are relevant to assessing the biodiversity value of ecological features. Clearly, many site designations provide clear indications of biodiversity value e.g. SPA, SAC (international) and SSSI (national). The EcIA Guidelines do not attempt to provide listings of values for all different types of ecological feature, due to the sheer number of variables that could affect the valuation and the tremendous range of interactions possible between these variables. The EcIA Guidelines recommend the use of 'professional judgement' to assign values to ecological features, based on available information from multiple sources, including advice from experts on the specific feature in the specific location where it is being considered. The Biodiversity Action Planning and prioritising process can be of particular help here. Although opinions may of course differ between professionals, the more evidence that is brought to bear to justify the valuation, the less the room for professional disagreement.

Care needs to be taken to properly assess not only existing value but both potential value and secondary or supporting value of ecological features. In other words, features that may intrinsically appear to be of fairly low biodiversity value may be subject to, for example, management plans or proposals anticipated to raise the value by restoring ecosystems to former states of integrity (e.g. under the terms of a local HAP, see above); or be very important in protecting features of high intrinsic value.

Impact Assessment

The EcIA Guidelines set out an approach to impact assessment that differs from previous commonly used approaches, and which has strong resonance with the terminology and approach of Appropriate Assessment (though some different meanings can apply to commonly used terms such as 'significance'). The EcIA Guidelines require the assessor to attempt to determine whether or not a given set of biophysical changes will lead to an impact that is significant in ecological terms or not, regardless of the value of the feature. By 'significant in ecological terms' is meant whether the ecological 'integrity' of a site or ecosystem, or the conservation status of a species or habitat in a given area, would be adversely affected (or sustainably restored/established for positive effects) or not. Once this decision has been made, and appropriate confidence levels attributed to the prediction, then an impact can be described as 'significant at the parish scale' if the feature is of parish value, at the national scale if of national value and so on.

The first step is the characterisation of the ecological baseline for the receptor, which may not be the same as the existing conditions. This needs to involve consideration of any trends or population fluctuations and consideration of the likely change in the status of the feature in the absence of the development, e.g. in relation to background trends such as climate change. Other developments for which planning consent has been granted and the effects of which might interact with those of the development under consideration (it is best to agree a list of these with the determining authority) must also be considered as far as reasonably possible.

The next step is to 'characterise' the likely impact as far as possible, due consideration being given to ecological resources used by the feature, random environmental processes, human influences and historical context, ecological relationships, ecological roles and functions and ecosystem properties. Characteristics of any impact should include definitions of its quantitative magnitude (e.g. numbers of individuals affected) and physical extent, likely duration, reversibility, timing and frequency.

Considering all of these factors, a judgement must be made for a site or ecosystem as to whether or not integrity would be affected/restored or not. Integrity is defined as the coherence of the site or the ecosystem's ecological structure and function across its whole area that enables it to sustain the habitat, complex of habitat and/or levels of populations of species for which it was classified (for a designated feature) or which would be 'acceptably characteristic of that site or ecosystem' (for an undesignated feature).

Similar assessments must be made for habitats and species in terms of conservation status. For habitats, conservation status is determined by the sum of influences acting on the habitat and its typical species that may affect its long-term distribution, structure and functions as well as the long-term survival of its typical species within a given geographical area. For species conservation, status is determined by the sum of influences acting on the species concerned that may affect the long-term distribution of abundance of its populations within a given geographical area.

It is important to note that whilst this method might appear to have limited descriptive power in terms of grade of impact on a feature, significant impacts can always be defined at the scale of sub-components of a feature, which whilst not likely to affect/restore the integrity or conservation status of the feature itself could be significant at the level of the sub-component.

Using this method, it is of paramount importance to attach confidence levels to predictions. The IEEM guidance recommends use of a four-level scale of confidence. For many receptors, and following the long-standing statistical tradition of the minimum acceptable significance level used in statistical tests, where the chance of an impact is estimated at 5% or less (1:20), then it might be reasonable to state the prediction as follows: *'certain/near-certain that the impact will be not-significant'*. Between a 5% and 50% likelihood of a significant ecological effect, the prediction might be expressed as *'possible though unlikely that the effect will be significant'*. Between a 50% and 95% chance, the prediction might be expressed as *'probable that the effect will be significant'*, and then for 95% of greater surety of a significant effect as *'certain/near certain that the effect will be significant'*. It is not possible to mathematically justify the category of confidence assigned, but it will generally be possible to exclude two of these by general reasoning and then choose the more precautionary of the remaining two confidence levels. Mitigation can be applied to *increase the confidence* in any potential impact being non-significant in practice; and the *shift in level of confidence of predictions* that would be effected by the mitigation should then be recorded in the EIA in the summary of effects of the mitigated scheme.

A more stringent probability level should apply in the case of designated sites, and for European sites, risk needs to be reduced to the point at which there could not be any measurable contribution of the project to detectable change in the features of a European site.

Mitigation, Compensation and Enhancement – and Consequences for Decision-making

At every stage of the EcIA process the ecologist preparing the ES needs to consider opportunities for mitigation of potential adverse impacts and incorporation of positive effects *by design* of the scheme. This is not only sensible and good practice but also a requirement of planning policy, as mentioned above.

Various terms are in use, and it is worth considering their definitions further. **Mitigation** is generally best defined in ecological terms as separate from compensation and enhancement, as failure to do so can give a false impression that all adverse effects can be readily nullified. Mitigation is best considered as avoidance or reduction/remedy. It is essential to ensure that mitigation measures for one potential impact do not have negative implications for other resources in addition to bio-diversity and nature conservation.

To avoid an adverse effect altogether, a developer might need to:

- locate development and access routes away from areas of ecological interest, including key commuting and dispersal routes
- protect such areas from encroachment during construction and occupation
- avoid working during sensitive periods, e.g. the bird-nesting season
- exclude species prior to construction.

To reduce/remedy the level of change brought about where an effect cannot be avoided, a developer might:

- modify the design to incorporate protection measures, e.g. silt traps
- incorporate disturbance barriers e.g. temporary screens to limit the effects of disturbance
- provide new habitat where there is very high confidence in its success and its use by the affected feature.

Where nothing can be done to reduce the impact on the feature, then it may be necessary to **compensate**. Actions that are perhaps best considered as compensation include habitat and species relocation and habitat creation (certain habitats). The effectiveness of habitat and species relocation is still subject to debate, and, while it may have been used in previous years, success has often been limited. Accordingly, it should only be attempted as a last resort. Ancient woodlands cannot be recreated, and while new planting of appropriate species can be instigated in their stead, this will in no sense replace them. Moreover, local planning authorities may not accept translocation of an old and valuable habitat as adequate mitigation even if it is biologically success-ful because of the loss of the historical context of the original location.

Compensation is also the term best used to apply to habitat creation off-site, as this is not necessarily going to benefit the local populations of species affected by the development, though it may help other individuals of the same species elsewhere. So by way of compensation measures, a developer might:

- remove and replace *in situ* important features, e.g. hedgerows or grassland turves
- provide artificial habitats where use can be very capricious, e.g. bat roosts
- relocate – provide appropriate receptor sites
- create off-site habitat, e.g. creation of new mudflats in compensation for the unavoidable loss of mudflats within a designated intertidal site, due to port development.

Biodiversity (Flora and Fauna)

Regardless of which of the above terms is applied to a given measure to nullify negative impacts, there is always a degree of uncertainty as to the likely success of proposed mitigation (the law governing monitoring of implementation and follow-up after care is weak). Accordingly, it is best practice to include a summary impact assessment of any scheme excluding any measures for ecological mitigation or compensation that are not clearly integral to the design and essentially subject to 'guarantee'. This assessment of the impact of a hypothetical unmitigated scheme is often required by EIA co-ordinators. The level of detail required in relation to each potentially affected feature will depend on both the value of the feature and the confidence that, for example, impact could be avoided by integral design of the scheme.

Enhancement refers to biodiversity gain that may not relate to any adverse effects of the scheme. As emphasised above, under the recent changes to planning policy for biodiversity, there is now a need to put considerable emphasis on the delivery of biodiversity enhancements through the development process and to fully document these through the Environmental Assessment process. It is important that the EcIA describes the rationale for, and proposed methods to realise and maintain, any habitat restoration, creation or enhancements that are proposed. The text should fully reference the relevant BAPs and regional and local strategies relating to biodiversity and taking all relevant cues from the surrounding 'signature' landscape. Where biodiversity enhancements are truly considered to be desired elements of scheme proposals for the multifunctional social, economic and general environmental benefits they may bring, rather than being measures taken solely to comply with biodiversity policy, then there is a strong case for them to be included in the description of the scheme in the planning submission, putting them on a par with any built elements. Such an approach would be in keeping with the shift towards holistic sustainable development planning.

In order to determine the nature and extent of mitigation, compensation and enhancement proposals that should be incorporated into the scheme proposals, the *likely consequences of any impacts for decision-making* by the determining authority must be considered. This assessment has to be made on the basis of consideration of *law and planning policy* at all relevant levels. Any feature included in the assessment is considered to be of a level of value considered worthy of mention in the EIA (see the previous discussion concerning the difference between triggers for EIA and features considered once EIA is being undertaken), and this is generally set by the lowest level of planning policy that is considered relevant, such as the presumption to protect features of local conservation interest that may be written into a Local Development Framework.

The mitigation, compensation and enhancement required for potential adverse impacts under law and policy varies in general in level and degree of effort required to ensure its successful implementation with the value of the feature. Nevertheless, it is good practice to establish systems to ensure the long-term success of any mitigation or compensation measures proposed, regardless of the value of the feature. A most useful tool in this regard is the inclusion of an outline Environmental Management Plan (EMP) in the ES that lists all of the measures proposed and defines the means of their long-term implementation. The plan should also detail what monitoring of the measures is

Biodiversity (Flora and Fauna)

proposed and how such monitoring would be resourced over the required timescale. Such an EMP can readily be referenced in any planning consent, thereby greatly improving the quality and detail of planning conditions.

A wide range of mitigation, compensation and enhancement measures have been developed in recent years, and experience of their effectiveness is still being gained.

Examples of mitigation measures at stages of development

Construction	*Examples*
Timing	Avoid nesting, breeding and flowering periods
Protection	Fencing off sensitive areas
Pollution control	Secure storage, sediment traps
Education	Briefing of site workers
Environmental management	Implementation of an EMP and the appointment of site environmental managers

Operation/occupation	
Preservation	Retention of valuable habitats and corridors
Design	Planting/creation of new habitat and the inclusion of a buffer zone around the site in the master plan
Pollution control	Provision of reed beds or sediment traps
Management	Ensuring long-term provision for and implementation of management

Restoration (if applicable)	
Design	New hedgerows, habitats and ponds
Management	Long-term site monitoring and aftercare

Sources of information

Type of information

Designated areas, habitats and species
Detailed survey data and local knowledge

Sources of information

Planning authority
Natural England
Environment Agency
Local Wildlife Trust
Local Biological Records Centre
Royal Society for the Protection of Birds (RSPB)
Botanical Society of the British Isles
British Trust for Ornithology
Natural history societies
Vincent Wildlife Trust
Local recorders, specialists and natural historians

Greenwich Millennium Site

Environment Agency objectives include enhancement of the River Thames edge throughout the London tideway. The Millennium scheme contributed to this by creating and planting riverbank tidal terraces at the Greenwich Peninsula. The Greenwich Village development has also incorporated a new biodiverse 'Ecology Park' as compensation for the loss of a reedbed once present on the peninsula, the conservation and enhancement of local biodiversity, for vital ecological education and the general amenity and pleasure of local residents and visitors, and to positively affect property values.

Key Features

- Early and thorough consultation and scoping, continued iteratively throughout the EIA.
- Surveys, methods of assessment and timescales vary with different species. Ecological assessment needs careful planning to ensure sufficient time in the development and authorisation programme. A clear statement of timing of surveys with an explanation of the reasons for any sub-optimal survey timing should be included in the ES.
- Brownfield sites may be of greater innate biodiversity value than many greenfield sites.

3.5   Soils and Agriculture, Contaminated Land and Geology

Introduction

The EIA Regulations state the need to describe and assess impacts on soils if they are likely to be significantly affected by a proposed development, and also include the need to estimate any soil pollution likely from a development. As discussed in Section 3.8, the definition of 'material assets' may be interpreted to include impacts on mineral resources and agricultural activities. The Department of Environment (DoE) 'good practice guide' (1995) defines soils as including the top and subsoil and underlying superficial deposits, and that loss of and damage to geological, palaeontological and physiographic features should also be assessed. The 'EIA Guide to procedures' (DETR 2000) states that the quality of agricultural land, solid geology, hydrogeology and minerals resources should also be taken into account.

Renewal of mineral permissions (Review of Old Mineral Permissions – ROMPs) requires EIA for their registration and review (EIA Regulations amended 2000).

Discussion

> **The interrelated functions of soils**
>
> - Storage, filtration and release of rainwater influencing flood risks.
> - Support for all terrestrial habitats, plant and animal communities.
> - Providing raw materials.
> - Providing a platform for built development.
> - Protection of archaeological remains.

As soils and geology greatly influence the vegetation, hydrology, groundwater, and land use in an area, effects are linked to landscape, flora, fauna, water, air, cultural heritage and material assets. Some geological formations and soils are also of importance as mineral resources, or for earth science (e.g. rock faces at worked-out mineral sites and coastal cliffs designated as SSSIs), archaeology and nature conservation (e.g. where caves provide habitat for bats). Ground conditions and their suitability for development are mainly determined by geological,

We know more about the movement of celestial bodies than about the soil underfoot

– Attributed to Leonardo da Vinci

Soil is a vital part of our environment and an essential resource for life

– Defra 2008. Soil Strategy for England, consultation draft

Key fact

Soils should be accorded the same priority in environmental protection policies as air and water

– Royal Commission on Environmental Pollution 1996. Sustainable Use of Soil

Key fact

Government guidance favours the reuse of brownfield land; such sites may not be suitable for sustainable development given contamination, access and biodiversity issues. Some brownfield sites have retained soils that can be used for landscaping and habitat creation topographical and soil conditions. Soils may be polluted by previous industrial or urban uses and contaminants may present risks to human health or the environment. They also influence catchment hydrology, flood risk assessments and the scope of sustainable drainage systems.

In the past, soils have often been taken too much for granted in policy-making and planning, without specific soil protection legislation or adopted government policies. A draft *Soils Strategy* for the UK has now been prepared, which addresses the particular concerns of the loss of soils to development and the reuse of contaminated sites. This strategy has been further developed by Defra's *First Soil Action Plan*, and the Environment Agency's *State of Soils in England and Wales*.

In recent years, there has been a significant relaxation in the narrowly focused protection of our best and most versatile agricultural land. The *Soil Strategy* and *Soil Action Plan* have introduced the need to protect the other interrelated functions of the soils, which are valuable in respect of a wider range of environmental objectives.

This more holistic approach recognises the key role of the soil in the environment, linking the atmosphere, geology, water resources and land use. The emphasis is on the protection of soils of particular value for the functions listed above, not just as agricultural land for food production.

Concern at the unnecessary loss of 'greenfield' sites to development when derelict sites are available in urban areas led to a national target for 60% of all new dwellings to be provided on previously developed land by the year 2008, as expressed in the revised PPS3 (2000) and the Urban White Paper (2001). PPS3 also introduced the 'sequential' approach to housing development, which prioritises the development of previously used sites in urban areas before the release of greenfield land. Brownfield and derelict land often has significant ecological value – greenfield land, by contrast, may have low ecological value.

Contaminated land is now defined by the Contaminated Land Regulations with regard to significant harm (to human health, buildings, livestock, water, flora and fauna) or pollution. It is assessed using a source, pathway, receptor model and an incomplete range of Soil Guideline Values (SGVs) available from a series of developing guidelines set out on the Defra and the Environment Agency websites. This model uses a **'suitable for use'** risk to human health approach. The nature and extent of the contamination and proposals for remediation should be included in EIA: contaminated land investigation and remediation can be expensive and time-consuming. Because of this, a phased approach is taken, progressing from desk studies to targeted site investigations and remedial strategies based on proposed end uses. Developers are often reticent to include details of surveys and remediation strategies for reasons of:

- confidentiality
- commitment to costs
- public perception and acceptability.

However, an ES with limited information may risk the success of the planning application: the ES must include sufficient information to enable assessment of impacts and satisfy the regulatory authority/ agency.

Key legislation and guidance

Environmental Protection Act 1990

Environment Act 1995

Contaminated Land Regulations 2000

CLEA Soil Guideline Values

PPS3: *Housing*

PPS7: *The Countryside*

PPS9: *Biodiversity and Geological Conservation*

PPG14: *Development on Unstable Land*

PPS23: *Planning and Pollution Control*

PPS25: *Development and Flood Risk*

Defra 2008. *UK Draft Soils Strategy consultation*

Defra 2004–2006. *First Soil Action Plan*

Environment Agency 2004. *State of Soils in England and Wales*

DETR Circular 02/2000: *Contaminated Land*

MPG7: *The Reclamation of Mineral Workings*

Ministry of Agriculture, Fisheries and Food 2000. *The Good Practice Guide for Handling Soils*

Key fact

The Environment Agency estimates that up to 300,000 ha of land are affected by industrial or natural contamination

Soils and Agriculture

Key fact

PPS23 states that the responsibility for providing information of whether land is contaminated rests primarily with the developer

case example

An ES for a major pipeline classified all soil types along the pipeline route through desk study and soil survey, and went on to identify significant potential impacts and mitigation measures for farm structure, soil excavation, handling, storage and reinstatement.

Regulators and consultees

Soils and agriculture:

Defra, farmers, National Farmers Union, landowners, Country Land and Business Association

Contaminated land:

Environment Agency, local and unitary authorities

Geology:

Minerals Planning Authority (county councils and unitary authorities), Coal Authority, British Geological Survey, Natural England, local Regionally Important Geological and Geomorphological Site (RIGS) group

case example

Outline redevelopment proposals for housing on a former munitions factory in Enfield, north London, were initially accompanied by an ES, which proposed a comprehensive reclamation strategy based on an initial field survey of ground contamination. Areas of greatest contamination, as identified by further detailed site investigations, were to be removed off site, and all contaminated materials to be removed from residential areas. Subsequently, new developers submitted revised remediation strategies for site development, which were eventually approved in 1997 amid local controversy. Local groups and the Environment Agency, given a special 'extended' remit by the government to offer good practice advice to the council, warned that the site surveys and precautions proposed for the 'capping' of contaminated soils in areas proposed for housing were inadequate. A subsequent report by London Friends of the Earth and Enfield Lock Action Group, and a Panorama TV programme, questioned the ability of the planning system to ensure the adequate remediation of risks to health and the environment from contaminated land which is being redeveloped when local councils can ignore specialist advice from the Environment Agency.

Soils tend to be an important topic for EIA where:

- soils need to be disturbed to enable a development (e.g. a pipeline or minerals workings), and later reinstated for continued use for agriculture, forestry, recreation or conservation
- a large volume of soils has to be excavated to create level footprints for developments in areas with relatively steep gradients – the beneficial use of this 'waste' material can create reclamation opportunities on brownfield sites elsewhere
- high-quality agricultural land (in absolute or relative terms within a given area) may be disturbed or lost to development
- existing land contamination is suspected or known.

Reviews of ESs have revealed that soils and geology appear to be considered among the least important issues in EIA. However, as indicated above, an understanding of the soils and geology of a site and the surrounding area is necessary for a range of other EIA topics recognising their interactions.

Regulators and Consultees

Soils and Agriculture

Defra is consulted on development proposals affecting agricultural land. Farmers and landowners (including their representatives where appropriate, e.g. the National Farmers Union, the Country Land and Business Association, and promoters of development) should also be consulted.

Agri-environment schemes aim to promote agricultural practices that conserve the landscape, wildlife and heritage features, both in Defra-designated Environmentally Sensitive Areas and in the wider countryside through the Countryside Stewardship Scheme.

Contaminated Land

The Contaminated Land Regulations 2000 require local authorities to inspect their areas and identify contaminated land which requires remediation. The Environment Agency is responsible for the most contaminated 'special sites', and is also a statutory consultee where development is within 250 m of a waste landfill site. Local authorities and the Environment Agency should therefore be consulted where land contamination is suspected.

The instability of land may be a material consideration for site development, and local authorities and mining organisations should be consulted where instability, e.g. on slopes or from previous mining activities, is suspected. Minerals planning authorities should also be consulted in areas where planning policies protect minerals resources from sterilisation by development. Geological and geomorphological features and biological sites (of which soil is an inherent part) of national importance are protected as SSSIs and designated by Natural England. Non-statutory Regionally Important Geological and Geomorphological Sites (RIGS) are identified by the county RIGS group.

Potential Effects

Most developments will affect soils and their functions in some way through loss (by building on land, and failing to conserve topsoils and subsoils together with increased erosion by rain and wind), or through physical and chemical damage of soils (largely compaction, loss of soil structure, and contamination). This includes soils which are stripped and stored for reinstatement. Compaction of soils by heavy vehicles during stripping, storage and reinstatement is common. This can reduce soil drainage, and lead to waterlogging, increased run-off and erosion. It also restricts root penetration and reduces plant growth. The nature of the soils present, the weather conditions and machinery used for soil handling will determine the likely severity of the impacts. Different soil types are more or less susceptible to damage. Clay and silty soils require drier conditions and more careful handling. The *Reclamation of Mineral Workings* and *The Good Practice Guide for Handling Soils* provide excellent advice on this.

The potential secondary effects of such soil impacts on water, land use, landscape, nature conservation and cultural heritage, and the implications for the development proposals, should also be considered. The loss of agricultural land to development can affect the viability of continued farming activities for farm holdings, and temporary disruption to farm access can be created by pipelines, transport routes and temporary roads. Increased public access to an area due to development may also lead to effects on a farm holding, through recreational activities, vandalism and fly-tipping, as well as positive effects of potential increased viability through farm diversification. The development of agricultural land may also affect features protected by landscape, wildlife or heritage designations, or have implications for the conservation of areas promoted by agri-environment schemes. Soil movement along pipeline spreads or other linear developments can also risk the spread of disease.

Development of land which is contaminated but not currently causing harm or pollution can lead to significant risks through public exposure or mobilisation of contaminants. As some of the liability associated with contaminated land may be passed on through land purchase, buyers of potentially contaminated land will need to carry out pre-purchase audits of such land to be fully aware of any such liabilities. Development near landfill sites can also be susceptible to the migration of landfill gas and leachate.

Geological issues can include the instability of slopes, the presence of geological faults, underground mine working and impacts on groundwater movement, underground cavities and potential for ground collapse, effects on coastal processes, the presence and potential sterilisation of mineral resources, and impacts on earth science conservation. In particular, development affecting coastal cliffs and erosion can have significant effects away from the site itself.

Methodology

Investigations are usually required to determine the ground conditions and underlying geology of a site to determine the stability of the land and the specific engineering requirements for building foundations, pipelines, minerals workings and waste disposal sites.

Key fact

All applications for development on 'greenfield' sites of over 150 houses or housing on over 5 ha must be notified to the Secretary of State

"

Contaminated land *'is land which appears to the local authority… to be in such a condition, by reason of substances in, or on or under the land, that* **significant harm** *is being caused or there is a significant possibility of such harm being caused; or pollution of controlled waters is being or is likely to be caused.' The Regulations further define 'significant harm'*

– Contaminated Land Regulations

"

guiding principle

Assessment of contaminated land is based on the '*suitable for use*' approach, which considers risks to human health and the environment

Soils and Agriculture

Early consideration of the likely significance of potential effects and the importance of the historical use of the land, the soils, geology and current (including any agricultural uses) is needed to determine the scope and level of baseline studies and impact assessments that are required.

Baseline Conditions

If only a brief description of soil types is required for an EIA, a desk study may be adequate to determine the general properties of soils. The Soil Survey and Land Research Centre (SSLRC) holds the national soil maps and accompanying booklets which describe the soil classifications and related geology and land uses.

Defra is responsible for the Agricultural Land Classification (ALC) system, which grades land as 1 to 5, with grade 3 being subdivided into 3a and 3b. Grades 1, 2 and 3a form the *'Best and Most Versatile Land'*.

Key fact

Small-scale published ALC maps do not differentiate between land classifications 3a and 3b, and consequently site surveys are often required

Small-scale ALC maps of land quality for strategic planning purposes only are available from Defra (although these do not differentiate between ALC grades 3a and 3b). The results of more detailed ALC surveys carried out for local authorities, and information on farm holdings and agricultural land uses on a parish basis, may also be available from Defra. The SSLRC publishes larger-scale soil maps suitable for farm management (not land use planning) purposes, but coverage is far from complete.

Where published soil and ALC information indicates that a development potentially involves the loss or disturbance of *'Best and Most Versatile'* agricultural land, site-specific surveys by specialist soil scientists may be needed to determine the precise ALC grades affected. It should be noted that the consultancies that carry out contaminated land studies do not necessarily employ such soil specialists. The Institute of Professional Soil Scientists has a website providing a comprehensive listing of competent professionals.

Soil surveys may also be needed to determine the soil types, topsoil and subsoil depths and volumes in more detail than is available from maps. This applies in particular to surface mineral sites. Field surveys usually involve a combination of hand auger boring over the site in a systematic grid pattern or focusing on specific areas of interest. Soil pits are dug for each of the main soil types identified to observe the subsoil structures. Soils surveys concentrate on the physical characteristics of soils, but samples may be taken for chemical analysis, particularly in respect of contamination studies.

If agricultural activities are to be significantly affected by a development, discussions and consultation should be held with affected farmers and landowners, to ascertain the land uses and activities affected.

guiding principle

Early discussion with the Environment Agency and the Local authority to agree to the appropriate level of site investigations can avoid later conflict and delays

An initial desk study of a site's history should reveal whether contamination by previous uses is suspected or considered likely: this comprises a *'time-series'* review of all available historic maps, site records from previous occupiers, local archives and histories. The public registers that local authorities are required to keep will identify all the known contaminated land in their areas once inspections have been undertaken. The National Land Use Database developed by the Department for

Communities and Local Government (DCLG) and others attempts to provide information on previously used and derelict or under-used sites considered suitable for residential development to local authorities to facilitate their redevelopment. The Environment Agency keeps records of former waste disposal sites. The series of DoE Industry Profiles distributed by Defra provides initial information to help identify and assess risks and remedial measures for a wide range of contaminative uses such as gas works and types of chemical works.

Site surveys will be required in areas to be developed that are suspected to be contaminated, to determine the nature and extent of contamination that may present risks to human health, water pollution, animals and plants. A systematic grid pattern of trial pits and boreholes at specified locations and depths are generally required. Analysis undertaken will vary according to type of contamination and the options for end-use.

The geology of an area can usually be determined through reference to the British Geological Survey (BGS) maps of solid and drift geology, and to mining and quarrying records held by the Coal Authority and others, although reliable records may only relate to the late 19th century onwards. Local authorities should also have access to good information on any land instability problems in their areas. Information on workable minerals resources will be held by the Minerals Planning Authority; the Environment Agency will hold maps showing the vulnerability of groundwater, and maps of geological SSSIs are available from Natural England. Local biological or environmental record centres usually have further information on RIGS sites.

Intrusive geotechnical surveys including boreholes at selected and representative locations will be required as appropriate to the proposed development and likely site conditions. Surveys should aim to determine both baseline conditions likely to be affected and future conditions likely to affect the development and future users of a site.

To determine the significance of contamination, the level of potential contaminants detected are commonly compared with the 'threshold' and 'action' levels established for a limited range of substances listed in the non-statutory Inter-Departmental Committee on the Redevelopment of Contaminated Land (ICRCL) 1987 guidelines. This has been superseded by the Defra on risk assessment and management of contaminated land under the new regulatory regime. Many developers have found it useful to use the more recent and comprehensive 'Dutch A–B–C values'. Guidance on the investigation of potentially contaminated sites is now available in BS 10175:2001.

Defra 2008. *Guidance on the Legal Definition of Contaminated Land*

Defra 2008. *The Way Forward. Soil Guideline Values*

Project Description

General considerations apply to many types of development, and include the area and nature (e.g. ALC/land quality) of permanent and temporary land take, the nature and location of permanent structures, the depth and nature of excavations, the nature of excavated materials, re-use of materials on site or disposal off-site, working methods for soil handling (stripping, storage and reinstatement), any requirements for re-use of soils, site restoration and after-use, the timescale and phasing of development and the season of working, potential for on-site or off-site soil treatment (e.g. to remove contamination), materials in contact with soils to avoid future contamination, access requirements for vehicles including temporary roads, and requirements for storage of fuels and materials.

Impact Prediction and Significance

The significance of direct losses of land and soil are usually dependent on the extent of the loss or disruption and grade of land affected. Temporary disturbance of soils, e.g. for pipelines, mineral and landfill sites, has been regarded as significant where the quality of the restored soil has deteriorated by an ALC grade. The significance of effects on soil should also be assessed with reference to secondary effects on groundwater infiltration, flood risks, cultural heritage, flora and fauna, and the landscape character. Effects from a development on the viability of farm holdings from land take or severance can be assessed using financial formulae.

Government guidance is that the redevelopment of contaminated land should be remediated to reduce risks to an acceptable level suitable for its current and intended use. SGVs, published by Defra and the Environment Agency, indicate levels of contamination which if exceeded could pose unacceptable risks to site users. They use the Contaminated Land Exposure Assessment (CLEA) model for land use.

Assessing the effects of a development on geological features and processes requires knowledge of similar cases and the application of sound scientific principles. Assessments of ground conditions and land instability need to take account of conditions outside the site boundary (i.e. often upslope or downslope of land within the site) and of potential variations in climate, as excessive rainfall or periods of drought can change ground and groundwater conditions.

Mitigation

Good practice techniques for soil handling (stripping, storage and reinstatement) can reduce the inevitable loss of and damage to soils (as a result of compaction, loss of soil structure, erosion and pollution) from development. This ensures that soils can be adequately reinstated for their previous uses or re-used as a growing medium within a development site for landscape planting and habitat creation. General requirements include limiting soil handling in wet weather, minimising the exposure of soils (especially on slopes), restricting heavy traffic movements to dedicated haul roads, fencing off land not required for development, and avoiding the mixing of topsoils and subsoils, loose tipping soils on reinstatement and ripping soils to decompact them, as necessary, and the prevention of pollution through adequate storage of fuels and other materials.

Mitigation for temporary disruption of agricultural activities can involve changes to the routes or timing of works, maintaining access to fields for farm machinery or livestock, and ensuring adequate protection and reinstatement of the soil, field drainage and boundaries, and taking account of any requirements of agri-environment schemes such as no fertiliser use. Adverse effects from increased public access may be reduced to some extent by waymarking, fencing or diversion of footpaths.

guiding principle

Contractors need to be consulted when drawing up detailed mitigation commitments for soils in the form of Soil Handling Strategies

Photograph courtesy of AC Archaelogy, reproduced with permission.
© *AC Archaelogy*

A contaminated site has been 'remediated' where the land is suitable for use and previous contamination does not cause any significant harm or pollution. To demonstrate that a site is remediated it must be ensured that each potential pollutant linkage is no longer significant by:

- removing the pollutant
- treating the pollutant
- breaking or removing the pathway that causes harm
- protecting or removing the receptor; or
- remedying the effect of any significant harm or pollution.

Treatment or containment/encapsulation options that avoid removing the contamination elsewhere (usually to landfill) are generally preferable, although a Waste Management Licence may be required for treatment, and the advice of the Environment Agency should be sought. Defra is producing a framework of model procedures for the selection of remedial measures in the redevelopment of contaminated land. Publications by Defra, the Environment Agency and the Construction Industry Research and Information Association (CIRIA) also describe best practice techniques for a range of '*in situ*' and off-site treatment options. Biological treatment methods are appropriate for certain contaminants, and are potentially more sustainable. However, the landtake and time for, for example, composting, needs to be integrated into the development schedule.

Careful design of a development is the best way of mitigating any significant impacts on geological features or processes, and avoiding significant risks to the development.

Sources of information

National Land Use Database
Department for Environment, Food and Rural Affairs (Defra)
Environment Agency
Soil Survey and Land Research Centre, Cranfield University
British Geological Survey (BGS)
Construction Industry Research and Information Association (CIRIA)

Key fact

The Contaminated Land Regulations use the source, pathway, receptor concept of a **pollutant linkage**, i.e. a linkage between a **contaminant** and a **receptor**, by means of a **pathway**. Contamination cannot cause pollution unless there is a pathway to the receptor. The Regulations give guidance on the types of receptor, the degree or nature of significant harm, and the degree of possibility of significant harm being caused

Further information

Royal Commission on Environmental Pollution 1996. *19th Report – The Sustainable Use of Soil*

DETR Circular 08/2000: *Town and Country Planning (Residential Development on Greenfield Land) (England) Direction 2000*

Environment Agency/National House Building Council 2000. *Guidance for the Safe Development of Housing on Land Affected by Contamination*

BS 5930:1999: *Code of Practice for Site Investigations*

BS 1377:1990: Methods of test for soils for engineering purposes

BS 7755: *Soil Quality* (many parts with various dates)

BS 10175:2001: *Investigation of Potentially Contaminated Sites: Code of Practice*

BS 8010-1:1989: *Code of Practice for Pipelines: Pipelines on Land*

BS 5837:2005: *Trees in Relation to Construction*

Key Features

- Soils have largely been taken for granted in the past in environmental planning, and the government is producing a soils strategy to attempt to increase the priority given to soil protection as a key part of sustainable development.

- Soils and geology may not always be major topics in their own right in an EIA. However, it is usually necessary in EIA to investigate the geology and types of soil on and around a site, to be able to determine not only the potential effects on the soil and geological resources in their own right but also to fully understand the interactions with other environmental issues.

- Government policies increasingly aim to minimise loss of soils and agricultural land to development and promote the safe redevelopment of contaminated land through the investigation and assessment of risks.

3.6 Water

Introduction

If the water environment is likely to be significantly affected by the proposed development, then the EIA Regulations require a description of the existing conditions or state, the likely significant effects and measures envisaged to prevent, reduce or offset such adverse effects on water.

The water environment includes consideration of environmental protection (both related to public health and the natural environment) and the use of natural resources.

Key legislation and guidance

Environment Act 1995

Water Resources Act 1991

Water Industry Act 1991

Land Drainage Act 1991

PPC Regulations 2000

Control of Pollution Regulations 1996

Groundwater Regulations 1998

Contaminated Land Regulations 2000

EU Water Framework Directive 2000 and UK Regulations 2003

PPG20: *Coastal Planning*

PPS23: *Planning and Pollution Control*

PPS25: *Development and Flood Risk*

Environment Agency 1997. *Policy and Practice for the Protection of Floodplains*

Environment Agency 1998. *Policy and Practice for the Protection of Groundwater*

Defra 2008. *Future Water, The Government's Water Strategy for England*

Aspects of the water environment and development

- Surface water
  - Watercourses (rivers and canals)
  - Reservoirs, lakes and ponds
  - Wetlands
- Groundwater
- Estuarine and coastal waters
- Flood risk management
- Flood defence (fluvial and coastal)
- Land drainage
- Infrastructure
  - Wastewater treatment and sewerage
  - Water supply
- Recreation and amenity
- Biodiversity
- Navigation and transport; hydropower

There is specific legislation and guidance relating to pollution control, water abstraction, flood management, land drainage, nature conservation and navigation, and these need to be addressed in parallel with the EIA process.

European legislation relating to water has been largely unified under the Water Framework Directive (2000/60/EC) (WFD). The selection criteria for screening Schedule 2 development draws special attention to the use of natural resources, the production of waste and pollution and the environmental sensitivity of the geographical areas likely to be affected by development, having regard to the absorption capacity of the natural environment, including wetlands and those areas in which environmental quality standards laid down in EU legislation have already been exceeded.

Discussion

Some significant water-related projects are subject to EIA under non-planning regulations. In particular, land drainage improvement works such as the repair or renewal of river control structures require EIA if the works are likely to have significant effects on the environment.

Works below the low-water mark, e.g. for new ports or harbours, marine fish farming, marine dredging or works under the Transport and Works Act 1992 (which can include interference with navigation or new waterways) all may require EIA and application to the appropriate authority (e.g. Defra, Department for Transport, Crown Estates).

Flooding is a natural process, and floodplains, by definition, act to contain the additional water from rivers in flood conditions. Development in floodplains will therefore be generally resisted by the Environment Agency, and developers will be required to provide for flood compensation elsewhere, fund flood defences or provide flood warning measures.

Key fact

The Environment Agency produces s105 maps (WRA91) to show flood risk areas

Redevelopment in the floodplain will be required to use Sustainable Drainage Systems (SuDSs) so as not to increase surface water run-off. Maintenance and adoption are the key issues for the implementation of SuDSs, and commitment should be made in the ES to this form of mitigation. Consideration of the application of SuDSs should be at the project inception stage, and include ecological and landscape designers within the project team.

guiding principle
New developments should use SuDSs wherever practicable

Key fact

PPS25 requires joint strategies with planners, drainage boards or authorities, sewerage undertakers and the Environment Agency to encourage the use of SuDSs

Planning Policy Statement 25 (PPS25), published in December 2006, sets out the government's policy on development and flood risk. Its aims are to ensure that flood risk is taken into account at all stages in the planning process, to avoid inappropriate development in areas at risk of flooding, and to direct development away from areas of highest risk. Where new development is, exceptionally, necessary in such areas, policy aims to make it safe, without increasing flood risk elsewhere, and, where possible, reducing flood risk overall. Complementary to PPS25 is the practice guide, and includes working examples through case studies (Communities and Local Government 2008).

The complexity of monitoring, regulating, using and protecting the water environment has led to a plethora of **water-related planning regimes**:

- Catchment Abstraction Management Strategies (CAMS)
- Catchment Flood Management Plans (CFMPs)
- Coastal Habitat Management Plans (CHaMPs)
- Coastal Zone Management (CZM)
- Estuary Management Plans (EMPs)
- River Basin Management Plans (RBMPs)
- Shoreline Management Plans (SMPs)
- Strategic Flood Risk Assessments (SFRAs)
- Water Level Management Plans (WLMPs)
- Water Cycle Strategies
- Water Resource Strategies

Water

> ### The EU Water Framework Directive 2000
>
> The WFD applies to all surface freshwater bodies (including lakes, streams and rivers), groundwaters, groundwater-dependent ecosystems, estuaries and coastal waters out to 1 mile from low water. The implementation of this Directive into UK regulations integrates the diverse Directives on the water environment, including bathing waters, dangerous substances, drinking water quality, ecological quality, freshwater fish and shellfish waters, groundwater protection, nitrate pollution from agriculture, surface water abstraction, surface water quality and urban waste water treatment.
>
> The framework requires River Basin Districts (RBDs) to be identified as the main unit for managing the water environment. Analysis will include the characteristics of each RBD, and review the environmental impact of human activities, and the economic use of water.

The issues relating to water management and proposed development are exacerbated by the predicted effects of climate change, which include:

- increased risk of flooding
- reduced groundwater recharge
- increased demand for public water supply and irrigation (this is further discussed in Section 3.7, 'Air, Climate and Odour').

Proposed development can offer the possibility of restoration of a watercourse; an enhanced water environment can facilitate regeneration and contribute to a wider Green Infrastructure Strategy.

Regulators and Consultees

Environment Agency:

- grants licences to abstract or impound water under the Water Resources Act 1991 (WRA91)
- sets discharge consents under WRA91
- sets Water Quality Objectives for rivers and manages water quality to meet with WFD objectives for good quality ecosystem status
- provides guidance and advice on PPC
- issues permits and regulates prescribed activities under PPC regulations (emissions to air, land and water)
- controls groundwater resources through Groundwater Regulations and WRA91 – groundwater vulnerability maps, Source Protection Zones and Nitrate Vulnerable Zones
- controls development within 8 metres of main rivers (or 15 metres on a tidal river) under WRA91 or construction of a structure that would affect the flow of an ordinary watercourse (Land Drainage Act 1991)
- supervises all matters relating to flood defence and flood warning
- provides an assessment of whether a water body is heavily modified or not.

Water companies – plc:

- provide wholesome water supply under WIA91

" We will work with all sections of the community to reduce flood risks through preventive planning, restoration of rivers and floodplains, better management of the disposal of surface water and better design of buildings

– Environment Agency 2000. An Environmental Vision "

Key fact

The Environment Agency will always insist on access provision alongside main rivers of at least 8 metres

- provide and maintain the sewerage system for the transfer of sewage to treatment works
- set and provide trade effluent standards and consents for discharges to sewers under WIA91.

Water companies – private:

- provide water supplies only.

Local authorities:

- regulate private water supplies
- regulate bathing waters (monitored on their behalf by the Environment Agency)
- undertake flood defence work on non-main rivers (outside Internal Drainage Board (IDB) districts)
- have powers to protect land against coastal erosion, encroachment or flooding by the sea (maritime authorities).

Defra:

- responsible for flood and coastal defence policy
- responsible for control of fisheries.

Others:

British Waterways
Port and Harbour Authorities
Port Health Authorities
Sea Fisheries Committees
IDBs
Natural England
Wetland and Wildfowl Trust
RSPB
angling, recreation, watersports, conservation and boat user groups.

Potential Effects

The potential effects on the water environment can conveniently be divided into those of physical effects, quantity (hydrological/hydrogeological) and quality (pollution).

Physical Effects

These include:

- canalisation of a river to increase channel capacity and rapid removal of floodwaters
- removal of ponds or lakes
- diversion of a watercourse
- construction of a dam, creating a new upstream reservoir and alterations to downstream flow regimes – with consequences for siltation in both the watercourse and the reservoir
- dredging to increase the depth of water
- construction of weirs as barrages preventing tidal effects, salinity and exposure or passage of migrating fish
- coastal defences affecting natural coastal processes of erosion and siltation/deposition.

> **guiding principle**
>
> Effects on the water environment are rarely in isolation: amenity and ecology are also affected. The indirect and cumulative effects must be remembered

Water

Quantity

Development can change the nature of the land and its ability to absorb or manage rainfall. Frequently, extensive paved areas and storm water drainage are included within development, which reduces the time taken for water to reach watercourses. Peak flows are increased and recharge of groundwater is reduced as a consequence. This in turn increases the risk and frequency of flooding downstream, causes erosion on site and downstream and reduces aquifer levels. This is particularly of importance for proposed development in floodplains.

Conversely, increased abstraction or changes to abstraction patterns from rivers or aquifers can lead to siltation and reduced flows from springs.

Developments in floodplains will require additional flood defence structures and changes to the profile, form or gradient of a river. This increases the risk of flooding upstream and downstream. Dredging or straightening of the river reduces habitat diversity and refuges for fish.

Reduction in aquifer levels can affect habitats dependent on water table levels. Similarly, pipelines can act as drains, diverting water from its natural catchment. New development can place additional demands on water resource requirements, further depleting aquifer levels, leading to potential drought conditions and supply restrictions. In certain geological conditions, rivers can dry up in summer.

Quality

Water quality is dependent on geology, topography and land use as well as discharges to the aquatic environment. Pollution occurs when the receiving environment can no longer absorb the concentration of pollutants discharged.

For any stretch of main river the Environment Agency sets Water Quality Objectives. which are based on the uses to which the river is put and to meet WFD objectives. Increased discharges could result in those objectives no longer being met, with a consequent effect on the users, e.g. potable abstraction by water companies, recreation groups, or on habitats and fisheries. In extreme cases, human health may be threatened. Pollutants include heavy metals, organic and inorganic wastes, suspended solids, toxic substances, oils and fuels, and heat.

Pollutants can enter the water environment by direct point source discharge from, for example, sewage treatment works, industry or agriculture. Land uses can increase run-off from diffuse sources, e.g. roads or agriculture. Leaching of pollutants from landfills or previously contaminated land can cause pollution of groundwater or watercourses.

The addition of an excess of nutrients, generally from sewage treatment or agriculture (in the form of fertilisers), can lead to eutrophication and algal blooms in surface waters. The excessive growth and life cycle of algae result in deoxygenation, causing fish kills and difficulties in water treatment processes. The presence of oil films on water surfaces can prevent the transfer of oxygen into the water, resulting in a similar

---

case example

Proposed Oil Pipeline

A proposed oil pipeline potentially crossed sensitive areas of the Norfolk Broads. Hydrogeological studies and ground surveys were required to select the appropriate route and technique to ensure that the pipeline would not affect these wetlands of international importance.

---

case example

Leeds Waterfront

The River Aire in Leeds had a legacy of industrial pollution. A partnership including Yorkshire Water, the Environment Agency and the local authorities restored the water quality of the river. This encouraged investors to redevelop the industrial warehouses fronting the river, promoting regeneration, and the waterfront is now a vibrant area in the city. The catalyst for the regeneration was the improvement to the water quality in the river.

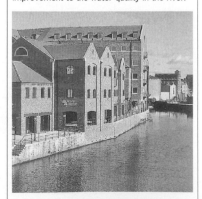

Photograph courtesy of Hugh Howes, reproduced with permission. © Hugh Howes

deoxygenation as well as the coating of water birds and creating aesthetic problems.

Vandalism or accidental and uncontained spillages, especially by chemicals or fuels and oils, are frequent but short-lived examples of pollution. However, once groundwater is polluted, it is difficult to remedy and can result in loss of an aquifer for potable supply.

Methodology

Baseline Studies

The scope of such studies is very much defined by the location of development in terms of catchment boundaries, proximity to the coast, and soil and groundwater characteristics. Considerable initial assistance and guidance can be obtained from the Environment Agency in respect of the range and extent of studies. Basic information about existing conditions, and Agency aspirations, objectives and concerns can be gathered from the Environment Agency website (www.environment-agency.gov.uk). These have identified, amongst other elements of the environment, discharges and abstractions, designations, habitats, water quality and objectives, aquifers and drainage patterns. Further detailed environmental data from routine monitoring programmes are available on request from the Agency or from the public register.

Scoping of the issues by consultation with the Environment Agency, water companies and others (see above) will identify the need for additional surveys as part of the baseline study. The Agency has produced guidance on the scoping of projects (2002). These surveys might include:

- river flow measurement
- groundwater (water table) measurement
- chemical and biological river surveys
- river corridor surveys
- geomorphological or fluvial audit surveys
- river habitat surveys
- fisheries surveys
- user surveys.

Flow measurement in rivers can include the employment of special equipment and the installation of temporary weirs. Groundwater measurement may involve boreholes, trial pits or piezometers for water levels. Any surveys have to be designed over an appropriate length of time to collect meaningful data.

Chemical river surveys initiated for the purpose of undertaking a project EIA have limited value: they are only spot checks unless integrated with a continuing programme of monitoring. Biological or fisheries surveys are of considerably more value since they will give a more accurate representation of the long-term health of the water environment. Responses to intermittent pollution may not be evident from a chemical survey. Biological surveys can also identify potential

Further guidance

Environment Agency 2002. *EIA: A Handbook for Scoping Projects*

Water pollution measurement

- Physical: temperature, suspended solids, odour
- Chemical: salinity, metals, pesticides
- Microbiological: coliforms, viruses
- Biological: fish, invertebrates, aquatic plants, non-native invasive species

Water

cumulative effects of discharge and synergistic effects of various pollutants. There are potentially conflicting requirements of water users, such as those of canoeists and anglers.

Project Description

All potential emissions to, or abstractions from, the water environment during both construction and operation of the proposed development should be described. This can include storage of fuels, water usage, and run-off from site activity and traffic during construction. The incorporation of water saving or recycling measures and the utilisation of SuDSs into the design should be reported.

Impact Prediction and Significance

Comparing the baseline conditions and trends with the activities and emissions of the proposed development will highlight those particular issues which are likely to be significant and require careful evaluation. Clearly, the significance of any predicted changes will be as measured against existing standards and objectives. If consent to discharge is (or will be) granted by the Environment Agency, the impact should be regarded by other regulators as acceptable. Any evaluation will need to take into account predicted changes due to climate change, i.e. sea level rise and increased severity and frequency of flooding. All development proposals require a Flood Risk Assessment (FRA) in accordance with PPS25, and masterplanning may require the preparation of a Water Cycle Strategy. In order to determine the acceptability of a proposed discharge or alteration to an existing consent, the Agency uses a formula based on the strength and value of the proposed or altered discharge and the assimilative capacity of the receiving watercourse.

In order to quantify the effects of proposed discharges, modelling of coastal or fluvial processes to understand the sensitivity of the receiving environment to changes in quality or flows may be necessary. Biological predictions are possible using RIVPACS (River Invertebrate Prediction and Classification System) and scoring systems to estimate the significance of change. Predictions of groundwater effects or movement can be made based on an understanding of the underlying geology. Once the predictions have been calculated, they can then be judged against the various relevant prevailing policies, guidance and standards.

If discharges are not possible or permitted to a watercourse or other waters, then discharge to the sewerage system may be an alternative to on-site treatment. Such a discharge will require the system to have capacity and the consent of the water company in accordance with the Water Industry Act 1991. Charges will be levied, and pre-treatment may still be required.

Mitigation

There is likely to be a range of negative impacts for an issue such as water, and a mitigation strategy should be developed. The available mitigation options are naturally numerous and wide-ranging depending on the nature of the impact, and may include:

Mitigation option	Typical objective
■ Restoration of original channel pattern	Increases the assimilative capacity of the watercourse
■ Introduction of new channel features, e.g. oxbows	Provides enhancement to habitat and aesthetic quality
■ Incorporation of sustainable drainage systems	Reduces flooding by alleviating rapid changes in flow regimes and watercourses within the catchment area; protects water quality; provides wildlife habitat
■ Reduction or elimination of particular chemicals from process or waste discharge	Protects the environment, reduces the need for treatment or transfer of flow to treatment works
■ Containment of storage areas/vessels within bunded areas	Reduces the risk of spillage during construction/operation
■ Use of sediment traps or interceptors and vegetated areas	Prevents blanketing of the river bed during in-stream work and reduces the levels of pollutants in run-off
■ Separation of clean and contaminated water	Reduces the volume to be treated
■ Re-use of heated water	Reduces the elevated temperature in receiving waters and the rates of growth of algae, etc.
■ Creation of flood storage areas	Maintains the capacity of the floodplain to regulate river flows

---

Sustainable Drainage Systems

SuDSs are methods of managing surface water drainage to balance the impacts (quantity, quality, amenity) of urban drainage on the environment. They aim to deal with run-off close to where the rain falls, to prevent flooding and reduce pollution. There are four general methods of control:

- filter strips and swales
- filter drains and permeable surfaces
- infiltration devices
- basins and ponds.

The variety of design options available allows designers and planners to consider local land use, land take, future management and the needs of local communities.

From DETR/CIRIA 2000. Sustainable Drainage Systems: Design Manual for England and Wales. Crown copyright: reproduced with permission of the Controller of Her Majesty's Stationery Office

---

case example

Two Rivers Retail Park, Staines

The redevelopment of a former trading estate for a retail development in conjunction with an Environment Agency flood protection scheme enabled the channelized watercourse to be restored and enhanced. The river now forms an attractive setting for the new development. By working in tandem, costs and responsibilities were shared between the Agency and the developer.

Photograph courtesy of Hugh Howes, reproduced with permission. © Hugh Howes

case example

Second Opening Bridge, Poole, Dorset

The ES for this project typifies potential environmental impacts of developments in, or close to, estuarine SPAs. For the bridge, the construction process, the presence of bridge piers and dredging could all potentially cause erosion of the sea bed, resulting in sediment in the water. Whilst some of this material could have been contaminated, it was determined (through hydrodynamic and sediment modelling) that there would be no impact on the shellfish beds in Poole Harbour, and the SPA would not be adversely impacted.

Further information

www.environment-agency.gov.uk

www.defra.gov.uk

DETR/CIRIA 2000. *Sustainable Drainage Systems: Design Manual for England and Wales*

DETR 2000. *A Guide to Water Quality*/NSCA 2000. *Pollution Handbook*

The River Restoration Centre. rr@cranfield.ac.uk

RSPB, NRA, Wildlife Trusts 1994. *The Rivers and Wildlife Handbook*

www.rspb.org.uk

CIRIA 2004. *Sustainable Construction*

Environment Agency 2002. *EIA Scoping for Projects*

TCPA 2004. *Biodiversity by Design*

"
It isn't pollution that's harming the environment. It's the impurities in our air and water that are doing it

– George W. Bush
"

Sources of information

Type	Source
Capacity of infrastructure	Water companies
River water quality	Environment Agency
Estuary surveys	
Groundwater	
Bathing water quality	
River flows	
Flood risk maps	
Discharge and abstraction	
Consents and licences	
Private water supplies	Local authority (environmental health department)

Key Features

- There is a plethora of regulations, plans, policies and associated regulators for the water environment, reflecting its complexity and interactions with other environmental elements.
- Development should avoid floodplains, wherever practicable.
- Flood risk assessments must be considered for all new developments.
- SuDS should be considered early and incorporated in the design of new or re-development, and arrangements identified for maintenance in the ES.
- Restoration of degraded, canalised or culverted watercourses can offer opportunities for environmental enhancement and regeneration.

3.7 Air, Climate and Odour

Introduction

Air and climate factors have to be examined if they are likely to be significantly affected by a development. This applies to developments covered by the EIA Regulations, and is increasingly the case on a voluntary basis for smaller developments. If significant effects are anticipated, the existing conditions need to be described together with the associated effects. In the case of air quality and climate, these effects arise from changes in emissions. Increasingly, consideration is also given to the impacts arising from introducing new exposure in areas of poor air quality, such as new housing near to busy roads in urban areas. Odour is not specifically referred to in the Regulations, but is listed in the DETR (2000) Guide to the Procedures as a consideration within the discussion of air and climatic factors.

The UK Air Quality Strategy provides the framework for air quality management and assessment in the UK. It considers improving and maintaining air quality as a joint responsibility, with industry, the transport sector, local authorities and individuals all asked to contribute. Under Local Air Quality Management (LAQM), local authorities are required to carry out a review and assessment of air quality in their area to identify whether objectives have been achieved. If the objectives are not expected to be met, then the authority is required to declare an air quality management area and prepare an action plan setting out how it intends to work towards meeting them. As a consequence, local authorities have a good understanding of air quality across their area, which is an invaluable source of information for air quality assessments.

PPS23 on PPC provides guidance on those situations when air quality is a material consideration in planning decisions. It emphasises the importance of the statutory air quality objectives and the need to take account of the presence of air quality management areas. It also makes clear that the planning system should complement and not duplicate the system under which permits are issued for the operation of industrial processes. These permits form part of the Integrated Pollution Prevention and Control (IPPC) regime, whereby process operators are required to obtain a permit from the regulator (either the Environment Agency or the local authority), before releasing emissions into the air. If a proposed IPPC installation requires planning permission, it is recommended that the operator should make both applications in parallel. The IPPC regulator can then start formal consideration early on and have a more informed input to the planning process. The regulator must also take account of any information related to the EIA Directive.

Discussion

At the local level, developments can alter the concentrations of locally acting pollutants, which might affect human health or sensitive ecosystems, or give rise to nuisance effects. They can also introduce people into areas where they might experience poor air quality due to existing pollution sources. Developments can also give rise to wider-scale impacts, which range from regional changes in ozone concentrations to contributions to global climate change. These wider-scale impacts are less straightforward to assess, and they are typically given scant attention. This is likely to change, given the growing concerns about emissions of carbon dioxide and other greenhouse gases as contributors to climate change, and the interactions between climate change and local air quality. The air quality assessment can highlight the scale of the change in emissions of greenhouse gases due to the development. This can lead to recommendations to minimise these emissions, as a contribution to providing a more sustainable development.

At the local level, developments can affect the microclimate; cause local warming due to high levels of thermal output and changes to land cover; cause cooling due to overshadowing; and affect local winds, creating wind canyons, eddies and downdraughts.

Regulators and Consultees

Initial consultation should be with the relevant local authority environmental health department. EHOs should be able to provide advice on key concerns or issues within the local area and provide access to local monitoring data. They can also advise on the approach to the assessment of air quality – which pollutants to examine, local sources and potentially sensitive receptors. It is advisable to agree the scope and approach to the assessment from the outset in order to avoid unexpected problems at a later date. (The Environment Agency and local authority are also

Key legislation and guidance

Air Quality Regulations 2000 and amended 2003

Pollution Prevention and Control Regulations 2000

PPG13: *Transport*

PPS23: *Planning and Pollution Control*

Secretary of State 2002. *LA-IPPC and LAPPC – Policy and Procedure for Permitting Installations*

Defra 2007. *The UK Air Quality Strategy*

Kyoto Protocol 1997

Further information

Defra 2006. *Climate Change: The UK Programme*

Defra 2003. *Local Air Quality and Management. Technical Guidance*

National Society for Clean Air 2006. *Planning Control: Planning for Air Quality*

Environment Agency 2008. *Climate Change Adaptation Strategy 2008–2011*

case example

Proposed Road Scheme

The ES for a bridge across the River Thames in London included consideration of the following effects:

- effects on concentrations of health-related pollutants alongside all roads significantly affected by the scheme
- effects on greenhouse gas emissions from the London road network
- assessment of dust and odours during the construction phase.

Regulators and consultees

Local authority environmental health department

Environment Agency

regulators and consultees for developments subject to authorisation under IPPC.)

Potential Effects

Air quality effects can arise during both construction and operation. During the construction phase, dust is likely to be a primary concern, albeit of a temporary nature. Construction traffic and plant may also release pollutants into the atmosphere; however, these emission sources are unlikely to result in significant long-term impacts.

Proposals for major developments such as for power stations, airports, motorways and major mixed-use developments (projects which are usually Schedule 1 developments) can lead to concerns about significant air quality impacts during their operation. For many development types, the principal concern during operation is likely to relate to emissions from traffic. The significance of the impact will depend on the level of traffic generated by the development, the proximity of traffic to sensitive receptors and the existing conditions. Increasingly, attention is also being focused on proposals that lead to new exposure to poor air quality, which can include exposure to existing sources of odour or dust from industrial or agricultural operations.

Odour is not often a concern, but can be an issue in relation to developments such as wastewater treatment works, landfills, chemical plants, oil refineries, food-processing factories and intensive-farming units, such as pig farms. Particular attention should be paid to developments that might affect air quality management areas, as even small changes are likely to be considered significant.

As discussed above, consideration should also be given to climate effects. In most cases, this aspect of the assessment relates to the contribution of the development to changed emissions of global warming gases. In some instances it is also necessary to consider the impacts of the development on the local microclimate, including the effects of tall buildings on wind conditions for pedestrians.

Methodology

Baseline Studies

Gathering baseline air quality data can be an expensive and time-consuming exercise; therefore, it is best to use existing sources of data wherever possible. Air quality data are now readily available on the internet at the UK Air Quality Archive website. Local authorities can also provide data, with this information increasingly being made available on the Internet. Such data provide up to date information, and often have the advantage of having been gathered over a number of years so that they can be used to identify historical trends. The disadvantage can be that the monitoring has not been undertaken at the locations, or for the pollutants, of concern for the EIA. The local authority air quality review and assessment reports will provide useful information on the air quality setting for the proposal and identify whether the development will be in or close to an air quality management area.

Where additional surveys are required, it is important to carry them out over a sufficient period, since air quality can vary considerably over short periods of time due largely to changing weather conditions. Seasonal factors also play a part and should be borne in mind when assessing air quality data. In addition to considering the timing of the survey, it is also necessary to determine which pollutants to survey, and how and where to monitor. These decisions will be influenced by the characteristics of the development and the sensitivities of the receiving environment. Where it is necessary to monitor over a limited period, which should ideally be no less than 3–6 months, then the results should be put in perspective by making comparison with results for a nearby long-term site. This will demonstrate how representative the monitoring period is.

Further information

UK Air Quality Archive website.
www.airquality.co.uk/archive

The UK Air Quality Strategy sets objectives for the control of air pollutants as follows:

Protection of health

- Benzene
- 1,3-Butadiene
- Carbon monoxide
- Lead
- Nitrogen dioxide
- Ozone
- Particulates (PM10)
- Sulphur dioxide
- Benzo-*a*-pyrene

Protection of vegetation and ecosystems

- Nitrogen oxides
- Sulphur dioxide

The above list highlights the principal pollutants of potential concern. An EIA will not necessarily consider all of these, but may need to consider others, such as metals, acids and dioxins, depending on the nature of the development. It will usually also be necessary to consider emissions of global warming gases, especially carbon dioxide and, on occasions, methane.

Once the data have been gathered, they can then be evaluated against the objectives set out in the Air Quality Strategy. In order to determine the impacts of the development, it is important to understand the quality of the receiving environment. Having established the existing baseline, it is necessary to predict what the baseline will be in the year of assessment. When predicting the future baseline, factors such as improvements in vehicle emissions should be taken into account, together with other developments that are proposed in the area that may give rise to significant air quality impacts.

If examining micro-climatic effects, data will need to be gathered regarding existing conditions, e.g. temperature, wind speed and direction, rainfall and shadowing. Where odour is to be assessed, existing sources of odour will need to be identified and odour levels assessed as appropriate.

Key fact

Traffic Impact Assessment

Data generated as part of the Traffic Impact Assessment (TIA) will need to be appropriate for the air quality assessment. It is therefore important to discuss data requirements with the project managers and traffic consultants at an early stage. Without such discussion, the TIA may generate data for locations, times of the day and years that are inappropriate for the air quality assessment as they are different types of study with different objectives

Project Description

In describing the project, it is important to highlight all potentially significant emissions to air during both construction and operation. Consideration should also be given to the impact of local sources on the development site, e.g. a food retail development next to an existing industrial source, or a proposed residential development next to a busy motorway or a wastewater treatment works. Sources will include traffic, plant and industrial processes. Information such as stack emissions, stack height and traffic generation will therefore need to be provided, as appropriate.

Impact Prediction and Significance

Predicting air quality impacts generally involves complex calculations and sophisticated computer modelling. Dispersion models can be used to model industrial emissions, including odours. Such models require information about the stack, the type and rate of pollutants to be emitted, meteorological conditions, the local terrain and the proximity of buildings. As with any model, the results obtained are only as good as the data entered, and it is important for the ES to provide details of all the inputs and assumptions made in carrying out the modelling, so that the validity of the modelling can be examined.

For many projects, traffic is the principal source of air pollutants, and in this instance a different approach to air quality prediction is required. The methodology set out by the Highways Agency in its *Design Manual for Roads and Bridges* (DMRB), Volume 11, is frequently used. The DMRB approach takes account of the number of vehicles, the proportion of heavy-duty vehicles, the distance from the road to the receptor, the speed of the vehicles and the effects of legislation on future emissions from vehicles. In certain circumstances, it may be appropriate to use more sophisticated models that take account more specifically of local meteorological conditions.

Whatever modelling is carried out, it will normally be necessary to add the predicted concentrations to the local background (see the baseline discussion above). It will also usually be necessary to verify the models against local monitoring data, especially if the predicted concentrations are close to the objectives.

Having predicted air quality levels with the development in place, it is then necessary to evaluate the significance of the impact by comparing the predicted levels with the existing situation and the predicted baseline for the year of assessment. Air quality should also be assessed against the relevant air quality standards. Impacts can be said to be significant if the development leads to exceedence of air quality standards, objectives or guidelines. Impacts may also be considered significant if there would be a serious deterioration in air quality, even without exceeding an air quality standard.

Guidance is provided by Environmental Protection UK on ways to describe the significance of air quality impacts. The assessment of significance will also need to take into account the sensitivity of the receiving environment such as schools, hospitals and SSSIs. In the case

case example

Proposed Energy Recovery Facility

The ES for this proposal included an assessment of the potential responses of vegetation and wildlife to sulphur dioxide, nitrogen dioxide, dioxins, furans and particulates. The proposed ERF was located in close proximity to an SSSI, SPA, candidate SAC and Ramsar site. Particular attention was paid to potential impacts on sphagnum flora and lichens.

of an impact in an air quality management area, even a very small increase is likely to be considered significant, and compensatory measures may be required from the developer.

Mitigation

Where significant adverse impacts are identified, then mitigation measures should be proposed within the ES. Examples of mitigation measures can be identified for each of the types of impact identified in this section.

Air quality:

- Promote greater atmospheric dispersion by raising the stack height, increasing the velocity of emission, etc. (noting potential increased visual impact).
- Modify industrial processes to use cleaner fuels or burn fuels more efficiently.
- Improve the quality of emissions through the use of scrubbers.
- Control the amount of traffic generated by the development proposals.
- Use mechanical ventilation to draw air into the building from a location away from the busy road.
- Apply a buffer zone around odour sources in which sensitive development does not take place.

Dust:

- Damp down materials and unpaved areas using water sprays.
- Use sheeting on lorries taking dusty materials to or from the construction site.
- Wash the wheels of vehicles before they leave the site.
- Cover temporary stockpiles with sheeting.
- Locate any temporary stockpiles away from sensitive locations.
- Regularly use a water-assisted dust sweeper on local roads to remove any material tracked out of the site.

Microclimate:

- Orientate buildings in such a way as to avoid overshadowing of existing dwellings or other sensitive areas and to prevent creating wind canyons.
- Select building and surfacing materials to avoid an excessive build up of heat.

Global climate:

- Use alternative technologies for providing heat and electricity, e.g. solar power or wind turbines.
- Insulate buildings and orientate them so as to reduce heating/ air-conditioning requirements.
- Encourage the use of alternative forms of transport to the car, e.g. walking, cycling and public transport.

Sources of information	
Type	*Source*
Assessment guidance	*Development Control: Planning for Air Quality* – updated guidance from Environmental Protection UK on dealing with air quality concerns within the development control process
	Horizontal Guidance for Odour – Technical Guidance Note IPPC H4 from the Environment Agency
Air quality data	UK Air Quality Archive
	Local authority (environmental health department)
	Meteorological Office
Energy conservation and efficiency	Future Energy Solutions
	Energy Saving Trust
Environmental assessment of buildings	Building Research Establishment Environmental assessment method (BREEAM)

Key Features

- Air quality modelling is a complex process. The inputs and assumptions on which modelling is based should be explicit in the ES.

- Impacts may range from changes to local air quality through to changes to emissions of global warming gases.

- Air quality assessments are often closely related to traffic assessments. Traffic assessments should provide the data required to assess emissions from vehicles; any measures proposed to reduce traffic generation will also have a positive effect on emissions.

- Changes in air quality can have an impact on flora and fauna. Air quality specialists may need to work with ecologists in order to determine the potential impacts of a development.

- In some circumstances, air quality data may be required by health specialists in order to contribute to an HIA of proposed development.

3.8 Cultural Heritage and Material Assets

Introduction

The EIA Regulations refer to the need to describe '*material assets, including the architectural and archaeological heritage*' if they are likely to be significantly affected by the development (Schedule 4, Part I). The Directive refers more simply to '*material assets and the Cultural Heritage*'. The phrase '*material assets*' is not well-defined, and has caused some difficulty.

The University of Bath *IEM Workbook* suggests some examples:

- property values
- loss of trading income
- severance of land ownership, particularly farmland

Material assets

"

this is a very broad all encompassing category which could cover almost every physical or non-physical sector of the environment that could be said to have material value ... there is no commonly accepted meaning of the term

– University of Bath 2008. *IEM Workbook* "

■ compulsory purchase at less than market price

■ sterilisation of mineral resources.

Clearly, the issue has to be remembered when scoping an EIA but, by definition, material assets frequently have an economic value, and such issues and disputes are more customarily resolved by commercial trans-actions, land valuation tribunals and compulsory purchase orders, and are not strictly a part of environmental impact. However, where, for example, agricultural activity or mineral extraction is involved, such issues should be addressed under the appropriate heading. Many schemes which potentially would sterilise mineral resources provide for their winning as part of the project programme (see Section 3.5).

Discussion

It has in fact become customary and common practice in EIA to focus on the effects on archaeology and wider cultural assets, and so this section is entitled 'Cultural Heritage', as coined in the Directive. Schedule 4, Part I refers also to the need to describe the range of emissions from the proposed development, including vibration, and the effects of vibration on architecture or archaeology should be given special attention (see Section 3.3). In addition to archaeology and the historic environment, an assessment of cultural heritage value would also need to consider other cultural factors, such as literary or artistic associations, where these are significant features of the site or its setting.

The selection criteria for screening Schedule 2 development draws special attention to the environmental sensitivity of the geographical areas likely to be affected by the development *'having regard to the absorp-tion capacity of landscapes of historical, cultural or archaeological significance'*.

The Regulations also interpret *'sensitive area'* as:

■ a property appearing on the World Heritage List of the 1972 UNESCO Convention for the Protection of the World Cultural and Natural Heritage

■ a scheduled monument within the meaning of the Ancient Monuments and Archaeological Areas Act 1979.

The DoE (1995) *A Good Practice Guide* clarified matters by treating cultural heritage and material assets as a single topic area. The term is described as embracing history, archaeology, architecture and urban design, and includes aspects not limited to material and economic value, extending them to human activities, ideas and spiritual and intellectual attitudes. Areas with particular associations with works of art or literature could well fall into this category.

The checklist of matters to be considered for inclusion in an ES in the *EIA: A Guide to Procedures* (DETR 2000) suggests the following:

■ **Information describing the site and its environment**: architectural and historic heritage, archaeological sites and features and other material assets; heritage coasts, conservation areas, listed buildings, scheduled ancient monuments and designated areas of archaeological importance.

■ **Assessment of effects on buildings and man-made features**: effects of the development on buildings, the architectural and historic

Cultural Heritage and Material Assets

heritage, archaeological features, and other human artefacts, e.g. through pollutants, visual intrusion or vibration (the effects on land include agriculture and mineral resource sterilisation).

- **Mitigating measures**: these might include recording of archaeological sites and measures to safeguard historic buildings or sites.

Regulators and Consultees

Initial consultation should be with the relevant county archaeologist. While not specifically listed in the Regulations as a consultee for EIA matters, the statutory consultee for heritage issues in England is English Heritage. Where development is likely to affect the site of a scheduled monument or any garden or park of special historic interest which is registered in accordance with Section 8C of the Historic Buildings and Ancient Monuments Act 1953 (register of gardens) and which is classified as Grade I or Grade II*, the consultee is English Heritage (the Historic Buildings and Monuments Commission for England). Development of land in Greater London which involves the demolition, in whole or part, or the material alteration of a listed building should also be referred to English Heritage.

Development within 3 km of Windsor Castle, Windsor Great Park or Windsor Home Park, or within 800 m of any other royal palace or park, which might affect the amenities (including security) of that palace or park, requires consultation with the Secretary of State for Media, Culture and Sport.

For listed buildings outside London, applications are made through the local planning authority. The principal point of contact for advice and guidance on the procedures is usually the conservation officer within the planning department.

For information regarding cultural heritage features, local authorities will often consult the National Trust, the Society for the Protection of Ancient Buildings, the Civic Trust, the Garden History Society, the Victorian Society or the Twentieth Century Society (formerly the Thirties Society), and will be able to advise on other national and local interest societies which may have particular information or may be able to advise on the significance, value and preservation of local features.

Potential Effects

Cultural heritage and those material or physical features representing it is irreplaceable, and it is therefore essential that any remains or features are identified before development takes place. Where nationally important features (whether scheduled or not) and their settings are likely to be affected by proposed development, there is a presumption in favour of their preservation *in situ*.

The possible effects on features of historic value can be summarised as follows:

- **Destruction**: e.g. demolition of listed building or disturbance of archaeological remains.

- **Visual or other intrusion**: e.g. impact on the character or setting of a building, conservation area or historic landscape which could include noise in a quiet setting.
- **Physical damage**: e.g. air pollution, water table fluctuations, vibration, recreational pressure for improved access, or loss of fauna and flora (especially for historic landscapes).

Methodology

The procedure for archaeological investigations (desk and field) is described in PPG16, *Archaeology and Planning*, which gives advice on handling archaeological remains under planning procedures. If the presence of such remains is suspected, planning consent may be withheld until sufficient information is made available to allow the local authority's archaeologists to formulate their advice. Provision of this information may involve commissioning historical map and documentary studies and/or the carrying out of site investigations. Further guidance is given in PPG15, *Planning and the Historic Environment*. This sets out the arrangement for assessing other aspects of the cultural heritage landscape, principally the built environment: World Heritage Sites, Historic Parks and Gardens, Historic Battlefields, Listed Buildings and Conservation Areas.

Other key guidance
PPG15: *Planning and the Historic Environment*
PPG16: *Archaeology and Planning*

Baseline Studies

These should focus on the type of effect the various stages of the development could have and the potential cultural value of the site, if any. The study commences with a desk study guided by preliminary consultation with the local authority's archaeologist. The Institute of Field Archaeologists (IFA) Guidance sets out sources of archaeological information which should normally be included in desk-based studies, including EIA. Sources which should be researched include the following.

National Monuments Record, held by English Heritage
This includes the National Archaeological Record for sites and monuments in England and the national library of aerial photographs as well as information on potential underwater sites or wrecks. (Similar records for Scotland and Wales are held by their respective Commissions.)

Heritage Environment Records (HERs), held by local authorities (England)
Regional Archaeological Trusts (Wales)
Regional and Island Councils (Scotland)
HERs – formerly known as Sites and Monuments Records (SMRs) – will normally contain a record of the known archaeological monuments (including scheduled monuments), sites and findspots together with references to further levels of information. The scope of HERs varies: some routinely include listed buildings, post-World War II sites of interest, etc., while others take a much more restricted view of what constitutes the archaeological record. The HER will be able to provide information on other surveys and historic landscape assessments relevant to the area of study. Any listing of known sites will be limited by the intensity of archaeological activity which has been undertaken, and the absence of recorded sites in certain areas does not necessarily indicate an absence of archaeological interest. HERs do not usually

Cultural Heritage and Material Assets

comment on the importance of individual sites or areas, and expert guidance and advice is necessary. Of further help in this respect are areas identified by county archaeologists as Areas of Archaeological Significance in local planning documents.

Listed Buildings

These are buildings or other features recognised as making an important contribution to the quality and character of the built environment. The listing is made by the Secretary of State at Defra, and is usually available from the local planning authority.

Conservation Areas

These areas are designated in accordance with their special architectural or historical interest and their character and appearance. All trees within Conservation Areas are subject to Tree Preservation Orders. Conservation Areas are recorded on local plans produced by the local planning authority.

Historic Landscapes

These do not have statutory protection in their own right but may be part of designated areas, e.g. a National Park and Area of Outstanding Natural Beauty (AONB). They should be identified on local planning documents produced by the local planning authority. Statutorily protected landscapes are designated by Natural England, which can provide further information. There are also non-statutory landscape designations, e.g. Areas of Great Historic Value (AGHV). Other factors which may define archaeologically or historically significant landscapes include clusters of sites forming archaeological landscapes, or field patterns incorporating boundaries which can be defined as being of historic significance in accordance with the criteria in the Hedgerow Regulations. Historic landscape characterisations, which summarise the origins, development and significance of landscapes, have now been completed for many areas of the country.

The Register of Parks and Gardens

The Register of Parks and Gardens of special historic interest is maintained by English Heritage and published in county volumes – the local planning authority will hold the relevant volume.

The Register of Historic Battlefields

The Register of Historic Battlefields in England is maintained by English Heritage.

Ordnance Survey

Early editions of Ordnance Survey and privately published maps are usually held in the County Record Office (which can advise on other useful sources) or reference library of the area concerned.

If the desk study and field walkover identifies the potential for a site of importance to the cultural heritage, further archive research or field investigation will be required. Field work, which may include geophysical study, trenching or trial pits, will be undertaken to a brief prepared in consultation with the local authority archaeologist.

Because PPG16 and best practice require a staged approach to archaeological assessment, it is possible that the desk study will result in a requirement for further levels of fieldwork prior to determination of the planning application. As this requirement cannot always be foreseen, there needs to be suitable allowance in the timetable and budgets to cover for this.

Evaluation

Sites, monuments and other features are all graded (with the exception of battlefields) according to a set of criteria. As an example, for the scheduling of Ancient Monuments the following are used:

- period
- rarity
- documentation
- group value
- survival and condition
- fragility or vulnerability
- diversity
- potential.

These criteria also provide a useful framework for evaluating locally important features.

Mitigation

The principal method of mitigation for a feature of cultural heritage importance is to identify it at an early stage in the project planning process (via effective scoping) and to avoid damage or disturbance and to leave a suitable buffer zone around it. If features are in close proximity to a development site, then protection should be provided during construction.

If disturbance cannot be avoided, then provision for further levels of investigation and recording, possibly excavation, may be necessary. If the feature cannot be left where it was found, then removal and relocation to an alternative site or to a museum may be appropriate. In the case of visual intrusion affecting the character of a site, then screening or other design measures should be considered. In urban situations, construction design should preserve the deposits *in situ*.

Preservation *in situ*, either by avoiding the sensitive area or limiting works (e.g. depths) to avoid impact, will always be the favoured option. Some elements of the built environment, e.g. milestones, can be moved. Where impacts are unavoidable, the notion of 'preservation by record' is enshrined in PPG16. This may involve archaeological recording in advance of construction by means of archaeological excavation or other recording, or during the course of construction as part of an archaeological watching brief maintained during the relevant phases of the development. The course of action will depend on the likely importance of the archaeological remains affected, and will need to be undertaken to a specification agreed by the local authority archaeologist. It does need to be borne in mind that some developments may have a beneficial impact in the removal of clutter from historically important streetscapes or landscapes, opening up of views, or opportunities for restoration, e.g. of earthworks.

case example

Water Main Construction

Determining archaeological potential by means of desk-based study and/or field investigation before commencement is likely to significantly reduce the likelihood of finding important remains during construction. No matter what level of prior investigation is carried out, however, it is still possible that unexpected archaeological sites may be encountered and disturbed. Here, a previously unknown 13th-century medieval pottery kiln discovered during pipe-laying works was excavated. Where such findings can be anticipated, investigation in advance of contractors' activities will allow sites to be more thoroughly investigated without risk to the development programme and budget.

Photograph courtesy of AC Archaelogy, reproduced with permission.
© *AC Archaelogy*

Where sites have potential but are otherwise of unknown quality, an archaeological watching brief should be maintained by an experienced archaeologist during construction and for time to be allowed in the programme for recording and relocation of any finds. Enhancement of knowledge of the archaeological record may also be developed as a result of the site investigations, e.g. by providing access as an educational resource.

Key Features

- Avoiding historic features and preservation *in situ* will always be the favoured mitigation option.
- There is no commonly accepted meaning of the term 'material assets'.
- Cultural heritage can include spiritual and intellectual attitudes as well as economic value.
- Because archaeology is so often hidden from view, time must be allowed in the EIA programme for the unexpected.
- A phased approach is required for archaeological assessment.
- Cultural heritage is irreplaceable.

Further information

Institute of Field Archaeologists

Council for British Archaeology

3.9   Landscape and Visual Impact Assessment (LVIA)

Introduction

Key fact

'Landscape' includes consideration of townscape and visual amenity

'Landscape' can be defined as ' ... *an area, as perceived by people, whose character is the result of the action and interaction of natural and/or human factors*' (European Landscape Convention 2000). In urban areas, human factors generally predominate, and the term '*townscape*', rather than '*landscape*', is often applied to reflect this differentiation. Visual issues relate specifically to the views of a landscape (or townscape) afforded to people. These separate but related issues form the basis for LVIA. It is important to note that the EIA Regulations require attention to be paid to emissions of light in the description of the development, and so night-time effects should be addressed.

Key legislation and guidance

Countryside and Rights of Way Act 2000

European Landscape Convention 2000

Rural and Urban White Papers 2000

PPS1: *Delivering Sustainable Development*

PPS7: *Sustainable Development in Rural Areas*

PPG15: *Planning and the Historic Environment*

Countryside Agency/Scottish Natural Heritage 2002. *Landscape Character Assessment: Guidance for England and Scotland* (and subsequent Countryside Agency Topic Papers)

Landscape Institute/IEMA 2002. *Guidelines for Landscape and Visual Impact Assessment*

Countryside Agency 2003. *Quality of Life Assessment Appraisals: Guidance for Facilitators and Practitioners*

The selection criteria for screening Schedule 2 development draws special attention to the environmental sensitivity of the geographical areas likely to be affected by the development, having regard to the absorption capacity of the natural environment, including landscapes of historical, cultural or archaeological significance (see also Section 3.8 on cultural heritage).

The Regulations include within the definition of sensitive areas the following:

- a National Park
- the Broads
- a World Heritage Site (UNESCO Convention for the Protection of the World Cultural and Natural Heritage)

■ an AONB designated as such by an order made by Natural
England in England (or the Countryside Council for Wales in
Wales) under the National Parks and Access to the Countryside Act
1949.

The checklist of landscape matters to be considered for inclusion in an
ES in *EIA: A Guide to Procedures* (DETR 2000) suggests the following:

Description of the site and its environment:
■ Landscape and topography.
■ Designations: National Parks, AONBs, Heritage Coasts, Regional
Parks, Country Parks and designated Green Belt.

**Assessment of effects on human beings, buildings and man-made
features**:
■ Visual effects of the development on the surrounding area and
landscape and on the settings of historic buildings.
■ Heritage sites, archaeological features and other human artefacts, e.g.
through visual intrusion.

Mitigating measures:
■ Site planning and aesthetic measures such as:
  – mounding
  – design/colour
  – soft and hard landscape
  – tree planting.
■ Assessment of the likely effectiveness of these measures.

Discussion

Landscape, in broad terms, is about the relationship between people
and places. As identified in the introductory section, this relationship is
manifested in the '*character*' of a place. In 2002, the Countryside Agency
(now Natural England) published guidance for the assessment of
character to enable a consistent approach to national, regional, local and
site-specific '**Landscape Character Assessment**'. Fundamentally, landscape impact assessment is concerned with evaluating the change in
landscape character that may result from a proposed development.
Landscape character assessment can make a contribution to the UK
priority actions for sustainable development with regard to natural
resource protection and environmental enhancement.

Visual impact assessment is specifically concerned with visual receptors (those who would have a view of a proposed development) and
any associated change in views as a result of changes to the landscape.
Visual receptors may include users of public rights of way, highways
and properties. A proposed development may also affect a valued setting, e.g. views relating to a Listed Building.

It should be noted that, unlike some of the other environmental aspects
considered as part of the EIA process, changes to the landscape and
associated views are generally tangible and readily apparent to the
public; as such, landscape and visual impacts often constitute the
principal issues for local communities and wider interest groups.

Key fact

Landscape Character Assessment is not a
tool to resist change – its role is to ensure
that change does not undermine what is
characteristic or valued about a particular
landscape

– Countryside Agency 2002. Landscape
Character Assessment

Landscape and Visual Impact Assessment (LVIA)

Regulators and consultees

Natural England

Local authorities (including National Park authorities): planning, landscape and conservation representatives

AONB partnerships

Environment Agency

English Heritage

National Trust

Garden History Society

Campaign to Protect Rural England

Other specialist interest groups and local communities

---

case example

Landraising Scheme, Berkshire

A landraising scheme for waste disposal was proposed in a relatively remote location in Berkshire. Despite thorough formal consultation, which elicited very little in terms of opinions of the proposal, the promoters were somewhat surprised when over 200 people turned up to a public meeting to voice their opposition. The scheme was even reported in a national tabloid newspaper. In the face of such concern, the scheme was withdrawn.

Regulators and Consultees

The statutory consultee for landscape issues in England is Natural England. However, this body is principally concerned with designated sites such as AONBs, and the onus for guiding determination of landscape matters is more likely to fall on the landscape officer for the relevant local planning authority. County and unitary planning authorities are the consultees for development in National Parks, where the National Park Board is the planning authority. Development affecting registered historic gardens or parks requires consultation with English Heritage.

Other consultees with an interest in landscape matters include the Environment Agency, which has a duty to consider the effects of development on the landscape, especially in respect of river valleys, coasts and wetlands, and the CPRE, which initiated a 'dark skies' campaign, and the National Trust. Parish councils, local residents and communities will be particularly concerned with landscape change in their locality.

Potential Effects

Direct effects on the landscape can occur through removal, alteration or addition of key features and defining characteristics. This may be through a change in landform, built form or landcover, as well as change in the prevailing management regime. Such changes may result in a loss of status in terms of national, regional or local designations.

The visual impact is a function of how visible a development is in its landscape context and the magnitude and range of this visibility. This is likely to affect most of those with views to the proposed development, or those who value the landscape for particular cultural reasons. Impacts can include not only the development itself but also emissions, e.g. steam plumes, or indirect effects, e.g. traffic movement. The potential of visual impact to harm the recreational use of landscape should also be remembered. However, the effect on the overall visual amenity can be one of enhancement as well as degradation.

Methodology

Guidance for LVIA was produced by the Landscape Institute and the Institute of Environmental Management and Assessment (IEMA), in 2002. Baseline landscape studies must, necessarily, consider the landscape character of a proposed development site and its local, regional and national landscape character context, as a foundation for evaluating any landscape change, and associated landscape impacts, that may result from a development. Where society places value on a landscape, for example through designation of an AONB, in a rural area, or Conservation Area in an urban area, appraising change in character provides the basis for evaluating implications for the integrity of that valued landscape (or townscape). The overall assessment of landscape impact (whether positive or negative) thus takes into account the implications of a development for landscape character and the value associated with it.

Baseline visual studies should identify those who would have views of a proposed development (visual receptors), e.g. users of a public footpath, and establish the views that are currently experienced. A Zone of Visual Influence (ZVI) may be mapped to indicate the area(s) over which a proposed development would be visible, within which visual receptors lie. Good photography and presentation of photographs is key to representing the views assessed. The Landscape Institute provides advice on the use of photography for LVIA (LI Advice Note 01/04).

Active involvement of the landscape and visual assessor in the design process is key to achieving a development that limits adverse landscape and visual impacts, and enhances the local landscape and associated views of it, wherever possible. The assessor will be a Chartered Landscape Architect, who will have design training (as well as assessment training), and will therefore be able to engage effectively with a project design team in order to achieve a development that is responsive to landscape (or townscape) context. An understanding of the temporal considerations regarding landscape development (with particular reference to vegetation) is key to both the design and assessment process.

Landscape and visual effects have to be considered on the landscape resource itself (both natural and man made) and on the way landscape is perceived by the public. Much of landscape impact assessment is based on professional judgement, and it is important that the methodologies, terminology and techniques used should be accurately explained and described, and any limitations of the assessment clearly identified. A structured approach, recording findings at stages of the assessment, should be maintained. Impartiality should be maintained as far as possible, distinguishing between facts and judgments; the worst case and precautionary principle should be applied, especially with respect to seasonal variations.

Since there are two types of impact, two separate but related methodologies are used; recording findings at stages of the assessment should be maintained.

1. Landscape character assessment. This, essentially, is a study based on the existing landscape character of a locality or district. Frequently, such studies will already have been carried out for the purposes of designation or identification of particular areas and their recognition in local development plans. It is important to clearly define the geographical extent of the studies from the beginning, and it should at least cover the whole contextual setting of the development (including construction as well as operational phases). The purpose is to identify areas of countryside with common and defining characteristics, e.g. rolling pastoral (agricultural) landscape with shallow river valleys and heather or conifer plantations on the hill tops.

Landscape and Visual
Impact Assessment (LVIA)

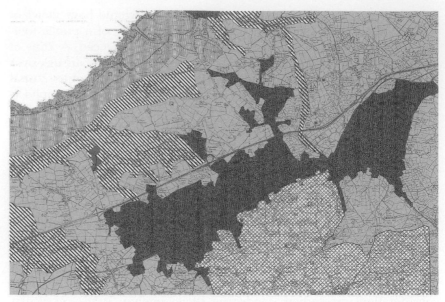

Granite Uplands

Urban

Agricultural Plateau

Steep Sided River Valley

Coastal

Landscape Character Illustration

Landscape character assessments require both objective recording (as in the example above) and a subjective valuation based on our appreciation of a particular landscape type, e.g. a comfortable, contained landscape but in which the regularity of the plantations is prominent.

Needless to say, landscape assessments need to be richly illustrated with photographs, sketches, maps or archive material. The Countryside Agency (now Natural England) Assessment approach takes three stages:

(a) *Landscape description*. This is based on field survey (baseline study), and describes what is there, i.e.

- landform – this is the physical structure, and is related principally to the underlying geology and consequent function of topography, rivers, soils and landform processes

- landcover – this relates to vegetation, and land use (such as arable or pasture, agriculture or urban uses)

- landscape elements – these include hedgerows, buildings, skylines and lines of slope, cultural associations, biodiversity and settlement patterns.

(b) *Landscape classification*. As noted above, this may have already been provided by a local authority, Natural England or others. The principal purpose is to identify areas of similar character and defining characteristics or features, and then to see how they relate to each other and how robust certain areas to any proposed changes in use or management would be. As the Countryside Commission stated *'landscape is more than just the sum of its parts'* (*Landscape Assessment Guidance*, CCP 423) so it is necessary to describe how individual elements relate to each other.

(c) *Landscape evaluation*. This is an assessment of the quality and value of the landscape summarising why it is or is not important. The Countryside Commission (CCP 423) produces Field Survey Sheets which may be utilised for the above process. At this stage it is essential to take the opinions of residents into account and to reach a consensus as to what is important and why. The more recent local authority landscape assessments significantly incorporate feedback from public consultation exercises.

2. Visual impact assessment. This determines the area from which a proposed development may be seen (the ZVI).

(a) *Zone of Visual Influence.* This is established by a combination of desk study using Ordnance Survey maps and contours and/or a digital terrain model computer programme, and field survey, which confirms the findings of the desk study. The field survey is also used to obtain photographs using the typical eye level view to illustrate the actual nature of the view. The desk study ZVI is refined by the field study, which can establish that intervening features such as woodland and buildings can limit the visual envelope.

(b) *Visual impact.* This entails using a number of discrete viewpoints which may be agreed with the landscape officer of the local authority or Natural England in advance. These should be chosen to represent particular key views that may be sensitive to change or designated areas from which policy may dictate that views should not be changed to any great extent. Distinction should be made between public and private views. Views at different seasons and including day and night-time vistas should be used. Key receptors and their sensitivity should be recorded. The impacts have to be illustrated, and this can be done by 'before and after' sketches, but their representation is most successfully achieved by using visually verified photomontages, for which considerable accuracy is required. Scale models can also be used, but they tend to accentuate 'birds eye' views, which of course are unrepresentative of the 'normal view'.

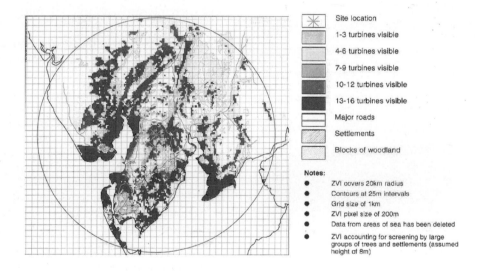

Example of a computer-generated ZVI

Site location
1-3 turbines visible
4-6 turbines visible
7-9 turbines visible
10-12 turbines visible
13-16 turbines visible
Major roads
Settlements
Blocks of woodland

Notes:
- ZVI covers 20km radius
- Contours at 25m intervals
- Grid size of 1km
- ZVI pixel size of 200m
- Data from areas of sea has been deleted
- ZVI accounting for screening by large groups of trees and settlements (assumed height of 8m)

3. Evaluation. Once the landscape and visual resource that may be affected by the proposed development, together with any recorded designated areas or areas covered by landscape policies, has been identified, the impacts and their significance can be predicted. Impacts may include the loss of particular elements or changes in character and views, and are always related to existing quality, sensitivity and enhancement potential. The significance of change is assessed by identifying impacts on the landscape character of an area or locality, the landscape resource and the visual resource.

Significance criteria include national, regional or local importance, sensitivity to change, rarity, uniqueness, representativeness, cultural association and effects on designated areas. The effects on designated areas should include a consideration of the importance of any change.

*Landscape and Visual
Impact Assessment (LVIA)*

To an extent, the question of 'significance' will be a judgement, but it is possible to quantify distance of views, numbers of people affected and whether they are residents or visitors. Such information can initially be gleaned from desk study, but can be enhanced by means of questionnaires or public exhibitions. Any subjective opinions should be clearly stated as such.

The evaluation should take into account the time taken for any mitigation such as tree planting to take effect and for any predicted changes which will take place, e.g. change of management regime, irrespective of whether the proposed development proceeds.

Mitigation

The principal aim of landscape mitigation is to 'design out' negative impacts, and requires close liaison within the team from an early stage. In other words, 'mitigation' starts at the commencement of the design process, including decisions relating to alternative site options. The opportunities to explore landscape enhancement options, especially where these will contribute to local authority aspirations for an area, should be considered.

Frequently, landscape design or management proposals may be perceived as a restoration of, or improvement to, the existing landscape. Even so, such restoration may involve impacts, e.g. dust or temporary soil storage, and such measures adopted to mitigate this should be described.

Care should be taken during consultation to ensure that what may appear to be 'derelict' landscapes are not actually valued for local or national reasons.

In developing the mitigation strategy, it is essential to set out the design objectives, e.g. screen, break line of sight or respect designations, and should be based on the landscape character and visual context of the area in which the development site is located. Mitigation for such effects can be approached by using the mitigation hierarchy:

Avoidance
- Achieved by locating elsewhere, alternative location within the development site, or overall design. If alternatives are considered but rejected, the reasons should be reported in the ES.

Reduction
- This reduces the landscape and visual impact to a point where a scheme which, whilst apparent, may not adversely affect the landscape or visual resource. Measures include screening by using existing vegetation or topography, new planting or bunds, and design of structures, their colour or finish. At all times, respecting the existing landscape pattern or structure maximises the effectiveness of such measures.

Remediation
- This includes new earth modelling, replacement of lost features or new planting.

Enhancement
- Offsite planting or other positive measures, e.g. river restoration or contribution to the overall green infrastructure strategy.

case example

Blaenavon

In the 1980s, schemes were prepared for the restoration of the derelict landscape of previous open-cast coal workings. These schemes never progressed, and in 2000 the area was included in the Blaenavon World Heritage Site as representing a historic landscape and evidence of the activities for which the area is important.

The effectiveness of the mitigation will need to be monitored, and measures to rectify any shortfalls identified and committed to in the ES. For example, a local authority may wish to ensure that proposed screening measures are implemented and are effective by regular monitoring. Landscape does not reach its maximum effectiveness overnight, and so management of planting is an essential requirement for the success of such mitigation.

Summary of Mitigation at Stages of Development

Pre-development	Advanced planting to assist screening Earth moving and formation of screen bunds
Design stage	Incorporate existing landscape features, e.g. water features, hedgerows or woodland belts, into the scheme design Grouping of buildings to minimise intrusion Design to reflect local architectural character or form, e.g. farm buildings, or create new complementary features New planting areas to screen important views Use colours and materials to reduce the prominence of buildings Introduce new landscape features consistent with the local landscape character, e.g. wetland habitats
Construction and operation	Protect and maintain existing landscape features Use low-level shrouded lighting consistent with security requirements
Restoration	Clear the site and restore or recreate habitats or woodland using local indigenous plant species.

Sources of information

Type	*Source*
Character Map of England	Natural England
Relevant designations	Natural England; English Heritage; local authorities
Countryside Stewardship	Natural England
AONB landscape guides	Natural England
Rights of Way	Local Authority
Common land	Land Registry
Environmentally Sensitive Areas (ESAs)	Defra
Soils	Soil Survey of England and Wales
Geology	BGS
Historic features	Ordnance Survey and private mapmakers
Aerial photographs	Ordnance Survey and private suppliers

Further information

Chartered Landscape Institute

IEMA

The Landscape Character Network (supported by Natural England)

Institute of Leisure and Amenity Management

English Heritage 2000. *Yesterdays World, Tomorrows Landscape*

National Trust 2000. *Archaeology and the Historic Environment: Historic Landscape Survey Guidelines*

Countryside Commission for Wales 2001. *Guide to Best Practice in Seascape Assessment*

Institute of Lighting Engineers 1997. *Guidance Notes for the Reduction of Light Pollution*

Countryside Commission 1997. *Lighting in the Countryside: Towards Good Practice*

"
EIA is now an integral and well established part of the UK land use planning process

– www.rtpi.org.uk
"

---

case example

Proposed Windfarm

This proposal was accompanied by an ES and supported by a planning statement. The Planning Statement discussed the need for wind energy and the strength of UK policy in favour of wind energy, and then identified national and local policy documents and debated their particular relevance to the proposal. It concluded with a discussion of the policy issues: Policy AT identifies access tracks as a key issue. The support statement explained how the impacts on the access tracks would be minimized and how the granting of planning permission would not breach Policy AT.

---

case example

Football Stadium Development

The land-use planning/policy context of this ES very briefly identified the land-use designation for the site and its surroundings such as Conservation Areas, Listed Buildings and SSSIs. This was followed with a review of relevant policy documents – national (PPSs), regional (RSSs) and local (development plan documents and Conservation Area briefs) – and focused on the principles which these sought to apply as being relevant to the proposed development. For example, Policy WD required that new residential development should provide facilities for recycling waste. At no point did the ES attempt to 'promote' the development.

Key Features

- An analysis of landscape character is fundamental to the assessment of landscape impacts.

- The separate but related discipline of visual impact assessment is specifically concerned with any change in views as a result of changes to the landscape.

- Landscape takes time to mature, and mitigation proposals must make clear the time taken to be effective.

- Landscape effects can interact with historic features and ecology.

- Landscape and visual effects are often the principal change perceived by the public as a result of development.

3.10 Planning Context

Introduction

Any proposed development, whether it requires planning consent or whether it falls under other consent regimes, will be subject to a range of planning policies relating to the locality. There may also be statutory designations and standards on and for the development site and its environs; these have been referred to in the previous sections. Since planning authorities are required to determine planning applications in accordance both with international and government guidance and with the development plan documents for the area, such applications will generally be accompanied by a supporting planning statement which will attempt to demonstrate compliance, or degree of compliance, with the applicable policies. It is not a requirement of the EIA Regulations that such compliance is repeated in an ES.

However, *EIA: A Guide to Procedures* (DETR 2000) does advise that the policy framework should be described. Any description should, therefore, demonstrate how such policies have been taken into account in formulating the project: frequently, a developer will examine the relevant local planning policies to identify a range of sites where the proposed development would be compliant. If this process is carried out, it is appropriate for it to be described in a section in the ES on alternatives.

In considering various international, national and local policies and guidance, it is useful to:

- record the status of the document (e.g. the date, whether adopted or non-statutory guidance)

- highlight key issues relevant to the development

- explain how the documents have been taken into account.

The planning review is not a 'promotional' element of the ES but should be balanced and impartial; separate planning support statements do not necessarily need to follow this approach.

Assessment of Effects

This requires a description of the existing land uses of the site and its surroundings – which broadly may be recorded in the local planning documents, including landscape descriptions and assessments. Comparison with the land-use requirements – which include, for example, temporary uses or access arrangements – of the project allows conclusions to be drawn by the regulatory authority officers. Of particular interest will be:

- land allocated in the statutory local development plan documents for specific uses, especially where these do not comply with the use being sought: mixed-use land for employment and residential use is held at a premium

- the site's relationship to the settlement boundary or limit of development, and whether it is previously developed land

- effects on adjacent sensitive land uses, e.g. residential, health care or educational (in some instances, a proposed land use will be incompatible with those existing on adjacent sites)

- sterilisation of mineral resources

- loss of agricultural land

- linking with an integrated transport system

- carbon footprints and natural resources efficiencies (e.g. in some areas, water supply and wastewater treatment may be a limiting factor for proposed development; in all areas, adaptation to predicted effects of climate change will be expected, such as the use of renewable energy sources).

The Planning and Compulsory Purchase Act 2004 requires the preparation of Regional Spatial Strategies (RSSs) and Local Development Frameworks (LDFs). Revisions to planning regulations and PPS12 in 2008 aim for greater flexibility to local authorities, e.g. it is now possible to include strategic site allocations in the core strategy.

Mitigation

In this context, mitigation is the selection of a site whose proposed use in the development plan document is compatible with that proposed by the developer. If the development, whilst otherwise acceptable, would sterilise minerals, then the prior mining of those minerals may well be an option to mitigate the otherwise negative impact. Water capacities for supply and the treatment of wastewaters can be limiting in certain areas such as the east and south east of England; developments that minimise water use or are water-neutral can be acceptable.

Reducing greenhouse gas emissions and adapting to the predicted effects of climate change are major factors in spatial and development planning; developments that include energy minimisation, and provide for on- or offsite renewable energy sources, will help to mitigate any negative effects of a proposal on existing infrastructure and resources. Similarly, waste minimisation and recovery/reuse would be expected to progress towards sustainable development objectives and targets. Another key mitigation option would be contributions to an integrated transport system, e.g. new cycle ways and footpaths, linkages and improvements to public transport.

Contributions to biodiversity improvements – new and/or restored habitats, especially promoting connectivity – will also facilitate development approvals: these are best if integrated within an overall green infrastructure strategy.

case example

Wastewater Treatment Works

The ES for this proposal included a policy context section. This looked briefly at the international treaties (e.g. the Ramsar Convention, EC Directives), national legislation and guidance (e.g. the Environmental Protection Act 1990, the UK Strategy for Sustainable Development, Circulars and PPGs/PPSs) and development plan documents. In all cases, it identified the particular status of the documents and drew out the relevant sections for the proposal. However, it also included a summary paragraph which attempted to demonstrate how the proposal was in accord with the policy context. This is acceptable, but phrases such as 'broadly in accordance with the provisions' might lead the reader to suspect (rightly or wrongly) that there are some elements which may not be in accordance with policy.

Sources of information

- International treaties and conventions
- Planning Policy Guidance and Statements
- Minerals Planning Guidance Notes and Minerals Policy Statements
- Regional Spatial Strategies
- County and Unitary Plans
- LDFs, including Area Action Plans and Site Allocations documents
- Minerals and Wastes Local Development Frameworks
- Planning briefs and masterplans
- Other supplementary planning documents e.g. green infrastructure

Review of Planning History

It is also helpful to consider the planning history of the site and, if appropriate, adjacent sites. While interpreting previous decisions would principally be of use in site selection and prior to submitting a planning application, it can also be used to demonstrate how the development's design had been modified or its impacts mitigated in order to overcome what had previously been identified as key issues. Nonetheless, every planning application should be treated on its merits – not only might design have been modified since previous applications but policy may have changed.

Summary of Compliance

The section in the ES reviewing planning context is best undertaken by considering each potential effect in turn. For each, there should be a clear statement on whether the development complies or not. There are not degrees of compliance. It is not appropriate to argue that the proposal would comply if certain mitigation action was taken – that action should already form part of the proposal. There should be a summary at the end of the section setting out the compliance. It is not appropriate for the ES to argue that non-compliance is acceptable because of other advantages of the scheme: that is a matter for the planning authority to consider. A full statement of compliance with policies from national down to local level can be both lengthy and tedious to read as part of the body of the text of the ES: it is good practice to place such information in a technical annex or appendix.

3.11   Integration and Synthesis

Introduction

The effects that a proposed development project may have on any one environmental topic are likely to have effects on other topics, and yet the interactions between them are rarely specifically addressed in EIAs. This may be associated with the lack of a standard method for assessing impact interactions, but it is often related to the practice of addressing each significant environmental topic separately in the ES. Scoping should identify potential interactions, although cumulative and indirect effects, as well as interactions, may also become apparent as the EIA progresses.

The EIA Regulations require a description of the interactions between effects, and an assessment of indirect and cumulative effects – these are often associated with interactions. For example, effluent discharges to a watercourse may affect flow regimes and water quality such that a habitat may be affected; traffic and air quality and noise are clearly interrelated with each other, and they affect the well-being and health of local communities and wildlife. The consideration of interactions is an essential part of **Cumulative Effects Assessment** (CEA).

As far as possible, the interactions between potential effects should be considered as part of the impact assessments carried out for each environmental topic and reported separately for clarity in the ES. Interactions between effects should also be considered for each stage of the project: construction, operation/occupation and decommissioning/restoration.

It can be useful for the reader if the ES summarises cumulative effects and interactions, intended mitigation measures, and any residual impacts in a final short section. This approach unifies the various environmental topics, thus acknowledging the complex interrelationships amongst environmental systems. It is inappropriate for an ES to reach conclusions as such, since the decision-making is carried out by others. The section may rather summarise impacts assessment and interactions, together with mitigation and how it will be achieved. Such an integrated and holistic approach follows the principles of sustainability.

The EIA Regulations require a description in the ES of the *interrelationships* between environmental factors likely to be significantly affected by the proposed development. When considering the effects of the development on the environment, the description of effects should cover:

- direct and indirect
- secondary
- cumulative
- short, medium and long term
- permanent and temporary
- positive and negative

Key fact

The integrated assessment of effects, including direct, indirect and cumulative, together with interactions, contributes towards sustainable development

guiding principle

Sustainability and sustainable development should not be confused – they are different

"

Environmental impacts are at the core of sustainability concerns

– Sadler, B. 1999 in Petts, J. *Handbook of Environmental Impact Assessment* "

Definitions

- *Impact*: a change to the environment attributable to the proposed development.
- *Effect*: the result of an impact on a receptor or resource.
- *Direct effect*: an effect arising from an impact attributable to an element or an activity of the project.
- *Indirect effect*: an effect which does not directly impact on a receptor or resource.
- *Secondary effect*: an effect which may arise as a consequence of another effect, often between different environmental topics.
- *Cumulative effect*: these may arise from:
  - interactions between different effects at the same location
  - interactions of different effects over time
  - additive or multiple impacts over time or space
  - effects of a number of developments.
- *Short/medium/long term*: there are no standard categories, but typical timescales may be 0–2/2–5/5–10 years. The environmental agencies are thinking in terms of 30 or 50 years; some planning authorities are thinking of more than the 10–20 years of a development plan, particularly with regard to climate change and energy issues.
- *Permanent effect*: an effect which is irreversible or likely to persist for the life of the development.
- *Temporary effect*: an effect which is limited either because the impact ceases or because the environment can assimilate it.

Integration and Synthesis

Cumulative effects can arise from actions and processes as follows:

- additive
- interactive
- sequential
- multiple
- synergistic
- threshold exceedence.

"

The changes that have been made to ecosystems (over the past 50 years) have contributed to substantial net gains in human well-being and economic development, but these gains have been achieved at growing costs in the form of degradation of many ecosystem services... The challenge of reversing the degradation... can be partially met... but will involve significant changes in policy...

– UN 2005. *Millennium Ecosystem Assessment* *"*

Valued Ecosystem Component (VEC)

VECs are used in CEA, and represent any part of the environment that is considered important by the developer, the public, scientists or the government involved in the assessment process. The importance may be determined on the basis of cultural values or scientific knowledge/concern

Further information

EC 1999. *Guidelines on the Assessment of Indirect and Cumulative Impacts.* www.europa.eu.int

Canadian Environmental Assessment Agency 1999. *Cumulative Effects Assessment Practitioners Guide.* www.ceaa.gc.ca

US Council on Environmental Quality 1997. *Considering Cumulative Effects Under the National Environmental Policy Act.* www.epa.gov

Canter, L. 1999. Cumulative Effects Assessment. In: Petts, J. 1999. (ed.) *Handbook of Environmental Impact Assessment*

IAIA 2008. *Assessing and Managing Cumulative Environmental Effects.* www.iaia.org

Key fact

The Royal Commission on Environmental Protection (RCEP) in Environmental Planning (2002) said that more advice is needed on '... *how exactly to analyse indirect and cumulative effects of development options*' (www.rcep.org.uk)

Cumulative Effects Assessment

Cumulative effects of human activities, such as climate change and loss of biodiversity, have led to notable scientists predicting that environmental deterioration may be reaching critical thresholds with irreversible loss of natural systems. The prediction of impacts affecting the global system are very difficult to estimate at the project level, and such matters may be better dealt with at the strategic plan and policy level through Strategic Environmental Assessment (SEA) (see Chapter 6).

Cumulative effects are the total effect on a given resource, ecosystem or human community of all actions taken, past, present and in the foreseeable future; they rarely correlate with political and administrative boundaries. Cumulative effects also come from existing activities, e.g. emissions and resource use from commerce, industry and transport movements. Therefore, CEA is perhaps better suited to assessing effects over wider spatial scales (e.g. global, national, regional and sub-regional) and temporal boundaries rather than a single project. The implementation of the European SEA Directive has promoted this approach at the strategic level of decision-making (see Chapter 6: SEA).

EIA Circular 02/99 states that CEA applies to the specific development, and the responsibility for determining the cumulative impacts of a proposal in combination with other existing or proposed '*developments*' is that of the planning authority. This assessment is based on information provided by developers. There can be issues when cumulative effects are identified – who is responsible for mitigation? CEA and consideration of interactions demonstrate a holistic and integrated approach that contributes towards the objectives of sustainable development.

Cumulative effects can result from multiple pathways, and can impact on both biophysical and socio-economic resources and systems. These effects may be significant even though the individual effects may be insignificant when assessed separately. There is no standard method for CEA in the UK; however, there is comprehensive guidance elsewhere, e.g. from the EU, Canada and the USA. CEAs typically build upon existing methods and approaches in EIA; a useful aspect is the consideration of VECs. In the UK, reliance is often put on professional judgement and expert opinion.

CEA methods and techniques include:

- questionnaires, interviews, panels and workshops
- checklists and matrices
- network, systems and causal chain analyses/diagrams
- modelling
- trends analysis
- overlay mapping and GIS
- carrying capacity and threshold assessment
- ecological and carbon footprinting
- forecasting and backcasting; horizon scanning

Sustainability and Sustainable Development

Sustainable development is the core principle underpinning the UK spatial and development planning system; PPS1 sets out how sustainable development will be delivered through planning. The second sustainable development strategy (Defra 2005, *Securing the Future*), covering the period to 2020, sets out a framework for policy in the UK founded on five guiding principles:

- living within environmental limits
- ensuring a strong, healthy and just society
- achieving a sustainable economy
- promoting good governance
- using sound science responsibly

It may be argued that sustainability is about whether or not to develop, whereas sustainable development presumes that development will progress. A key aspect of the revision of the UK sustainable development strategy was the change in principles from '*respecting environmental limits*' to '*living within environmental limits*'. This recognises that environmental sustainability is fundamental to the delivery of sustainable development. With the strategic context for environmental decision-making now guided by the requirements of the European Strategic Environmental Assessment Directive (see Chapter 6: SEA), decision-making at the project level EIA should become more focused. The cross-cutting characteristics of the priority actions and guiding principles may help with considerations of interrelationships between environmental topics in SEA and EIA.

Environmental sustainability is concerned with the regenerative and assimilative capacities of natural systems. The EIA Directive and Regulations require consideration of '*the... regenerative capacity of natural resources in the area; and the absorption capacity of the natural environment...*', indicating clear links between EIA and sustainability. The aims of the SEA Directive include '*...to promote sustainable development*', setting the strategic context for environmental assessment and sustainability.

Key fact

Sustainability and sustainable development are often used interchangeably, but they are different

Sustainability Appraisal (SA) methods have evolved from SEA methods, and are used during the preparation of development plan documents and for locational choices for development. These methods tend to be criteria-based, with objectives against which progress towards sustainable development can be assessed. In England and Wales, the requirements of the European SEA Directive are subsumed within the requirements for SA of spatial and development plans (see Chapter 6: SEA).

Key fact

EIA has a role to play in securing sustainable construction and operation (and decommissioning, if appropriate) as elements of mitigation

The interrelationships of sustainable development within EIA are likely to be addressed throughout the ES with the appropriate planning context for particular issues. Mitigation and enhancement proposals can be aligned with sustainability objectives of other plans and programmes. Some ESs now include a section on sustainable development; however, it is felt that this is beyond the requirements of the EIA Directive and Regulations, and details are more appropriately presented in a sustainability report that might accompany a planning application, together with other supporting information. Local planning authorities are increasingly requesting sustainability assessments of major projects,

Further information

Office of the Deputy Prime Minister 2005. *Sustainability Appraisal of Regional Spatial Plans and Local Development Frameworks*

Barton, H. *et al.* 2003. *Shaping Neighbourhoods: Health, Sustainability and Community*

BRE Sustainability Checklists for developers. www.bre.co.uk

Department for Business, Enterprise and Regulatory Reform 2008. The Strategy for Sustainable Construction. www.berr.gov.uk

UK Sustainable Development Commission. www.sd-commission.org.uk

DCLG 2006. *Planning for the Protection of European Sites: Appropriate Assessment* (draft guidance)

Association of Public Health Observatories. The HIA Gateway. www.apho.org.uk

and a number of methods and sustainability standards have developed, e.g. the Sustainability Checklist for Developers (SEEDA 2006, www.seeda.co.uk). The mitigation and enhancement commitments in an ES may be secured through s106 agreements (see Section 3.10, 'Planning Context'). The proposed Community Infrastructure Levy will be set by local authorities, and may be at different rates according to development type; revenue will be used to support local infrastructure.

Links with Other Assessment Processes

The evolving practice of sustainability appraisal and assessment has developed an improved understanding of cross-cutting issues, e.g. climate change, and potential actions for resolving problems. This experience has transferred to EIA practice, and may help with assessing the interrelationships between topics in environmental assessment, as required by both the EIA and the SEA Directives. Practical synergies have also been found with carrying out the impact assessment requirements for the European Habitats Directive; this, together with other requirements for assessment, e.g. equality and health, has led some plan-makers to use Integrated Assessment. However, different processes have a specific role at particular stages of decision-making.

Habitats Regulation Assessment/Appropriate Assessment (HRA/AA) is required for plans and projects likely to have a significant effect on a European or internationally important site for nature conservation. The UK Regulations (2006) require HRA/AA of spatial and development plans.

Health Impact Assessment (HIA) typically examines how factors such as transport, employment, housing and the built environment can affect health and well-being. The core determinants of health are age, sex, hereditary and individual lifestyle factors; social and community influences, living and working conditions and general socio-economic, cultural and environmental conditions are also major contributors.

Chapter 4

Development Types

Environmental Impact Assessment (EIA) is site-specific, and the extent of potential impacts is dependent on the quality and characteristics of the receiving environment. However, development types tend to have characteristics also, and these may suggest typical environmental impacts. This chapter is presented in checklist format for easy reference, and lists key potential impacts, mitigation, monitoring, environmental management and further guidance for a range of development types. It also draws attention to the opportunities for environmental enhancement from development proposals.

4.1   Introduction

A number of development types drawn from the principal sectors of activity in the UK are addressed in this chapter. For each, the key characteristics of the development are listed, together with the legal requirement for EIA. The main scope of the EIA is indicated as a checklist of issues/terms of reference. This is only intended as a guide, since the actual scope for any one EIA will be determined through the scoping exercise and will be site-specific. The likely impacts are shown with potential mitigation options: examples are indicated, but there will be many more creative solutions to resolving potential environmental problems. Key legislation, guidance, key consultees and further sources of information are listed.

Within the context of environmental studies, development is often seen as detrimental to the environment. However, development can offer opportunities for environmental enhancement. Government policy supports the principle that it is reasonable to expect developers to contribute towards the cost of infrastructure – and this may include environmental benefits. Adapting to the predicted effects of climate change is vital to the planning of any project; potential benefits may accrue from contributions to ecosystems services, efficient use of natural resources and material assets, including green infrastructure. It is essential for developers that this is considered early in project planning.

guiding principle

EIA is site-specific but includes consideration of alternative locations and effects outside the site boundary

Further information

Department for Communities and Local Government (DCLG) 2007. Planning Policy Statement: Planning and Climate Change. www.communities.gov.uk

Construction Industry Research and Information Association (CIRIA). www.ciria.org

Sustainable Construction. www.sustainable-construction.org.uk

Green Infrastructure. www.greeninfrastructure.eu

4.2   Characteristics of Projects

Every Environmental Statement (ES) should provide a full factual description of the project. Developers are also required by the 1999 EIA Regulations to include an outline of the main alternative approaches to the proposed development and the main reasons for their choice. Strategic Environmental Assessment (SEA) should have already considered *'reasonable alternatives'* at the strategic planning level, and there will be some developments for which there are no meaningful alternatives.

The EIA Regulations require that the characteristics of projects must be considered having regard to:

Characteristics of
Projects

■ the size of the project
■ the cumulation with other projects
■ the use of natural resources
■ the production of waste
■ the risk of accidents and hazardous materials
■ pollution and nuisances.

The screening and scoping stages of the EIA process will have
described the project to an increasing degree. The level of detail
required for the final ES is as follows.

Project Description

■ Site setting and context of development:
  - general description of the proposed site location to include
    topography, catchment, land use and transport.
■ Purpose and physical characteristics of the development:
  - area of site at all phases of the project including temporary
    contractors' compounds or laydown areas and access
  - design, size and height of buildings, structures, roads,
    landscaping, utilities.
■ Project features should include all stages:
  - construction
  - operation/occupation
  - decommissioning
  - restoration.
■ Operational characteristics of the development:
  - traffic (private, delivery, occupiers) generated
  - employees, visitors, residents, occupiers including construction
    workers
  - type and volume of materials, energy and resources used
  - frequency and duration of intrusive activities
  - energy consumption or production
  - emissions by type, quantity and quality – water, air, soil, noise,
    vibration, light, heat, radiation
  - residues such as wastes and methods of treatment – recycling,
    reuse.
■ Alternatives: sites, processes, options.

*The description should make full use of maps, figures, drawings, sketches or
photomontages to illustrate the proposed development, locality and setting.*

4.3   Minerals Extraction

Characteristics of Minerals Extraction Projects

- Risk of pollution, accident and nuisance.
- Temporary use of the land.
- Restoration commitment is essential and long-term.
- Commitment to an Environmental Management Plan (EMP) is important.
- Opportunities for environmental, recreational and amenity enhancement for local communities.
- Alternatives may be limited to consideration of processes and phasing, since minerals can only be exploited where they are found.

Scope of EIA

The main considerations for minerals extraction are the scale of the development, emissions to air, discharges to water, risk of accident, and transport. Depending on the type of minerals development, environmental issues typically include visual intrusion, noise, dust, discharges to water, ecology, risk of accident and transport.

Mining, especially opencast, is very much a temporary use of the land and its resources; landscape architects have used the term 'landscape on loan' to describe (or perhaps downplay) its potential effects above ground. Therefore, the temporary nature of impacts are as important as the permanent or 'on restoration' proposals.

Because of the long-term nature of these temporary impacts, environmental management is of particular importance, and the mining and extraction industry has in recent years led the field in its practical application. Since the exploitation of minerals is only temporary, mitigation must focus on restoration proposals.

Since minerals can only be exploited where they are found, alternative sites are not an option. However, alternative routings for traffic, and alternative process and infrastructure location still apply. (Renewal of Minerals Permissions (ROMPs) are subject to EIA for registration and review – EIA Regulations as amended 2000.)

Key Consultees

- Local authorities: planning, highways, conservation, environmental health
- Minerals and Waste Planning Authority
- Environment Agency
- Conservation, heritage and community groups
- Coal Authority
- Health and Safety Executive
- English Heritage
- Natural England

EIA Regulations Projects Schedule

Schedule 1

Quarries and opencast	over 25 ha
Peat extraction	over 150 ha

Schedule 2

Quarries, opencast and peat extraction

Underground mining

Fluvial dredging for minerals

Deep drillings

Surface industrial installations for extraction of coal, petroleum, natural gas, ores and bituminous shale (see also Section 4.4) over 0.5 ha

---

Other key legislation and guidance

Minerals Planning Guidance nos 3, 7, 11

Minerals Policy Statements nos 1 & 2

PPS 23 Planning and Pollution Control EIA and Habitats (Extraction of Minerals by Marine Dredging) Regulations 2007

Groundwater Regulations 1998

Minerals Extraction

Potential issues/ EIA terms of reference	Potential impacts on the environment
Population	Accidents from traffic Public health Social effects on existing communities Nuisance
Noise and vibration	Noise from blasting and drilling Noise from traffic
Ecology	Damage or loss to terrestrial or aquatic habitats or species Hedgerows
Land and soils	Subsidence Erosion or damage to soil Risk of pollution Effects on agriculture
Water	Hydrological disturbance to aquifers or watercourses Elevated suspended solids in watercourses Risk of pollution
Air and climate	Dust from blasting Dust and pollution from traffic
Cultural heritage	Loss or damage to historic buildings, features or their settings
Landscape	Visual impact Changes to landscape character
Use of resources	Waste management

Potential options for mitigation	Opportunities for environmental enhancement
Different mining technologies Alternative locations for infrastructure Traffic management and timing Environmental management Environmental liaison officer	New local road layouts Traffic calming New access and Rights of Way Recreation and amenity areas
Timing of operations Acoustic barriers	–
Avoidance	Creation of new or additional habitats Connections to green networks
Separation and storage of soils Environmental management Access for agricultural users	Restoration to more appropriate land use
Environmental management	Restoration of watercourses Contributing to the natural functioning of floodplains
Timing of operations Use of rail or water transport Damping down roads and vehicles	–
Avoidance Pre-development survey Watching brief	Education
Screening of operations, e.g. mounding and planting	New woodlands New hedgerows
Waste management plan	Recycling and reuse

Commitment to Restoration

Since restoration to an agreed standard is critical to the consenting of minerals extraction, regulatory bodies will require assurance of a commitment to such restoration. Some bodies frequently request payment of a bond prior to commencement of operations which is forfeited if restoration is not carried out (the bond can then be used by the regulator to undertake the restoration). If appropriate, phased restoration in the case of progressive quarrying or opencast mining can be implemented.

Restoration can include enhancement of the environment by planting of new woodlands (especially in advance of operations); improvement of watercourses; new hedgerows; new Rights of Way/access (including 'country park'-type options for the local community); soil management; and new roads and highways. Restoration may not always be to put back what was there before, e.g. agricultural land can be restored as lakes and wetlands: there can be opportunities for creative environmental design.

Middleton Hall, Staffs

Photograph courtesy of Hanson, reproduced with permission. © *Hanson*

Progressive development and restoration of sand and gravel quarries can make a positive contribution to nature conservation and public access. At Middleton Hall, Hanson's restoration is managed by the Royal Society for the Protection of Birds (RSPB) as a 170 ha wetland nature reserve

Key fact

Preparation of an EMP and compliance through operations should be a requirement of any mineral development

Further information

Walsh, F., Lee, N. and Wood, C. 1991. *Environmental Assessment of Open Cast Coal Mines*

CIRIA 1994. *Environmental Assessment, Special Publication 96*

Environment Agency 2002. *Scoping Guidelines for the EIA of Projects*

British Geological Survey

Minerals UK

Monitoring

- Archaeological watching brief during soil stripping.
- Monitor for noise and dust in accordance with environmental health officer (EHO) requirements.
- Water quality of discharges and groundwater levels.
- Compliance with the agreed traffic management plan.
- Compliance with:
  - predicted visual impact
  - ecological effects
  - land restoration
  - planting.

4.4 Energy

Characteristics of Energy Projects

- Safety and risk management is essential.
- Includes fuel supply, production and transmission.
- Renewable energy projects offer sustainable development opportunities.
- Non-renewable projects can affect climate change.
- Range of specific EIA Regulations under separate legislation.

Photograph courtesy of BP Exploration, reproduced with permission. © BP

Scope of EIA

Power stations need to be sited close to the source of energy (feedstock) and to cooling waters. They are, therefore, often sited in similar locations, and potential cumulative impacts need to be addressed. In the case of waste to energy or combined heat and power plants, the energy source is likely to be principally domestic or commercial waste requiring the plant for economic reasons to be sited in or near urban areas, when air pollution and traffic will be a major concern.

For non-renewable projects, full Life Cycle Analysis is required. Fuel extraction, energy production and transmission processes with construction, operation and restoration phases for each should be addressed.

Windfarms frequently raise concerns of the effects on ecology, landscape and noise. In all instances, transmission lines result in visual impact, as will above-ground pipelines.

The effects of the discharge of cooling water on the receiving aquatic environment have to be carefully considered, and schemes designed to minimise any impacts.

Key Consultees

- Health and Safety Executive
- Local authorities: planning, highways, environmental health
- Environment Agency
- Health Protection Agency
- Conservation, heritage and community groups
- English Heritage
- Natural England
- Department for Business, Enterprise and Regulatory Reform
- Coal Authority

EIA Regulations Projects Schedule

Schedule 1

Crude oil refineries

Thermal power stations and other combustion installations over 500 t

Nuclear power stations

Nuclear fuel production, processing, reprocessing

Storage and disposal of radioactive waste

Extraction of petroleum and natural gas over 500 t/day, over 500,000 m^3/day (see also Section 4.3)

Pipelines for the transport of gas, oil or chemicals over 800 mm diameter and over 40 km length

Storage of petroleum, petrochemical or chemical products over 200,000 t

Schedule 2

Production and transport of electricity, steam and hot water over 0.5/1.0 ha

Storage of gases and fossil fuels over 500 m^2 within 100 m of controlled waters

Industrial briquetting of coal and lignite over 1000 m^2

Processing and storage of radioactive waste over 1000 m^2 requires consent under the Radioactive Substances Act 1993

Hydroelectric energy production over 0.5 MW

Windfarms with more than two turbines or a hub height over 15 m

Key fact

The first EIA was for the trans-Alaska oil pipeline

Energy

Potential issues/ EIA terms of reference	Potential impacts on the environment
Population	Public health Risk of accidents Displacement (hydropower schemes) Transport nuisance and risk of pollution
Noise and vibration	Construction noise, especially drilling Low-frequency noise (windfarms) Noise from traffic Production and processing noise
Ecology	Temporary disturbance – construction Risk of spillages (pipelines) Bird strike and effects on bats (windfarms) Intertidal communities (barrages)
Land and soils	Effects on agriculture (pipelines) Temporary soils storage
Water	Cooling water discharges Risk of pollution Effects on hydrology and hydrogeology
Air and climate	Cumulative effects of emissions Climate change Dust during construction
Cultural heritage	Loss or damage to historic features or their settings
Landscape	Visual impact (especially windfarms)
Use of resources	Renewables can lead to positive effects Waste management, storage and treatment

Potential options for mitigation	Opportunities for environmental enhancement
Health and safety plan Pollution contingency plan Hazard, risk and environmental management Traffic management plan	Recreation and amenity from hydropower and barrage schemes New local road layouts Traffic calming
Timing of construction Acoustic barriers Avoidance of populated areas	–
Avoidance of habitats Adherence to agreed methods Creation of alternative habitats	Creation of new habitats Linkages to green networks
Maintenance of access for agricultural users	–
Environmental management Process design Water reuse	Restoration of watercourses Creation of wetlands
Use of renewable options contributes to climate change targets	Use of rail or waterborne transport
Avoidance Pre-development survey Watching brief	Education
Avoidance of sensitive areas Screening	New woodlands/hedgerows
Use of renewable options Waste management	Recycling and reuse

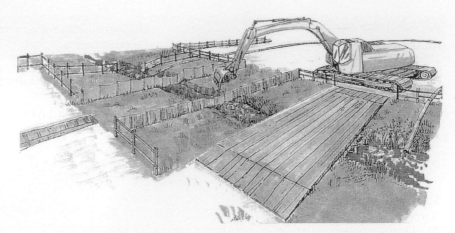

Extract from an ES demonstrating working methods of pipeline construction

case example

Gas pipeline

A proposed gas pipeline had to cross a wetland of international importance. Whilst a route was selected to cross the wetland by underground directional drilling at the narrowest point, detailed studies were required to determine the impact of the crossing on the adjacent aquatic environment and associated fauna and flora. Working methods were specified, and a commitment was made in the ES to ensure compliance.

Other key legislation and guidance

Large Combustion Plant Directive (revised) 2001

The Nuclear Installations Act 1965 (as amended) (for Licensed Nuclear Sites)

Electricity Act 1989

Environmental Protection Act 1990

Water Resources Act 1991

Radioactive Substances Act 1993 (amended)

Petroleum Act 1998

Pollution Prevention and Control Act 1999 and Regulations 2000

Offshore Petroleum Production and Pipelines (Assessment of Environmental Effects) Regulations 1999

Nuclear Reactors (EIA for Decommissioning) Regulations 1999 (as amended)

Public Gas Transporter Pipe-line Works (EIA) Regulations 1999

Electricity Works (EIA) Regulations 2000

Pipe-line Works (EIA) Regulations 2000 (as amended)

PPS22: *Renewable Energy*

British Wind Energy Association 1994. *Best Practice Guidelines for Wind Energy Development*

Department of Trade and Industry (DTI) 1992. *Guidelines for the Environmental Assessment of Cross Country Pipelines*

Environment Agency 2002. *Scoping Guidelines for the EIA of Projects*

Further information

Department for Environment Food and Rural Affairs (Defra) 2006. *Action in the UK – The UK Climate Change Programme*

National Grid

Health Protection Agency

Environment Agency National Groundwater and Contaminated Land Centre

Pipeline Industries Guild

Health and Safety Executive 2002. *COSHH: A Brief Guide to the Regulations*

Defra 2005. *IPPC: A Practical Guide*

DTI 2006. *The Energy Challenge: Energy Review Report*

Environmental Protection UK 2007. *Pollution Handbook*

Office of the Deputy Prime Minister 2004. *Planning for Renewable Energy: A Companion Guide to PPS22*

Commitment to Construction Techniques and Environmental Management Plans

It has long been recognised that long-distance, below-ground pipelines can have potentially damaging effects if careful working methods are not followed. Apart from safety aspects and pollution risk in the event of fracture, pipelines can act as a drain and affect hydrological features; a barrier to wildlife; and, if not properly restored, can be visually apparent and reduce habitat or agricultural land quality. For this reason, pipeline promoters made an early commitment to the principles of environmental management planning.

For each project, an EMP has to be produced to ensure that valued features are protected, working methods are employed and restoration to the required standard is carried out. It is customary to include an outline in the ES of these proposals so that they can be conditioned and monitored by the authorising authority and so that contractors have an indication of environmental constraints.

Monitoring

- Routine discharges of radiation to the environment.
- Cooling water quantities and characteristics, especially temperature and disinfectants.
- Noise and emissions to air.
- Restoration compliance.

4.5   Wastes Management

Characteristics of Wastes Management Projects

- Only some 25% of wastes generated in the UK is controlled waste – the rest comes from agriculture (20%) and mining/quarrying/demolition.
- Waste management is based on the hierarchy of reduce, reuse, recycle.
- A key feature is energy recovery or production of compost from waste.
- For 'temporary' projects such as landfill or landraising, a commitment to restoration is important and can result in enhancement, especially of mineral workings.

Scope of EIA

The range of methods of waste management leads to very different effects. Landfill or landraising, usually based on a completed mineral project, will entail a continuation of the same type of activities in terms of movement of plant and materials. New hazards may arise such as landfill gas, leachate, odour and noise – visual impact is frequently an important issue. The EIA has also to consider the length of time the scheme will last and the restoration proposals and commitments.

Other waste management facilities such as incineration, chemical treatment, waste transfer or recycling stations require built development, plant and possibly exhaust stacks. Incinerators may emit harmful gases and chemicals from incomplete combustion. In all instances, though, traffic noise and movement is likely to be a key issue.

Proposed landfill sites based on worked-out and abandoned mineral sites have to pay particular attention to ecological issues since such sites are frequently colonised by rare or protected species; bats in particular favour caves or fissures in mineral workings.

The location of sites for storage or disposal of wastes is always contentious due to the public perception of nuisance and health risk.

Key Consultees

- Health and Safety Executive
- Environment Agency
- Local authorities: planning, waste, highways, environmental health, conservation
- English Heritage
- Natural England
- Conservation, heritage and community groups.

The UK Waste Strategy 2007 is based on five key objectives:

- decouple waste growth (in all sectors) from economic growth and put more emphasis on waste prevention and re-use
- meet and exceed the Landfill Directive diversion targets for biodegradable municipal waste in 2010, 2013 and 2020
- increase diversion from landfill of non-municipal waste and secure better integration of treatment for municipal and non-municipal waste
- secure the investment in infrastructure needed to divert waste from landfill and for the management of hazardous waste
- get the most environmental benefit from that investment, through increased recycling of resources and recovery of energy from residual waste using a mix of technologies

---

EIA Regulations Projects Schedule

Schedule 1

Incineration, chemical treatment and landfill of hazardous waste

Incineration and chemical treatment of non-hazardous waste exceeding 100 t/day

Schedule 2

Installations for the disposal of waste not included in Schedule 1

Sludge deposition sites

Key fact

The Duty of Care is a statutory requirement that all producers or keepers of waste must prevent it causing pollution or harm

Key fact

The UK now recycles a third of its waste, a 300% increase since 1997.

– Environmental Services Association 2009 *Will Waste Strategy Review Provide a Roadmap to European Standards?*

Wastes Management

Potential issues/ EIA terms of reference	Potential impacts on the environment
Population	Perceived and actual public health risks Disturbance to amenity Nuisance (vermin, litter, etc.) Traffic generated during construction, operation and restoration Transboundary pollution transfer
Noise and vibration	Increased noise levels Traffic noise including reversing alarms
Ecology	Loss of habitat and protected species from restoration of minerals workings
Land and soils	Land contamination Temporary loss of agricultural land
Water	Leachate from landfill Pollution of surface or groundwaters
Air and climate	Landfill gas Odour (perceived or actual) Dust and particulates Pollutants from incomplete combustion
Cultural heritage	Loss of heritage features and settings
Landscape	Change or loss of valued landscape Visual impact (e.g. incinerator, stack or landraising)
Use of resources	Loss of potential resources Transboundary pollution transfer

Potential options for mitigation	Opportunities for environmental enhancement
Good operational management Community liaison Site design and facilities Traffic management plans	Restoration of derelict land Recreational and amenity afteruse
Good operational management Acoustic screens and housings	–
Avoid sites of ecological interest Relocation as a last resort	Restoration to more varied habitat and biodiversity Strengthen linkages to green networks
Soils storage, handling and management	Composting for soil restoration Restoration of derelict land to appropriate use
Landfill design Leachate collection and treatment	Restoration of watercourses
Good operational management Site design Gas scrubbing Negative pressure at sources of emissions	Waste to energy
Avoid sites of heritage interest Archaeological watching brief	–
Screening Site design Planting	Restoration of degraded landscape
Waste minimisation Domestic waste separation Recycling and reuse Composting	Waste to energy

Wastes Management

Other key legislation and guidance

The Directive on Waste (75/442/EEC, as amended by Directive 91/692/EEC)

Hazardous Waste Directive 1991

Integrated Pollution Prevention and Control (IPPC) Directive 1996

Landfill Directive 1999

Waste Incineration Directive 2000

Waste Electrical and Electronic Equipment (WEEE) Directive 2002

Environmental Protection Act 1990

Radioactive Substances Act 1993 (amended)

Environment Act 1995

Landfill Tax Regulations 1996 and Landfill Tax (Qualifying Material) Order 1996

Waste Management Licensing Regulations 1994

The Special Waste Regulations (amended) 2001

PPS10: *Planning for Sustainable Waste Management*

PPS23: *Planning and Pollution Control*

Defra 2007. *Waste Strategy for England 2007*

Further information

Environment Agency 2002. *Scoping Guidelines for the EIA of Projects*

Defra 2005. *IPPC: A Practical Guide*

Environmental Protection UK 2007. *Pollution Handbook*

Environment Agency. www.environment-agency.gov.uk

Chartered Institute of Wastes Management (CIWM)

Waste online. www.wasteonline.org.uk

case example

Landfill ES

A landraising operation in the green belt on the edge of a major conurbation had been operated successfully for many years with landfill gas management and leachate treatment. Access was good and, being near to the city, this contributed to the satisfactory operation of the site. It was proposed to extend the scheme and provide a materials recycling facility (MRF). The mitigation proposed was to plant extensive woodland to link with a new urban forest together with restoration of a channelized watercourse. An agreement was entered into to manage the woodland for 100 years for the benefit of the local community as a Country Park – demonstrating the commitment to mitigation.

Cumulative Impacts

The EU Landfill Directive has reduced the quantity of waste that can be taken to landfill, and the capacity of landfill sites in the UK is limited. Other methods of waste treatment and management continue to be explored and adopted. One of the options has been to consider the need for incineration, which has the added bonus of utilising the heat from waste combustion for energy generation. However, incinerators can emit toxins such as dioxins and heavy metals, giving the technique a poor public image. If the waste management industry is to pursue the incineration option, including local Combined Heat and Power, it will be necessary to consider the *cumulative impacts* of these plants, especially in the more populated areas. Recycling policy and targets, together with increased awareness, have led to more waste recycling centres with concomitant EIAs that similarly require addressing cumulative effects.

Monitoring

- Archaeological watching brief.
- Monitor for noise and dust in accordance with EHO requirements.
- Water quality of leachate, surface water and groundwater.
- Compliance with the agreed traffic management plan.
- Compliance with predicted:
  - visual impact
  - ecology
  - land restoration
  - planting.
- Stack emissions in accordance with Pollution Prevention and Control (PPC) requirements.

Restored landfill

4.6 Water

Characteristics of Water Projects

- Includes dams, reservoirs, water mains and pipelines, treatment works, and coast and river flood protection.
- See also Section 4.4 – hydroelectric and barrage schemes.
- Incorporation of sustainable drainage systems, where appropriate, into other development types.
- New and improved infrastructure can provide major environmental and social benefits.
- In UK planning – issues with water companies, regulators (Environment Agency and Ofwat) and local planning authorities (LPAs).
- Compliance with other Directives is often required; wastewater schemes should also consider the effects of sludge production.

Scope of EIA

Of particular interest in water schemes is careful consideration of alternatives. This can range from decisions on whether to defend a coastline to demand management to avoid the need for a reservoir. Development of reservoirs, in particular, can involve the enforced resettlement of communities and the loss of cultural heritage assets: this can provoke strong opposition, and the principles promoted by the World Commission on Dams (2000) can help to avoid confrontation. The cumulative impacts, which can have transboundary effects, are important to address.

New sewerage or wastewater treatment schemes in previously unsewered or overloaded systems in urban environments can create substantial temporary disturbance. The siting of new treatment plants will often be contentious, primarily due to the perception of nuisance (odour and noise) – despite their evident benefits.

The provision of coastal defences frequently leads to competing views between landowners and conservationists. In all cases, thorough consultation is essential.

Key Consultees

- Local authorities: planning, environmental health, conservation, highways
- Environment Agency
- Port health authorities
- Sea fisheries committees
- Conservation, heritage and community groups
- Defra
- Natural England
- English Heritage

EIA Regulations Projects Schedule

Schedule 1

Groundwater abstraction or recharge where the volume is 10 million m^3/year or more

Water transfer schemes between river basins

Wastewater treatment plants with a capacity exceeding 150,000 population equivalent

Dams where water stored exceeds 10 million m^3

Schedule 2

Groundwater abstraction, water transfer, wastewater treatment plants and dams not included in Schedule 1

Canalisation and flood relief works exceeding 1 ha

case example

Wastewater treatment plants have been built under car parks or underground without causing nuisance to local residents.

Key fact

Water needs to be considered within the context of strategic planning such as river basin management planning

Key fact

The Environment Agency will not give land drainage consent to development proposals which include culverting of surface water

case example

Technologies for water treatment are such that imaginative design solutions can be used for locations in small, urban and sensitive areas.

Water

Potential issues/ EIA terms of reference	Potential impacts on the environment
Population	Social effects on existing communities Public health Actual effect often beneficial Nuisance Traffic during construction
Noise and vibration	Noise from construction Noise from operation – plant and activities
Ecology	Damage or loss of habitat and biodiversity
Land and soils	Effects on agriculture Contamination
Water	Temporary discharges/risk of pollution during construction Hydrology – change of flow Pollution incidents and run-off
Air and climate	Odour (perceived or actual) Dust and particulates during construction
Cultural heritage	Loss of buildings, features or settings
Landscape	Visual impacts of dams, treatment works and coastal defences Temporary effects of pipelines
Use of resources	Loss of water resource

Potential options for mitigation	Opportunities for environmental enhancement
Backstop dams to protect communities Relocation and resettlement Traffic management plans Haul routes below the proposed water level of new reservoirs	Recreation and amenity on new lakes and restored rivers Improved bathing waters Improved fisheries
Acoustic screens/housings Quiet machinery and plant	–
Avoidance of valued areas Backstop dams to protect features Translocation	Improved/additional ecological features River restoration Contribution to natural functioning of floodplains
Soils storage, handling and management	–
Containment measures Provision of compensation water Sustainable drainage systems	River restoration Improved fisheries Improved water quality
Odour control measures Alternative technologies	–
Backstop dams to protect features Archaeological watching brief	–
Design dams to integrate into setting Reduce scale of plant Screening, mounding Avoidance of sensitive locations	Additional woodland to contribute to green infrastructure River restoration
Recycling and reuse Energy efficient plant Waste to energy	Sustainable water management Provision of treated sewage sludge for soil conditioning Potential for hydropower

Water

Other key legislation and guidance

Urban Waste Water Treatment Directive 1995

Water Framework Directive 2000

Bathing Waters Directive 2006

Shellfish Hygiene Directive 1991

Shellfish Waters Directive 2006

Freshwater Fish Directive 1978

Wild Birds 1979 and Habitats Directive 1992

Water Resources Act 1991

Water Industries Act 1991

Land Drainage Act 1991

Environmental Protection Act 1995

Water Act 2003

Water Resources (EIA) Regulations 2003

The Urban Waste Water Treatment (amended) Regulations 2003

The Water Environment (Water Framework Directive) Regulations 2003

PPS23: *Planning and Pollution Control*

PPS25: *Development and Flood Risks*

Defra 2008. *Future Water. The Government's Water Strategy for England*

Further information

River Basin Management Plans (RBMPs)

Coastal and Shoreline Management Plans (CMPs and SMPs)

Environment Agency 2002. *Scoping Guidelines for the EIA of Projects*

Water companies

Royal Society for the Protection of Birds (RSPB)

Chartered Institution of Water and Environmental Management (CIWEM)

Centre for Ecology and Hydrology (CEH)

Sustainable Drainage Systems

Development alters the existing state of drainage in an area with impermeable surfaces such as roads/roofs directing surface water from a site, which can result in local flooding and pollution. The sustainable management of surface and groundwater regimes has a role to play in the achievement of sustainable development. Sustainable drainage is the practice of controlling surface water run-off as close to its origin as possible before discharging into a watercourse or the ground.

There are a wide range of sustainable drainage options available, and the Environment Agency can advise on the most suitable application depending on the characteristics of the receiving environment. Examples include rainwater recycling; filterstrips and swales; filter drains and permeable porous surfaces; infiltration; and basins and ponds.

Sustainable drainage has many benefits relating to a variety of environmental issues such as reducing flood risk, minimising diffuse pollution from run-off, reducing pollution to aquifers, minimising erosion and damage to habitats, maintaining or restoring natural flow regimes to receiving watercourses, and maintaining groundwater recharge.

Monitoring

- Consented Discharges
- Licensed Abstractions
- Bathing Water quality
- Odour/noise
- Compensation flows.

River restoration (during construction and then after). Many local drainage and flood alleviation schemes in the 1950s–1970s resulted in the straightening or culverting of rivers. New works associated with rivers should consider the restoration of rivers to their original courses, which also provides for enhanced assimilative capacity of pollution loads by the provision of reed beds, meanders and off-line ponds

4.7 Housing and Mixed-use Development

Characteristics of Housing and Mixed-use Projects

- The government seeks to reduce dependence on the car by planning for mixed use.
- Mixed use includes residential, commercial and recreational.
- Housing demands are increasing due to demographic changes and the requirement for single-occupancy accommodation. Therefore, housing may be the greatest potential cause of environmental impact from new development.
- Requirement to meet affordable housing targets.
- The key characteristics are associated with transport and energy.

Scope of EIA

The scope is dependent on location: if rural and under development pressure, issues focus on loss of greenfield sites; in urban areas, issues are about regeneration and increased density; whilst on the urban fringe, issues can be about integration and access.

The local development documents will identify land use and relevant environmental issues. Government requirements to use brownfield sites rather than greenfield sites can cause conflict with sustainability issues for accessibility and ecology. Derelict and contaminated sites can be isolated from good transport links and may be of greater ecological value due to lack of disturbance than greenfield sites, which themselves have suffered from intensive agriculture. Development in the floodplain will be resisted.

All stages of development – site preparation, construction and occupation – need to be considered, and design should be led by sustainable principles (e.g. BREEAM, Code for Sustainable Homes). Early consideration of a community/residents' management plan is useful, especially when habitats or flood risk management (sustainable drainage systems) measures are required.

Key Consultees

- Local authorities: planning, waste, highways, environmental health, conservation
- Environment Agency
- Utility companies
- Development agencies
- Chambers of Commerce
- Commission for Architecture and the Built Environment
- English Heritage
- Natural England
- Conservation, heritage and community groups.

Key fact

'Housing' as such is not mentioned in the EIA Regulations but is taken to be included within 'urban development projects'

"

For LPAs, 'the priority for development should be previously developed land, in particular vacant and derelict sites and buildings'

– PPS3, *Housing*
"

EIA Regulations Projects Schedule

Schedule 1

Schedule 2

Infrastructure projects if the development area exceeds 0.5 ha

- Industrial estates
- Urban development projects, including the construction of shopping centres and carparks, sports stadiums, leisure centres and multiplex cinemas

Housing and Mixed-use Development

Potential issues/ EIA terms of reference	Potential impacts on the environment
Population	Integration with existing communities Disturbance and loss of amenity Competing settlements/neighbourhoods Increased traffic generation leads to congestion – highway capacity Provision of new transport links/nodes/systems Increased risk of accidents; increased car parks
Noise and vibration	Noise levels from traffic, site clearance, demolition and construction, e.g. piling, can affect both humans and wildlife Effect on listed buildings from vibration
Ecology	Loss and fragmentation of habitats and disturbance to species Severance of wildlife corridors
Land and soils	Loss of geological Site of Special Scientific Interest (SSSI) exposures Disturbance of contaminated land Loss of best agricultural land
Water	Surface water run-off; effects on groundwater and river flows Pollution from storage and accidents Water supply, sewerage and sewage treatment provision Floodplain and coastal encroachment
Air and climate	Effects of dust and emissions on population and sensitive habitats and species, buildings and structures Contribution to climate change
Cultural heritage	Loss or damage to historic features or their settings Loss or degradation of local identity
Landscape	Visual impact Loss of valued landscape character
Use of resources	Loss and consumption of natural resources Contribution to climate change Production of waste

Potential options for mitigation	Opportunities for environmental enhancement
Community input into design development and requirements for the provision of facilities Traffic calming; traffic routing Restrict private car use/ownership Contribution to integrated sustainable transport network	Improved recreation/leisure facilities Public open space Improved transport links and facilities Physical fitness Highway improvements – cycle/walkways Car-free areas
Timing of activities; traffic routing Quiet equipment/machinery Acoustic barriers; double glazing	Reduction of existing noise levels by alternative traffic routings and insulation
Avoiding sensitive areas Phasing construction to avoid breeding or migration Relocation of species, translocation of habitats Creation of new habitats	Improvement to biodiversity integrated within provision of open space or buildings: green infrastructure Community involvement in ecological management
Design to avoid or treat contaminated land Recreation of geological exposures Soils storage and management	Enhance exposures Decontamination of brownfield sites
Sustainable drainage systems Grey water recycling Flood storage area provision Pollution control measures via EMP	Restoration of degraded rivers and natural functioning of floodplains Habitat creation; provision of amenity Sewage treatment for unsewered areas
BREEAM design standards Code for Sustainable Homes Site selection and orientation of buildings Construction methods and site control	Reduction in energy demand contributing to climate change targets Increased use of renewable energy
Avoidance Pre-development investigations On site monitoring and watching brief	Restoration or improvement of setting
Site selection Building or structure heights/design Screening – planting, bunds Colour and material selection	Improvement of setting Creation of new woodlands Public open space provision
Use of recycled materials for construction Waste minimisation, recycling and reuse	–

Housing and Mixed-use Development

case example

New Settlement South of the M4

Wokingham District Council was required to make an allocation in the emerging local plan for a new settlement of up to 5000 houses. Three alternative sites were promoted by potential developers for inclusion in the plan. Each proposal was accompanied by an ES, and the District Council sought to ensure that the ESs were of equal quality so that the sites could be compared by the inspector on their merits rather than be jeopardized by inadequacies in the ES.

Achieving an urban renaissance is ... about creating the quality of life and vitality that makes urban living so desirable. We must bring about a change in urban attitudes

– Urban Task Force 1999. *Towards an Urban Renaissance*

Other key legislation and guidance

Local Government Act 2000

PPS3: *Housing*

PPS7: *Sustainable Development in Rural Areas*

PPS13: *Transportation and Land Use*

PPS23: *Planning and Pollution Control*

PPS25: *Development and Flood Risk*

Further information

DETR 2000. Urban and Rural White Papers

Urban Task Force 1999: *Towards an Urban Renaissance*

DCLG: New Deal for Communities

Barton, H. *et al*. 2002. *Shaping Neighbourhoods*

Building Research Establishment Environmental Assessment Methods (BREEAM)

Sustainable Construction: Practical Guide for Planners and Developers. www.sustainable-construction.org.uk

Environment Agency 2002. *Scoping Guidelines for the EIA of Projects*

House Builders Federation (HBF)

Town and Country Planning Association (TCPA)

Royal Town Planning Institute (RTPI)

Energy Saving Trust

DTI 2006. *Code for Sustainable Homes*

Green roof for habitat and water management: Gallie Craig Coffee House in Stranraer, Scotland

Photograph courtesy of Alumasc, reproduced with permission. © Alumasc

Promotion of Sustainable Development: Key Features

- Energy-efficient construction and buildings; renewable energy targets.
- Integrated sustainable transport.
- Waste minimisation, recycling and reuse.
- Local Combined Heat and Power.
- Avoidance of floodplains or provision of compensation flood storage.
- Sustainable drainage systems.
- Grey water recycling, where appropriate.
- Provision of open space; contribution to green infrastructure.
- Enhancing biodiversity, ecological networks, creation of habitats.
- EMPs (construction and occupation).

Monitoring

- Community Management Plans.
- Monitoring for noise and dust in accordance with EHO requirements.
- Traffic Management Plan compliance.
- Flood storage facilities and sustainable drainage management.

4.8 Transport

Characteristics of Transport Projects

- Often linear (roads, railways and canals) and long distance.
- Can apply to on-line widening of existing routes or the development of new routes.
- New routes are often highly contentious, leading to polarisation of public opinion.
- Locally, new roads can create air and noise pollution and severance; globally, traffic contributes to climate change.
- Bypasses can resolve congestion in towns and villages but can also lead to their isolation.
- Traffic effects are associated with most types of development.

Scope of EIA

The scope of EIA studies associated with roads and bridges is clearly set out in the Department for Transport's *Design Manual for Roads and Bridges*, Volume 11.

Specific methods have been developed for Traffic Impact Assessment (TIA). However, the scope of a TIA is different from that required for the ES, and close liaison between the traffic, air and noise consultants is especially important. These assessments have to take into account future use of the routes, i.e. the level of traffic and emissions in the 'baseline/opening year' and a 'future year'.

Surface water run-off from roads has implications for receiving watercourses; water quality and hydrological assessments are required, together with construction of flood storage and pollution control processes. Existing roads and railways are often havens for wildlife, given the relatively undisturbed nature of verges and sidings; derelict railway sidings, in particular, can have developed valued habitat for rare or unusual species. Consideration has to be given to both vertical and horizontal alignments when developing a new transport corridor – alignment, as well as acoustic bunds, can have unacceptable visual impacts.

The scope of the EIA should also include factors of physical fitness (encouraging cycling and walking) and journey ambience (traveller stress and views) in accordance with government policy PPS13 and to integrate into a sustainable transport strategy.

Key Consultees

- Local authorities: planning, highways, conservation, environmental health
- Civil Aviation Authority
- Port and harbour authorities
- Navigation authorities
- Public transport operators
- Ramblers Association
- Residential Boat Owners Association
- Conservation, heritage and community groups
- British Waterways
- Network Rail
- Natural England
- English Heritage
- Sustrans
- Highways Agency
- Living Streets

Key fact

One of the longest public inquiries in UK planning history was associated with Terminal 5 at Heathrow Airport

Key fact

Legislation has had, and will continue to have, a significant effect on reducing pollutant emissions from vehicles. This will continue to more than outweigh the predicted general increase in traffic, such that air quality will continue to improve. In the case of greenhouse gas emissions, these have been harder to control, and traffic growth has outweighed any reductions in emissions. Emissions have therefore been increasing. The future balance of traffic growth and reductions in emissions is hard to predict, but a small overall decline is expected.

EIA Regulations Projects Schedule

Schedule 1

Railways and airports (runway length 2100 m or more)

Motorways and express roads (EU traffic artery)

Inland waterways and ports (vessels over 1350 t)

Trading ports and piers (vessels over 1350 t)

Schedule 2

Railways and international transhipment facilities and terminals (not in Schedule 1)

Airfields (not in Schedule 1)

Roads, harbours and port installations (not in Schedule 1)

Inland waterways, canalisation and flood-relief works

Tramways, elevated and underground railways

Potential issues/ EIA terms of reference	Potential impacts on the environment
Population	Severance and isolation Loss or degradation of amenity Public health Risk of accidents Delays during construction
Noise and vibration	Piling, tunnelling and blasting Vehicle movement and aircraft take-off/landing
Ecology	Habitat loss, fragmentation or damage Disturbance Loss or damage to wildlife corridors
Land and soils	Landtake Sterilisation of minerals Damage or contamination
Water	Contamination from run-off Effects on groundwater or surface water flows and levels
Air and climate	Dust and particulates Gaseous emissions: ■ global/climate change ■ local air quality
Cultural heritage	Damage to listed buildings from vibration Effect on the setting and amenity of listed buildings and features
Landscape	Effect on the character of valued or historic landscape Removal of features Restriction to views – visual intrusion Opening of views
Use of resources	Demand for construction materials

Potential options for mitigation	Opportunities for environmental enhancement
Change of alignment Footbridges and underpasses Traffic management and calming Public transport provision and cycleways/walkways	Improved amenity, tranquility and accessibility Physical fitness Safety improvements Removal of light pollution Improved journey times
Noise insulation Construction methods Change of alignment Acoustic bunds Restrictions on night-time movements	Improved quality of life for bypassed villages and towns
Change of alignment Protection of valued areas and features Timing of construction Maintaining ecological networks Translocation, tunnels for wildlife	Creation of new habitats Restoration of watercourses Sustainable drainage systems Green infrastructure
Alignment to minimize landtake Negotiation for land exchange Extract minerals prior to construction Soils storage and handling	–
Sustainable drainage systems Provision of flood storage EMP	Ecological and amenity value from sustainable drainage systems Blue infrastructure
EMP Wheelwashing, sheeting of lorries Vehicle and aircraft fuel efficiencies	Improved emissions quality from reduced congestion Electric vehicles, trains and trams (depending on the power source)
Change of alignment Preservation *in situ* Excavation and recording Archaeological watching brief	–
Change of alignment Screening – mounding and planting Quality of design	Improved traveller views
Reuse of materials Energy efficiency during construction	Fuel saving by improved routes

case example

On appeal for an outline application for a business park it was ruled that an unacceptable development could not be approved just because a Green Transport Plan was proposed. The site was inaccessible by public transport and remote from settlements, so walking and cycling were not realistic options; private cars would remain the main form of transport. While the applicants proposed a Green Transport Plan in the ES, there was concern about how effective this could be.

Other key legislation and guidance

Transport and Works Act 1992
Transport Act 2000
Road Safety Act 2006
Transport and Works (Assessment of Environmental Effects) Regulations 2000
The Highways (EIA) Regulations 1999 (as amended)
The Harbour Works (EIA) Regulations 1999 (as amended)
PPS13: *Transportation and Land Use*
Department for Transport (DfT) 2007. *Manual for Streets*
Environment Agency 2002. *Scoping Guidelines for the EIA of Projects*
DfT 2006. *Full Guidance on Local Transport Plans*
Institute of Economic Affairs 1993. *Guidelines for the Environmental Assessment of Road Traffic*
Highways Authority 1993. *Design Manual for Roads and Bridges*, Volume 11. *Environmental Assessment*
Institution of Highways and Transportation 1994. *Guidelines for Traffic Impact Assessment*

Further information

DfT 1999. *Sustainable Distribution: A Strategy*
DfT 2000. *Transport 10 Year Plan*
DfT 2004. *The Future of Transport*. White Paper
DfT 2007. *Tomorrow's Roads – Safer for Everyone: The Second Three-year Review*
Royal Commission on Environmental Pollution 1997. *20th Report Transport and the Environment*
The Institution of Highways and Transportation
Inland Waterways Association
Transport Research Laboratory
Sustrans

A New Approach to Appraisal (WebTAG)

The requirement for integrated transport has led to new appraisal methods for all transport projects that require government approval, from multi-modal studies to highway schemes (A New Deal for Transport, 1998). In response, the DfT has initiated the 'Transport Analysis Guidance' website (WebTAG) to provide detailed guidance on the appraisal of transport projects and wider advice on scoping and carrying out transport studies.

The site brought together and superseded DfT documents such as *The Guidance on the Methodology for Multi-modal Studies* (GOMMMS) and *Applying the Multi-Modal Approach to Appraisal to Highway Schemes* (The Bridging Document).

The appraisal process should consider the objectives of environment, safety, economy, accessibility and integration. The environment objective then considers 10 subobjectives: noise, local air quality, greenhouse gases, landscape, townscape, biodiversity, heritage of historic resources, water environment, physical fitness and journey ambience. Worksheets are prepared to summarise the results of each appraisal; these are then combined into an overall Appraisal Summary Table (AST).

Travel Plans and Local Transport Plans

A Travel Plan is a package of initiatives for employers to tackle different aspects of transport, including commuter journeys, business travel and fleet management.

Local Transport Plans (LTPs) are for local authorities to help better integrate transport policy and embrace the full range of transport issues.

Monitoring

- Archaeological watching brief.
- Noise, dust and air quality during construction, as in EMP.
- Water discharges and receiving waters.
- Compliance with the agreed Traffic Management Plan.
- Compliance with predicted impacts, e.g. visual impact.
- Compliance with requirements or conditions, e.g. planting.

Chapter 5

Environmental Management

Environmental management reduces the risk of pollution to the environment and improves the sustainable management of environmental resources. This chapter introduces the role of environmental management in Environmental Impact Assessment (EIA) and explains how commitments to mitigation and environmental protection can be made in a systematic and transparent way.

Contents

5.1   Introduction

5.2   Definitions

5.3   Discussion

5.4   Approaches

5.1   Introduction

This chapter describes the relationship between EIA and environmental management during construction, operation/occupation and restoration – which is generally controlled via an Environmental Management Plan (EMP). As stated in Chapter 2, the implementation of the proposed and agreed mitigation measures, monitoring and follow-up arrangements, and management of impacts, can be managed through an EMP. The EMP has links to Environmental Management Systems (EMSs), which are more usually adopted for industrial activities, commercial processes and their organisational procedures, since both are aimed at the management of environmental risk and the improvement of environmental performance. EMSs may be independently audited against a formally accredited system such as EMAS or ISO 14001. The maintenance of an EMS by the developer, operator and/or contractor facilitates the environmental management of site preparation, construction and later activities, since appropriate procedures are already in place and are part of the organisation's policies, protocols and culture. The inclusion of an EMP, in draft or outline, in the ES, or operation of an EMS by the developer, will provide additional reassurance to the regulators and the public. As stated in Chapter 2, the environmental commitments of the project, managed through the EMP, need to be secured in contract documentation and arrangements for construction and later project stages, in order to be implemented. The requirement for an EMP can also be specified by local planning authorities through conditions on planning permission or by legal agreement. Thus, there are crucial links between a project EMP and an organisation's EMS, and between the ES, planning requirements and contractual arrangements, which need to be carefully planned and managed.

5.2   Definitions

Since environmental management in relation to Environmental Impact Assessment (EIA) is a relatively recent concept, a number of terms are being used by different institutions and organisations. These are some of those in most common use:

- EMP (Environmental Management Plan): a generic term, and refers to the construction period but can also more generally refer to arrangements for environmental management during occupation/operation.

Further information

ISO 14001: *Environmental Management Systems*

European Eco-Management and Audit Scheme (EMAS)

Charles, P. and Connolly, S. (eds) 2005. *Environmental Good Practice on Site*

www.bsi-global.com

www.ciria.org.uk

IEMA 2008: *Environmental Management Plans*

An ES outline EMP provides:
- Checklist for regulators
- Commitments to mitigation
- Starting point for tender specification

A Contract EMP provides:
- Communication systems
- Environmental policy statements
- Method statements
- Definition of environmental responsibilities, personnel and training
- Auditing and monitoring

■ EAP (Environmental Action Plan): another term for EMP, used by the Environment Agency and others, to manage implementation of a project's environmental commitments.

■ CEMP (Construction (or Contract) Environmental Management Plan): to be prepared by contractors before they commence on a development site; often part of contract documentation.

■ SEMP (Site Environmental Management Plan): prepared by site owners or operators for long-term environmental maintenance and management of the site.

■ HEMP (Handover Environmental Management Plan): prepared by the contractor on completion of construction for future environmental maintenance and management.

5.3   Discussion

As discussed in Chapter 2, various practitioners and commentators recognise the usefulness of providing in the ES an indication of how the construction and operational activities will be managed insofar as they may potentially affect the environment.

The EMP is developed and designed through consultation between the design team, regulators and competent authorities, and the local community, and can be secured by inclusion or reference within appropriate contract documentation and/or through planning condition or legal agreement. It achieves the following objectives:

■ to identify predictions, activities and commitments in the ES which may require specific conditions/agreements, consents or licences from the competent authorities

■ to ensure that contract documentation (see below) and detailed design addresses the relevant mitigation measures agreed during the EIA process and that the contractors allow for this in the tendering process – in this respect, the EMP should be prescriptive yet flexible enough to allow for innovation

■ to provide specific Method Statements for procedures when working near sensitive areas

■ to ensure that the developers/operators are clear about the mitigation commitments and means of their implementation

■ to ensure that systems are in place to resolve any potential problems associated with the site activities

■ to comply with relevant legislation, standards and guidance.

As noted in Chapter 2, the extent to which mitigation measures can be reliably described in an Environmental Statement (ES) will depend on the type of contract awarded and how the project and contract/s are managed. This will also determine when it is most appropriate and useful to define the EMP, and how the EMP will be managed. Many contracts are procured via the Design and Build process. This requires the contractor's team to take responsibility for the preparation of the ES and the EMP in parallel, thus ensuring integration of environmental risk minimisation into the design and build activities. It may also be linked, for example, to Considerate Constructors Schemes, which have been adopted as codes of practice in some cities. Other forms of contract may give opportunities for the EMP to be defined earlier or later in the project.

case example

New Neighbourhood, Gloucestershire

A strategy for environmental monitoring and management during the construction phase of a proposed new neighbourhood of 1900 homes was agreed through the EIA process and secured in outline planning conditions, and is being implemented through adherence to an outline CEMP strategy, which describes the precautions required to avoid and mitigate environmental effects in this sensitive location. Housing developers (through agreement) and main infrastructure contractors (through contractual requirement) are responsible for implementing the strategy as it relates to their specific sites and contracts. The CEMP strategy is overseen by the applicants' environmental consultants, who provide overall co-ordination, environmental briefings, site inspections and monitoring, with the aim of ensuring good practice and compliance with legislation and the environmental commitments agreed in the EIA and planning conditions.

EMPs have tended to focus on pollution prevention and control and the protection of the natural environment. However, they may also be used to promote sustainable use of resources including energy and construction materials. The EMP, therefore, has the added function of not only incorporating the mitigation of those environmental issues identified in Chapter 3 but also encompasses other issues which may be raised during consultation. These can be of particular local concern, e.g. waste and litter, vermin and pests, sustainable construction, and wider global issues of energy use. The ES can, therefore, make a commitment to sustainability principles and progress towards sustainable development objectives.

Considerate Constructors Scheme
- Considerate
- Environment
- Cleanliness
- Good neighbour
- Accountable
- Respectful
- Responsible
- Safe

5.4 Approaches

This section provides a model outline of the contents of the various EMPs. This outline can be used as a checklist in an ES to ensure that commitments are made and methods of implementation are identified. All sites, development types and contracts differ to a degree, so it can be adapted to suit the particular circumstances.

CEMP

Consultation and Liaison Arrangements

The EIA process will have covered considerable consultation with local residents and other interested parties as well as the regulatory authorities. This section describes how this can be maintained through the duration of the project. The construction team may set up a local environmental liaison group to advise and monitor environmental concerns during construction activities and programming. This is particularly important to advise local businesses or residents of any particularly disturbing activities, e.g. noise or traffic movements. It also provides details of contacts in the event of any complaints and procedures for responding.

Method Statements

These include all the measures agreed during the EIA with the regulatory authorities. They may address the following activities:

- soil handling, storage and reinstatement
- reinstatement of habitats
- waste management plan
- noise prevention and abatement
- protection of existing habitats and species
- implementation of new planting and seeding
- landscape and ecology management plan
- use of herbicides
- public rights of way
- pollution control and contingency procedures
- construction compounds, haul routes, borrow pits, lay down areas and batching plants

Example contents of a CEMP

1 Consultation and liaison arrangements
2 Method statements
3 Environmental policy
4 Environmental responsibilities and personnel
5 Training
6 Auditing and monitoring

Key fact

Appointing a project environmental liaison officer can help resolve any problems with the local community

- archaeological management
- drainage features
- working times
- traffic management plan
- energy and other resources use.

Specific contents of some of the above include the following:

Site Waste Management Plan. This is a legal requirement for all construction projects over £250,000 in England from 2008 under regulations brought in by the Clean Neighbourhoods and Environment Act 2005. It provides a structure for systematic waste management at all stages of a project's delivery, in accordance with waste management licensing and 'duty of care' legislation. It identifies types and quantities of wastes arisings, their management, documentation, treatment/ disposal, and the parties responsible. Local authorities and the Environment Agency will enforce Site Waste Management Plans, and they will impose penalties for failure to make, keep or produce a plan.

Pollution Control and Contingency Plan. This identifies sensitive or vulnerable receptors and natural features, e.g. watercourses, and working methods to minimise environmental risk. It includes detailed procedures for the storage and use of materials, fuels, lubricants and any other environmentally hazardous substances and incident notification procedures for regulators. Requirements for pollution control equipment and protection measures for sensitive areas are identified.

Traffic Management Plan. This details the agreed and approved routes for each stage of the construction to minimise disturbance and to ensure that public highways are maintained in a safe condition. This, therefore, ensures road safety (e.g. avoidance of school access), road cleanliness (removal of mud from road) and minimal traffic disruption.

Archaeological Management. This includes arrangements for any advance works, archaeological watching briefs, protection of archaeological features, phasing of archaeological activities and archaeological recording.

Environmental Policy

This records the environmental policies of the contractor/developer and any certification under an accredited EMS, e.g. EMAS or ISO 14001, and compliance with industry codes of practice. This demonstrates that the relevant organisations are committed to the highest standards of environmental performance and compliance with legislative requirements.

Environmental Responsibilities and Personnel

The responsibilities for environmental management for the project and job descriptions for environmental staff should be defined, to ensure that responsibilities of the different parties are clear and that staff have relevant knowledge, experience and authority to monitor, audit and rectify any environmental issue. Personnel can include the overall site environmental liaison officer, contractors and developers' own site managers and environmental managers, environmental co-ordinators, specialists and other advisors.

Training

Site personnel, appropriate design staff and relevant visitors should receive induction training in accordance with the EMP; a record of competence and training given should be maintained. This will particularly apply to any subcontractors.

Auditing, Monitoring and Follow-up

Arrangements should be defined for:

- how the site activities are monitored and by whom
- the frequency of such audits and checks
- who undertakes them and is responsible
- follow-up reporting and procedures to action and manage issues and unforeseen impacts
- communications with the local planning authority, environmental regulators and other stakeholders.

SEMP/HEMP

These plans provide for the longer-term maintenance and management relating to environmental issues of the site. They describe the strategies for maintenance of all environmental areas and record how these will be achieved together with appropriate timetables and programmes. Such management can be undertaken by a range of organisations, but is often contracted to specialist companies. Of particular concern is to involve residents or occupiers in the formulation and implementation of these plans. Such plans include (but are not limited to):

- monitoring and maintenance of new planting
- management of existing hedgerows and woodlands
- maintenance of pollution control systems, including oil interceptors
- maintenance of domestic sewage treatment plants
- maintenance of public open space and footpaths
- maintenance of sustainable drainage systems, especially flood alleviation ponds
- monitoring (e.g. water quality, species, habitats, noise and air quality)
- energy and water resource use
- waste management.

> ## *Key features of Environmental Management*
>
> - An EMS gives confidence to regulators and the community.
> - Environmental management reduces the risk of pollution and improves the sustainable management of resources.
> - Environmental management provides commitment to implementation of mitigation and follow-up monitoring and management in the ES.
> - EMPs are relevant for a variety of developer/contractor/regulator relationships.

Protection of environmental resource during construction
Photograph courtesy of AC Archaelogy, reproduced with permission. © AC Archaelogy

Chapter 6

Strategic Environmental Assessment

This chapter provides an overview of Strategic Environmental Assessment (SEA). It explains what SEA is, why it is required and when it should be applied. The process of undertaking an SEA is briefly described, with reference to examples and guiding principles. The links between SEA and Environmental Impact Assessment (EIA) are also discussed.

Contents

6.1   What is SEA?

SEA is a process used during the preparation of policies, plans and programmes that aims to provide a high level of protection for the environment and to promote sustainable development. Many definitions have been proposed since the early 1980s: Sadler and Verheem's definition in 1996 is particularly useful:

Sadler, B., Verheem, R. *SEA: Status, Challenges and Future Directions*, 1996

'SEA is a systematic process for evaluating the environmental consequences of proposed policy, plan or programme initiatives in order to ensure that they are fully included and appropriately addressed at the earliest appropriate stage of decision making on a par with economic and social considerations.'

So, SEA is about making better decisions at a strategic level, by ensuring that environmental and broader sustainable development issues are included at a stage in planning and policy-making when options are still open. It has been suggested that an SEA has to demonstrate it has addressed four key elements of the SEA process:

- Key stakeholders are fully engaged and their participation in the decision-making process has been actively promoted.

- The SEA is addressing the key environmental and sustainable development issues that are relevant to strategic-level decisions (in contrast to project-level more-detailed concerns).

- The precautionary principle is applied: negative impacts are minimised and positive impacts are optimised.

- Environmental limits are understood, so that planned actions will not cause irreversible adverse effects.

Key fact

SEA is a strategic level activity: it assesses policies, plans and programmes while they are still being developed with the potential to improve the outcomes or actions that result from the plan-making

SEA is required for plans and programmes that '*set the framework for future development consent for projects*'

– EU SEA Directive

6.2   The Need for SEA

Recognition of the global nature of environmental problems, together with increasing awareness of sustainable development and environmental carrying capacities, indicated that project EIA may occur too late in the planning process to ensure that all alternatives and impacts were adequately considered. Thus, SEA developed from the 1980s to address these issues and better set the context for project EIA; in Europe it was delayed by focusing on the project EIA legislation.

The Purpose of SEA

Key legislation and guidance

EU Directive 2001/42/EC

The Environmental Assessment of Plans and Programmes Regulations 2004 (Statutory Instrument 2004 No. 1633)

The Planning and Compulsory Purchase Act 2004

PPS1: *Delivering Sustainable Development*

Defra 2005. *Securing the Future – UK Government Sustainable Development Strategy*

Office of the Deputy Prime Minister (ODPM) 2005. *A Practical Guide to the Strategic Environmental Assessment Directive*

Environment Agency 2004. *SEA Good Practice Guidelines*

Department of Health 2007. *Guidance on Health in SEA* (draft)

Department for Transport 2004. *SEA – Core Guidance for Transport Plans and Programmes*

Countryside Commission for Wales *et al.* 2004. *SEA and Biodiversity: Guidance for Practitioners*

Environment Agency, Natural England, UKCIP 2007. *SEA and Climate Change: Guidance for Practitioners*

Royal Society for the Protection of Birds 2007. *SEA: Learning from Practice*

ODPM 2005. *Sustainability Appraisal of Regional Spatial Strategies and Local Development Documents*

"

The objective of the Directive is to provide for a high level of protection of the environment and to contribute to the integration of environmental considerations into the preparation and adoption of plans and programmes with a view to promoting sustainable development by ensuring that an environmental assessment is carried out of certain plans and programmes that are likely to have significant effects on the environment

– EU SEA Directive
"

Key fact

The UK guidance provides a list of indicative PPs subject to SEA. Responsible Authorities (plan-makers) must confer with the statutory Consultation Bodies (English Heritage, the Environment Agency, Natural England) when arriving at a screening determination. The conclusions drawn, including the rationale for not requiring SEA, must be made available to the public

In Europe, the requirement for SEA now stems from the European Directive 2001/42/EC 'On the Assessment of the Effects of Certain Plans and Programmes on the Environment'. The Directive is known as the Strategic Environmental Assessment (SEA) Directive, even though the word '*strategic*' is not mentioned. This is because the plans and programmes (PPs) referred to as requiring '*environmental assessment*' are considered to occur at a strategic level of decision-making. The Directive is transposed into UK law by a series of Regulations, which reproduce the Directive without adding any further requirements, although some adaptations to meet UK-specific circumstances are made.

The language and intent of the SEA Directive is closely linked to the EIA Directive, as discussions for both began simultaneously with the intention that project level and strategic actions would be covered by one Directive. The particular types of plans and programmes that are required to undergo SEA are set out in Articles 2 and 3 of the Directive. Determining whether the Directive applies to any given PP is guided by the screening process. Specifically, the Directive applies to PPs that are:

■ subject to preparation and/or adoption by an authority at the national, regional or local level or which are prepared by an authority for adoption through a legislative procedure by Parliament or the government, and

■ required by legislative, regulatory or administrative provisions.

The Directive is mandatory for PPs:

■ which are prepared for agriculture, forestry, fisheries, energy, industry, transport, waste management, water management, telecommunications, tourism, town and country planning or land use; and

■ which set the framework for future development consent for projects listed in Annexes I and II to the EIA Directive (85/337/EEC); and

■ which are likely to have a significant effect on the environment or

■ require an assessment under the Habitats Directive (92/43/EEC).

6.3 The Purpose of SEA

Regulation provides the key driver for SEA and its purpose; the European SEA Directive aims to provide a high level of protection for the environment and promote sustainable development. This is achieved by providing a structured process of assessment that can be applied to ensure that environmental and sustainability considerations are taken into account when PPs are developed.

SEA provides a framework to help decision-making; it requires us to understand the environment, to know where the vulnerabilities and sensitivities lie, and to seek out solutions that integrate environmental concerns with broader social and economic needs. Integration is key – and good SEA should seek to dispel the conflict situation (between the environment and other priorities) that has previously characterised assessment processes.

> **Guiding principles**
>
> SEA emphasizes:
>
> - collecting and presenting information on the environmental baseline and current environmental challenges and their future evolution
>
> - predicting significant environmental effects of the plan or programme, including those of strategic alternatives
>
> - addressing adverse environmental effects through mitigation measures
>
> - consulting the public and authorities with environmental responsibilities as part of the assessment process
>
> - monitoring the environmental effects of the plan or programme during its implementation.

From ODPM 2005. A Practical Guide to the SEA Directive. Crown copyright: reproduced with permission of the Controller of Her Majesty's Stationery Office

Clearly, in any plan-making process, SEA, and the information it provides, is not the only input that decision-makers are required to deal with. However, practitioners are increasingly identifying that SEA has the ability to challenge assumptions, allow a more informative consideration of alternatives and crucially – to be an influential component in any final decision that is made. The mandated engagement processes and the participation of stakeholders is an instrumental part of the process. If SEA is demonstrably influential, then it is achieving its purpose.

6.4   SEA Procedures

Getting Started

It is the duty of the Responsible Authority who is preparing and adopting the plan or programme to undertake the SEA. In practice, the preparation of an SEA may be carried out in-house, contracted to specialist SEA consultants, or carried out by a team of internal staff (who understand the detail locally and to build capacity) and external consultants (who can contribute wider experience and independence to the process). Given the importance of starting SEA early and integrating it with the plan-making process, it is crucial that the two parties work effectively together. When choosing the appropriate team for SEA, it is helpful to consider the following factors:

- choose your consultants carefully – do they understand your approach/key environmental issues specific to your area?
- look at examples of previous SEA work undertaken
- refer to examples of good practice published
- ensure that flexibility and responsiveness is integral to the team working.

All SEAs should be tailored to the task in hand, and the level of detail ought to reflect the nature of the plan or programme under

Key fact

Addressing the requirements of the SEA Directive is necessary for all Regional Spatial Strategies (RSS) and Development Plan Documents (DPDs) as part of the Sustainability Appraisal (SA) process required by the Planning and Compulsory Purchase Act (2004) in England and Wales; Scotland does not subsume SEA requirements within SA.

the European Directive (2001/42/EC) is probably the best known framework law that establishes a minimum common procedure for certain plans and programmes

– Dalal-Clayton and Sadler 2005

An SEA need not be done in any more detail, or using any more resources, than is useful for its purpose

– ODPM 2005. *A Practical Guide to the SEA Directive*

SEA should be open, transparent and inclusive. Good engagement will provide useful information to planners and expedite the time taken from planning to implementation.

consideration. For consistency and rigour it is useful for those preparing the SEA to follow the typical core stages, as set out in the figure below:

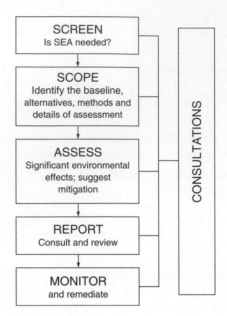

The UK SEA guidance (ODPM 2005) identifies five core stages to the process:

SEA: core stages	
Stage	**Detail**
Stage A	Setting the context and objectives, establishing the baseline, and deciding on the scope
Stage B	Developing and refining alternatives and assessing effects
Stage C	Preparing the Environmental Report
Stage D	Consulting on the draft plan or programme and the Environmental Report
Stage E	Monitoring the significant effect of implementing the plan or programme on the environment

Screening

The European Directive lists plans and programmes for which SEA is mandatory if they are likely to '*have a significant effect on the environment*' as described above. In practice, the screening process depends upon the likely significance of effects on the environment. It was decided in England and Wales that SA/SEA should be mandatory for spatial and development plans, in consideration of their likely significant effects on environmental factors; in Scotland, SEA remains a separate process and is not subsumed within the SA process.

SEA screening (and scoping) requires consideration of tiering, i.e. the way in which high-level, strategic actions set the context for lower-level activities. The SEA should have a scope proportionate to the importance of the issues, recognising the potential for addressing them at other tiers in the decision-making hierarchy.

Scoping – Stage A: Setting the Context and Objectives, Establishing the Baseline and Deciding on the Scope

Scoping the SEA focuses on the issues to be addressed and how they will be assessed and, as such, it shares similarities with the approach taken for EIA (see Chapter 2). It involves looking at the geographical, temporal and thematic extent of the PP and determining the level of detail required. The UK guidance sets out five key tasks in this stage:

- identify other relevant PPs and environmental protection objectives
- collect baseline information
- identify environmental problems
- develop SEA objectives
- consult on the scope of the SEA.

Clearly, a core part of scoping involves evidence gathering. PPs rarely exist in isolation; most are influenced to a greater or lesser extent by other PPs or by strategies, policies and legislation that set the framework for action. Examining other relevant PPs means that potential synergies can be identified, and inconsistencies and/or constraints can be dealt with. Practice suggests that SEAs being developed within a plan hierarchy can make good use of extant, relevant PPs reviews to avoid duplication of effort.

Gathering and describing the baseline contributes to defining the character of the plan area; it helps identify environmental challenges and provides a future basis for predictions and monitoring. The baseline should provide an understanding of the current and likely future status of the environment in the absence of the strategic plan being assessed. In considering the value and sensitivity of the receiving environment, trends and comparisons are important in SEA.

Good practice principles for scoping

- Focus on collecting information that is relevant to the plan scale and scope; avoid collecting excessive data.
- Focus on the strategic level information.
- Take advantage of linkages between plans to share information and avoid duplication of data collection.
- Remember to consider how the environment will evolve without the plan or programme development.
- Look at the information you already have before embarking on new data collection.
- Be aware of data gaps and report them where they occur; be explicit about the limitations of your data.
- Consider the synergies and conflicts between plans.
- Consider the potential cumulative effects both within the plan and between plans.

The SEA Directive does not specify an assessment approach such as using SEA objectives and indicators. However, practice has demonstrated that an objectives-led approach provides a robust and coherent framework for assessment and subsequent monitoring activities.

SEA Procedures

Objectives and indicators

- Use stakeholder engagement
- Aim for no more than 15–20 objectives
- Make objectives relevant to the characteristics of the plan area
- Find synergies with other indicators and minimise numbers
- Consider being bold and creative

---

case example

SA/SEA of the South West Regional Spatial Strategy

The assessment framework is founded on six headline sustainability objectives and asking the questions 'Will the RSS...'

- *improve health?*
- *support communities that meet people's needs?*
- *develop the economy in ways that meet people's needs?*
- *provide access to meet people's needs with least damage to the environment?*
- *maintain and improve environmental quality and assets?*
- *minimize consumption of natural resources?*

– www.southwest-ra.gov.uk

---

case example

SEA of Scotland River Basin Management Plan

Examples of SEA objectives:

- to manage waste in a way that reduces emissions to air, land and water
- to support the development of alternative renewable energy supplies
- to reduce the movement of waste

– www.sepa.org.uk

Statutory consultees for SEA

Natural England

English Heritage

Environment Agency

---

case example

DTI Off-shore Energy Licensing

The Department of Trade and Industry (now the Department for Business, Enterprise and Regulatory Reform) set good practice standards with extensive consultation in SEA for offshore licensing for oil and gas.

– www.offshore-sea.org.uk/site/

The SEA Directive requires that the Environmental Report shall include information *'that may reasonably be required taking into account current knowledge and methods of assessment'*. It further requires information to be provided *'...including on issues such as...'* biodiversity, population, human health, fauna, flora, soil, water, air, climatic factors, material assets, cultural heritage, landscape and their interrelationships. An issue amongst practitioners is that a concern of plan-makers to minimise risk of challenge to the SEA process means that it is rare for SEAs to scope out any of *'SEA topics'*.

It is mandatory for the Responsible Authority to consult with the Consultation Bodies on the scope of the Environmental Report. While the Directive does not require wider consultation with the public and other stakeholder groups, good practice tends towards this. Given the valuable feedback and input to the iterative process of SEA that can result, this practice is to be welcomed and encouraged.

Assessing – Stage B: Developing and Refining Alternatives and Assessing Effects

After consultation on the scope of the SEA, the next stage is to predict and evaluate the significant environmental effects of the evolving plan and its alternatives. The UK SEA guidance sets out six key tasks in this stage:

- testing the plan or programme objectives against the SEA objectives
- developing strategic alternatives
- predicting the effects of the plan or programme, including the alternatives
- evaluating the effects of the plan or programme, including alternatives
- mitigating adverse effects
- proposing measures to monitor the environmental effects of the plan or programme implementation.

The main aim of testing the evolving plan objectives against the SEA objectives is to ensure that plan objectives are in accordance, and do not conflict with, environmental and sustainable development principles. A compatibility matrix is typically prepared.

It is the role of the plan-maker to consider different solutions or options: these may typically be the proposed plan, *'business as usual'* or it could involve a series of alternatives. The task of the SEA is to consider the relative merits of the options as presented from an environmental (and sustainable development) perspective. This information can then inform the decision-making process. Being able to demonstrate that alternatives have been properly considered is a key part of meeting the SEA Directive requirement.

Predicting and evaluating the effects of the plan is best achieved using assessment matrices to demonstrate transparency. The core of the prediction process involves asking a number of key questions.

- How will the environmental baseline change if the plan or its alternatives are implemented?

■ What is the likely nature of this change? What is the geographical scale? Over what time period will it occur? Will the changes be permanent, temporary, positive or negative, probable or improbable, frequent or rare? Will the changes have secondary, cumulative and/ or synergistic effects? (UK SEA guidance, ODPM 2005)

The approach here is likely to be mixed, using both quantitative and qualitative information; it should be grounded by evidence where possible, and assumptions should be clearly stated.

Annex II of the SEA Directive sets out specific criteria for determining the likely significance of effects:

Evaluating the effects of a draft plan or programme

1. The characteristics of plans and programmes having regard in particular to:
   - the degree to which the PP sets a framework for project and other activities, with regard to the location, nature, size and operating conditions or by allocating resources;
   - the degree to which the PP influences other PPs including those in the hierarchy;
   - the relevance of the PP for the integration of environmental considerations in particular with a view to promoting sustainable development;
   - environmental problems relevant to the PP;
   - the relevance of the PP for the implementation of Community legislation on the environment (e.g. PPs linked to waste management or water protection).

2. Characteristics of the effects and of the area likely to be affected, having regard in particular to:
   - the probability, duration, frequency and reversibility of the effects;
   - the cumulative nature of the effects;
   - the transboundary nature of the effects;
   - the risks to human health or the environment (e.g. due to accidents);
   - the magnitude and spatial extent of the effects (geographical area and size of the population likely to be affected);
   - the value and vulnerability of the area likely to be affected by: special characteristics or cultural heritage; exceeded environmental quality standards or limit values; intensive land use;
   - the effects on areas or landscapes which have a recognised national, Community or international protection status.

Reproduced from 'ANNEX II Criteria for determining the likely significance of effects referred to in Article 3(5). Directive 2001/42/EC of the European Parliament and of the Council of 27 June 2001 on the assessment of the effects of certain plans and programmes on the environment.' Official Journal of the European Communities, 21/07/2001, L197/30–L197/37.

Mitigation is an integral element of the SEA process. If potential significant adverse effects are indicated, suggestions for mitigation should be made, and typically these are associated with changes to outline strategic thinking or detailed wording of policy. SEA is only one factor informing decisions in plan preparation; however, iterative interaction

SEA Procedures

between the plan and SEA teams can facilitate creative solutions to environmental problems. The mitigation hierarchy is similar to project EIA, and the Directive requires prevention, reduction and, finally, offsetting. SEA considers both adverse and beneficial effects; good practice seeks to enhance positive effects.

The final element of stage B involves developing proposals to monitor the environmental effects of implementation (required by Article 10 of the Directive). In order to be effective, monitoring needs to be considered from the outset of the SEA process during the development of the SEA objectives. This will give greater certainty that the proposed indicators (and possible) targets proposed are relevant and appropriate.

The monitoring framework should be focused on *'significant effects'*, and can be used to answer key questions:

- Were the predictions of environmental effects accurate?
- Have there been any adverse environmental effects, and do these fall within acceptable limits?

Monitoring of predicted beneficial effects should also be addressed, and good practice tends to seek synergies with other monitoring requirements for cost/resource effectiveness. In practice, planning authorities are selecting indicators and targets that are already used for performance monitoring of plans such as quality and quantity of groundwater, water use and flood risk.

Reporting – Stage C: Preparing the Environmental Report

Preparing the Environmental Report is a specific and key requirement of the Directive. The report needs to document the process of SEA, its key findings and how it has influenced the plan-making. Whilst this may involve substantial detail, it is important to remember that the Environmental Report is a publicly available consultation document. As such, it must be accessible, informative and crucially understandable to a wide range of stakeholders. In practice, technical details and working matrices are presented separately in appendices, with the main report text typically less than 50 pages. As with EIA, a non-technical summary is required. The Environmental Report is published alongside the draft of the plan being prepared as part of the formal consultation process.

The Environmental Report documents the methods and findings of the SEA process; it needs to be presented in a form suitable for the decision-makers, stakeholders and the public. It is likely to include the following:

- methods used (data, assessment, mitigation, consultation)
- context and background (problems, uncertainty)
- alternatives considered
- assessment of significant environmental effects and mitigation proposed
- proposals for monitoring that the effects of the plan are as predicted
- a non-technical summary.

Consulting – Stage D: Consulting on the Draft Plan or Programme and the Environmental Report

The Environmental Report is made available at the same time as the draft plan, and is an integral part of the consultation process. Views and opinions expressed during the consultation phase should be taken into account, and inform the final preparation before adoption of the plan. The results of consultation and how they have been addressed should be documented. The European SEA Directive requires that plan-makers should report the difference the SEA has made with *'a statement summarising how the environmental considerations have been integrated into the plan . . .'*.

The lists of consultees will change and evolve as the SEA progresses through scoping, assessment and formal reporting – issues may develop further or cease to be relevant. It is important to ensure that the right participants are involved at the appropriate levels, and relevant stages, of the SEA; and according to the scale and nature of the plan or programme. For example, it can be difficult for local groups focused on local issues to take a more strategic view with regard to a regional or national level plan.

Monitoring – Stage E: Monitoring the Significant Effect of Implementing the Plan or Programme on the Environment

The SEA process includes an iterative feedback review during implementation of the plan. In this way, the environmental performance of the plan can be reviewed and remedial action taken as necessary where any adverse effects are identified. The monitoring agreed after consultation reporting stage C should be used, and this can be usefully integrated with the monitoring regime for the plan itself. Integration of the SEA monitoring in this way helps to mainstream environmental and broader sustainable development issues within plan-making.

Responsible Authorities have an obligation to ensure that everyone has equal access to the information, and opportunity to comment

6.5   SEA Methods

Development of an SEA framework of objectives, indicators and targets is a commonly used approach to carrying out SEA. This acknowledges the strategic nature of the assessment and allows for integration of both qualitative and quantitative factors. At the strategic level, prediction and evaluation of effects on the environment may be difficult, since the actions and impacts are often indirect, cumulative and synergistic or antagonistic; information may be incomplete or not available at the relevant spatial or temporal scales.

There is a wide range of methods and techniques available for use in SEA; in practice, the most commonly used methods in the UK rely on expert judgement. The use of methods and techniques depends upon a number of factors, including the tier of plan- or programme-making (national, regional or local), the sector, and the stage of the assessment process; in practice, budget and timescale are key factors. An overview of methods and techniques is provided in the table below (developed from ODPM 2005, *A Practical Guide to the SEA Directive*):

Key fact

The SEA process '. . . is most effective when started as early as possible, ideally at the same time as the preparation of the plan or programme. SEA will often involve an iterative process . . .'

– ODPM 2005. *A Practical Guide to the SEA Directive*

SEA Methods

Methods and techniques used in SEA	Comment
Expert judgement	Widely used at all stages of SEA
Checklists, objectives and impact matrices (see also MCA below)	Widely used at all stages of SEA
Indicators and targets	Key factors particularly used in monitoring
Public participation and consultation; communication and reporting	Advisory group, workshop, visioning, questionnaire, survey, interview, public meeting, website, newsletters, exhibitions, TV and radio, newspapers, leaflets, telephone, reports
Ecological and carbon footprinting	Methods increasingly being developed and used
Carrying capacities, threshold assessment	Developed from environmental capacity concepts, especially useful for cumulative and comparative assessments
Forecasting and backcasting; visioning; horizon scanning	Particularly used in cabinet and policy SEAs; and for long-term effects such as climate change
SWOT analyses	Useful for scenario testing (options/alternatives)
Geographical information systems (GIS), overlay mapping	Widely used for constraints and opportunities analyses in spatial and sectoral planning; useful for presentations and reports, communication; GIS can be expensive
Network/causal chain analysis	Useful for scoping and engaging with stakeholders
Multi-criteria analysis (MCA)	Usually not related to economic considerations; use of weightings complicates the method and implies precision or scientific rigour that is not necessarily inherent in SEA
Cost–benefit analysis (CBA)	Usually economically based and used in decision-making for plans such as flood risk management; generally not preferred by SEA practitioners since it introduces economic bias
Risk assessment; Best Available Technique (BAT) and Best Practicable Environmental Option (BPEO)	Can be difficult at the strategic level but widely used at the project level, and links with other assessments (e.g. Health Impact Assessment) and regulatory regimes

Annex II outlines criteria for determining the likely significance of effects according to:

■ the characteristics of PPs

■ the characteristics of the effects and of the area likely to be affected.

In practice, it is useful to use Cumulative Effects Assessment (CEA) (see also Section 3.11 on integration) to help with decision-making on the difficult and cross-cutting issues such as climate change, movement and transport, energy, water and waste resource efficiencies, and aiming for net biodiversity gain.

6.6   SEA and EIA

There were certain criticisms of project EIA historically, including the following:

■ limited consideration of alternatives

■ limited assessment of cumulative impacts

■ lack of contribution to the achievement of wider global environmental and sustainable development aims.

These concerns, together with the perceived weakness of environmental aspects in policy-, plan- and programme-making, led to the distinction that generally became made in the 1980s between project- and higher-level tiers of decision-making for environmental assessment. The term 'EIA' was retained for project-level assessment, and SEA was introduced for the higher-level tiers of decision-making, and widely referred to as policies, plans and programmes (PPPs).

SEA sets the context/framework for the future assessment of development projects that may require EIA. SEA helps with the preparation of EIA, for example:

■ synergistic effects of several projects

■ global impacts such as greenhouse gas emissions and biodiversity

■ induced impacts, e.g. a new road can induce both new traffic and new developments such as out-of-town shopping centres.

In practice, SEA may be more proactive, aiming to both prevent negative impacts and enhance positive impacts through an iterative and ongoing dialogue with plan-making; project EIA focuses on mitigating negative environmental impacts through early and iterative integration into the design process. SEA may address a broad range of potential alternatives covering different sectors and spatial applications; the alternatives considered in project EIA relate to location, process selection, and design details.

Environmental assessment changes depending on where it is in the tiers of decision-making, and this may be summarised in the following table:

> *SEA may deal with different fiscal, regulatory or organisational and spatial development options. Project EIA, by contrast, deals with detailed decisions that are normally concerned with the location and design of a project*
>
> – Fischer 2007

SEA and EIA

	SEA	EIA
Decision-making level	POLICY ⟹ PLAN ⟹ PROGRAMME ⟹ PROJECT	
Nature of action	Strategic, visionary, conceptual	Immediate, operational
Scale of impacts	Macro, cumulative, unclear	Micro, localized
Timescales	Long–medium term	Medium–short term
Alternatives	Area wide, political, technological, fiscal, regulative	Specific locations, design, construction, operation
Data	More qualitative	More quantitative
Rigour of analysis	More uncertainty	More certain
Assessment	More professional judgement, benchmarks of objectives and criteria, industry good practice	More specific methods, legal requirements and industry standards
Role of practitioner	Mediator for negotiations, user of stakeholder values	Advocator of values and standards, user of stakeholder values
Public perception	More vague and distant	More reactive and 'NIMBY'

Adapted from Fischer (2007) and Wood (2003)

Appendices

1. Further Guidance: Key Consultees and Sources of Information

2. Schedule 2 Projects: Thresholds and Criteria

3. Schedule 3: Selection Criteria for Screening Schedule 2 Development

4. Schedule 4: Content of Environmental Statements

5. Review Criteria

6. Bibliography

7. Organisations

8. Training Courses

Appendix 1

Further Guidance: Key Consultees and Sources of Information

Name:	Botanical Society for the British Isles (BSBI)
Address:	Botanical Society of the British Isles, Botany Department, The Natural History Museum, Cromwell Road, London SW7 5BD
Website:	www.BSBI.org.uk

Name:	British Trust for Ornithology (BTO)
Tel.:	01842 750050
Address:	BTO, The Nunnery, Thetford, Norfolk IP24 2PU
Website:	www.bto.org

Name:	British Waterways
Tel.:	0845 671 5530
Address:	Head Office and Customer Service Centre, 64 Clarendon Road, Watford, Hertfordshire, WD17 1DA
Website:	www.britishwaterways.co.uk

Name:	Construction Industry Research and Information Association (CIRIA)
Tel.:	020 7549 3300
Address:	Classic House, 174–180 Old Street, London EC1V 9BP
Website:	www.ciria.org.uk

Name:	Countryside Council for Wales (CCW)
Tel.:	08451 306229
Address:	Countryside Council for Wales, Maes y Ffynnon, Penrhosgarnedd, Bangor, Gwynedd LL57 2DW
Website:	www.ccw.gov.uk

Name:	Centre for Ecology and Hydrology (CEH)
Tel.:	01491 838800
Address:	Maclean Building, Benson Lane, Crowmarsh Gifford, Wallingford, Oxfordshire OX10 8BB
Website:	www.ceh.ac.uk

Name:	Communities and Local Government
Tel.:	020 7944 4400
Address:	Communities and Local Government, Eland House, Bressenden Place, London SW1E 5DU
Website:	www.communities.gov.uk

Name:	Campaign to Protect Rural England (CPRE)
Tel.:	020 7981 2800
Address:	CPRE National Office, 128 Southwark Street, London SE1 0SW
Website:	www.cpre.org.uk

Name:	Department of Agriculture and Rural Development, Northern Ireland
Tel.:	02890 524999
Address:	Dundonald House, Upper Newtownards Road, Belfast BT4 3SB
Website:	www.dardni.gov.uk

Name: Department of Environment, Northern Ireland
Tel.:   02890 540540
Address: Department of Environment Headquarters, Clarence Court, 10–18 Adelaide Street, Belfast BT2 8GB
Website: www.doeni.gov.uk

Name: Department of Environment, Northern Ireland – Planning Service
Tel.:   02890 416700
Address: Planning Service Headquarters, Millennium House, 17–25 Great Victoria Street, Belfast BT2 7BN
Website: www.planningni.gov.uk

Name: Department for Business Enterprise and Regulatory Reform
Tel.:   020 7215 5000
Address: Ministerial Correspondence Unit, Department for Business, Enterprise and Regulatory Reform, 1 Victoria Street, London SW1H 0ET
Website: www.berr.gov.uk

Name: Department for Transport (DfT)
Tel.:   020 7944 8300
Address: Department for Transport, Great Minster House, 76 Marsham Street, London SW1P 4DR
Website: www.dft.gov.uk

Name: English Heritage
Tel.:   08703 331181
Address: Customer Services Department, PO Box 569, Swindon SN2 2YP
Website: www.english-heritage.org.uk

Name: Environment Agency
Tel.:   08708 506506
Address: National Customer Contact Centre, PO Box 544, Rotherham S60 1BY
Website: www.environment-agency.gov.uk

Name: Joint Nature Conservation Committee (JNCC)
Tel.:   01733 562626
Address: JNCC, Monkstone House, City Road, Peterborough PE1 1JY
Website: www.jncc.gov.uk

Name: Natural England
Tel.:   0114 241 8920
Address: Head Office, Natural England, 1 East Parade, Sheffield S1 2ET
Website: www.naturalengland.org.uk

Name: Natural Environment Research Council (NERC)
Tel.:   01793 411500
Address: NERC, Polaris House, North Star Avenue, Swindon SN2 1EU
Website: www.nerc.ac.uk

Name: Office for National Statistics
Tel.:   08456 013034
Address: Customer Contact Centre, Room 1.015, Office for National Statistics, Cardiff Road, Newport NP10 8XG
Website: www.statistics.gov.uk

Name: Planning Inspectorate
Tel.:   01173 726372
Address: The Planning Inspectorate, Registry/Scanning, Room 3/01 Kite Wing, Temple Quay House, 2 The Square, Temple Quay, Bristol BS1 6PN
Website: www.planning-inspectorate.gov.uk

Name: Royal Society for the Protection of Birds (RSPB)
Tel.:   01767 680551
Address: The Lodge, Potton Road, Sandy, Bedfordshire SG19 2DL
Website: www.rspb.org.uk

Name: Scottish Environment Protection Agency (SEPA)
Tel.:   01786 457700
Address: SEPA Corporate Office, Erskine Court, Castle Business Park, Stirling FK9 4TR
Website: www.sepa.org.uk

Name: Scottish Natural Heritage
Tel.:   0131 316 2600
Address: Silvan House, 3rd Floor East, 231 Corstorphine Road, Edinburgh EH12 7AT
Website: www.snh.org.uk

Name: The Wildlife Trusts
Tel.:   01636 677711
Address: The Kiln, Waterside, Mather Road, Newark, Nottinghamshire NG24 1WT
Website: www.wildlifetrusts.org

Name: Wildfowl and Wetlands Trust
Tel.:   01453 891900
Address: Slimbridge, Gloucestershire GL27 7BT
Website: www.wwt.org.uk

Name: World Wide Fund for Nature (WWF)
Tel.:   01483 426444
Address: Panda House, Weyside Park, Godalming, Surrey GU7 1XR
Website: www.wwf.org.uk

The above list of key consultees and sources of information is not intended to be exhaustive. There are many other organisations and societies more specific to certain subject areas, concentrating on particular flora and fauna, for example, or certain aspects of built heritage or history. Other consultees and organisations will become 'key' depending upon the locality in question. Departments of local authorities will often be consultees, and Local Agenda 21 groups or local community groups are likely to be active and interested in spatially specific impacts.

Appendix 2

Projects to which the Town and Country Planning (Environmental Impact Assessment) (England and Wales) Regulations 1999 Apply: Schedule 2 Projects

1. In the table below:
   'area of the works' includes any area occupied by apparatus, equipment, machinery, materials, plant, spoil heaps or other facilities or stores required for construction or installation;
   'controlled waters' has the same meaning as in the Water Resources Act 1991[1];
   'floorspace' means the floorspace in a building or buildings.

2. The table below sets out the descriptions of development and applicable thresholds and criteria for the purpose of classifying development as Schedule 2 development.

[1]1991 C. 57. *See* section 104.

From DETR 2000. *Environmental Impact Assessment: A Guide to Procedures.* Crown copyright: reproduced with the permission of the Controller of Her Majesty's Stationery Office

Table

Column 1 Description of development	Column 2 Applicable thresholds and criteria	Column 3 Indicative thresholds and criteria
The carrying out of development to provide any of the following:		

1. Agriculture and aquaculture

Column 1	Column 2	Column 3
(a) Projects for the use of uncultivated land or seminatural areas for intensive agricultural purposes;	The area of the development exceeds 0.5 hectare.	Development (such as greenhouses, farm buildings, etc.) on previously uncultivated land is unlikely to require EIA unless it covers more than 5 hectares. In considering whether particular development is likely to have significant effects, consideration should be given to impacts on the surrounding ecology, hydrology and landscape.
(b) Water management projects for agriculture, including irrigation and land drainage projects;	The area of the works exceeds 1 hectare.	EIA is more likely to be required if the development would result in permanent changes to the character of more than 5 hectares of land. In assessing the significance of any likely effects, particular regard should be had to whether the development would have damaging wider impacts on hydrology and surrounding ecosystems. It follows that EIA will not normally be required for routine water management projects undertaken by farmers.
(c) Intensive livestock installations (unless included in Schedule 1);	The area of new floorspace exceeds 500 square metres.	The significance or otherwise of the impacts of intensive livestock installations will often depend on the level of odours, increased traffic and the arrangements for waste handling. EIA is more likely to be required for intensive livestock installations if they are designed to house more than 750 sows, 2000 fattening pigs, 60 000 broilers or 50 000 layers, turkeys or other poultry.
(d) Intensive fish farming;	The installation resulting from the development is designed to produce more than 10 tonnes of dead weight fish per year.	Apart from the physical scale of any development, the likelihood of significant effects will generally depend on the extent of any likely wider impacts on the hydrology and ecology of the surrounding area. Developments designed to produce more than 100 tonnes (dead weight) of fish per year will be more likely to require EIA.
(e) Reclamation of land from the sea.	All development.	In assessing the significance of any development, regard should be had to the likely wider impacts on natural coastal processes beyond the site itself, as well as to the scale of reclamation works themselves. EIA is more likely to be required where work is proposed on a site which exceeds 1 hectare.

2. Extractive industry

Column 1	Column 2	Column 3
(a) Quarries, open-cast mining and peat extraction (unless included in Schedule 1); (b) Underground mining;	All development except the construction of buildings or other ancillary structures where the new floorspace does not exceed 1000 square metres.	The likelihood of significant effects will tend to depend on the scale and duration of the works, and the likely consequent impact of noise, dust, discharges to water and visual intrusion. All new open cast mines and underground mines will generally require EIA. For clay, sand and gravel workings, quarries and peat extraction sites, EIA is more likely to be required if they would cover more than 15 hectares or involve the extraction of more than 30 000 tonnes of mineral per year.

Environmental impact assessment handbook

Table (continued)

Column 1 Description of development	Column 2 Applicable thresholds and criteria	Column 3 Indicative thresholds and criteria
2. Extractive industry (continued)		
(c) Extraction of minerals by fluvial dredging;	All development.	Particular consideration should be given to noise, and any wider impacts on the surrounding hydrology and ecology. EIA is more likely to be required where it is expected that more than 100 000 tonnes of mineral will be extracted per year.
(d) Deep drillings, in particular: (i) geothermal drilling; (ii) drilling for the storage of nuclear waste material; (iii) drilling for water supplies; with the exception of drillings for investigating the stability of the soil.	(i) In relation to any type of drilling, the area of the works exceeds 1 hectare; or (ii) in relation to geothermal drilling and drilling for the storage of nuclear waste material, the drilling is within 100 metres of any controlled waters.	EIA is more likely to be required where the scale of the drilling operations involves development of a surface site of more than 5 hectares. Regard should be had to the likely wider impacts on surrounding hydrology and ecology. On its own, exploratory deep drilling is unlikely to require EIA. It would not be appropriate to require EIA for exploratory activity simply because it might eventually lead to some form of permanent activity.
(e) Surface industrial installations for the extraction of coal, petroleum, natural gas and ores, as well as bituminous shale.	The area of the development exceeds 0.5 hectare.	The main considerations are likely to be the scale of development, emissions to air, discharges to water, the risk of accident and the arrangements for transporting the fuel. EIA is more likely to be required if the development is on a major scale (site of 10 hectares or more) or where production is expected to be substantial (e.g. more than 100 000 tonnes of petroleum per year).
3. Energy industry		
(a) Industrial installations for the production of electricity, steam and hot water (unless included in Schedule 1); (b) Industrial installations for carrying gas, steam and hot water;	The area of the development exceeds 0.5 hectare. The area of the works exceeds 1 hectare.	EIA will normally be required for power stations which require approval from the Secretary of State at the Department of Trade and Industry (i.e. those with a thermal output of more than 50 megawatts). EIA is unlikely to be required for smaller new conventional power stations. Small stations using novel forms of generation should be considered carefully in line with the guidance in PPG 22 (Renewable Energy). The main considerations are likely to be the level of emissions to air, arrangements for the transport of fuel and any visual impact.
(c) Surface storage of natural gas; (d) Underground storage of combustible gases; (e) Surface storage of fossil fuels;	(i) The area of any new building, deposit or structure exceeds 500 square metres; or (ii) a new building, deposit or structure is to be sited within 100 metres of any controlled waters.	In addition to the scale of the development, significant effects are likely to depend on discharges to water, emissions to air and risk to accidents. EIA is more likely to be required where it is proposed to store more than 100 000 tonnes of fuel. Smaller installations are unlikely to require EIA unless hazardous chemicals are stored
(f) Industrial briquetting of coal and lignite;	The area of new floorspace exceeds 1000 square metres.	As paragraph 4 – Production and processing of metals.
(g) Installations for the processing and storage of radioactive waste (unless included in Schedule 1);	(i) The area of new floorspace exceeds 1000 square metres; or	EIA will normally be required for new installations whose primary purpose is to process and store radioactive waste, and which are located on sites not previously authorised for such use. In addition to the scale of any development, significant effects are likely to depend on the extent of routine discharges of radiation to the

Table (continued)

Column 1 Description of development	Column 2 Applicable thresholds and criteria	Column 3 Indicative thresholds and criteria
3. Energy industry (continued)		
	(ii) the installation resulting from the development will require an authorisation or the variation of an authorisation under the Radioactive Substance Act 1993.	environment. In this context EIA is unlikely to be required for installations where the processing or storage of radioactive waste is incidental to the main purpose of the development (e.g. installations at hospitals or research facilities).
(h) Installations for hydroelectric energy production;	The installation is designed to produce more than 0.5 megawatts.	In addition to the physical scale of the development, particular regard should be had to the potential wider impacts on hydrology and ecology. EIA is more likely to be required for new hydroelectric developments which have more than 5 megawatts of generating capacity.
(i) Installations for the harnessing of wind power for energy production (wind farms).	(i) The development involves the installation of more than 2 turbines; or (ii) the hub height of any turbine or height of any other structure exceeds 15 metres.	The likelihood of significant effects will generally depend on the scale of the development, and its visual impact, as well as potential noise impacts. EIA is more likely to be required for commercial developments of five or more turbines, or more than 5 megawatts of new generating capacity.
4. Production and processing of metals		
(a) Installations for the production of pig iron or steel (primary or secondary fusion) including continuous casting; (b) Installations for the processing of ferrous metals: (i) hot-rolling mills; (ii) smitheries with hammers; (iii) application of protective fused metal coats; (c) Ferrous metal foundries; (d) Installations for the smelting, including the alloyage, of non-ferrous metals, excluding precious metals, including recovered products (refining, foundry casting, etc.); (e) Installations for surface treatment of metals and plastic material using an electrolytic or chemical process; (f) Manufacture and assembly of motor vehicles and manufacture of motor-vehicle engines; (g) Shipyards; (h) Installations for the construction and repair of aircraft; (i) Manufacture of railway equipment; (j) Swaging by explosives; (k) Installations for the roasting and sintering of metallic ores.	The area of new floorspace exceeds 1000 square metres. The area of new floorspace exceeds 1000 square metres.	New manufacturing or industrial plants of the types listed in the Regulations, may well require EIA if the operational development covers a site of more than 10 hectares. Smaller developments are more likely to require EIA if they are expected to give rise to significant discharges of waste, emission of pollutants or operational noise. Among the factors to be taken into account in assessing the significance of such effects are: • whether the development involves a process designated as a 'scheduled process' for the purpose of air pollution control; • whether the process involves discharges to water which require the consent of the Environment Agency; • whether the installation would give rise to the presence of environmentally significant quantities of potentially hazardous or polluting substances; • whether the process would give rise to radioactive or other hazardous waste; • whether the development would fall under Council Directive 96/82/EC on the control of major accident hazards involving dangerous substances (COMAH). However, the need for a consent under other legislation is not itself a justification for EIA.

Table (continued)

Column 1 Description of development	Column 2 Applicable thresholds and criteria	Column 3 Indicative thresholds and criteria
5. Mineral industry		
(a) Coke ovens (dry coal distillation); (b) Installations for the manufacture of cement; (c) Installations for the production of asbestos and the manufacture of asbestos based products (unless included in Schedule 1); (d) Installations for the manufacture of glass including glass fibre; (e) Installations for smelting mineral substances including the production of mineral fibres; (f) Manufacture of ceramic products by burning, in particular roofing tiles, bricks, refractory bricks, tiles, stoneware or porcelain.	The area of new floorspace exceeds 1000 square metres.	As for paragraph 4.
6. Chemical industry (unless included in Schedule 1)		
(a) Treatment of intermediate products and production of chemicals; (b) Production of pesticides and pharmaceutical products paints and varnishes, elastomers and peroxides;	The area of new floorspace exceeds 1000 square metres.	As for paragraph 4.
(c) Storage facilities for petroleum, petrochemical and chemical products.	(i) The area of any new building or structure exceeds 0.05 hectare; or (ii) more than 200 tonnes of petroleum, petrochemical or chemical products are to be stored at any one time.	
7. Food industry		
(a) Manufacture of vegetable and animal oils and fats; (b) Packing and canning of animal and vegetable products; (c) Manufacture of dairy products; (d) Brewing and malting; (e) Confectionery and syrup manufacture; (f) Installations for the slaughter of animals; (g) Industrial starch manufacturing installations; (h) Fish-meal and fish-oil factories; (i) Sugar factories.	The area of new floorspace exceeds 1000 square metres.	As for paragraph 4.

Table (continued)

Column 1 Description of development	Column 2 Applicable thresholds and criteria	Column 3 Indicative thresholds and criteria
8. Textile, leather, wood and paper industries		
(a) Industrial plants for the production of paper and board (unless included in Schedule 1);	The area of new floorspace exceeds 1000 square metres.	As for paragraph 4.
(b) Plants for the pre-treatment (operations such as washing, bleaching, mercerisation) or dyeing of fibres or textiles;		
(c) Plants for the tanning of hides and skins;		
(d) Cellulose-processing and production installations.		
9. Rubber industry		
Manufacture and treatment of elastomer-based products.	The area of new floorspace exceeds 1000 square metres.	As for paragraph 4.
10. Infrastructure projects		
(a) Industrial estate development projects;	The area of the development exceeds 0.5 hectare.	EIA is more likely to be required if the site area of the new development is more than 20 hectares. In determining whether significant effects are likely, particularly consideration should be given to the potential increase in traffic, emissions and noise.
(b) Urban development projects, including the construction of shopping centres and car parks, sports stadiums, leisure centres and multiplex cinemas;	The area of the development exceeds 0.5 hectare.	In addition to the physical scale of such developments, particular consideration should be given to the potential increase in traffic, emissions and noise. EIA is unlikely to be required for the redevelopment of land unless the new development is on a significantly greater scale than the previous use, or the types of impact are of a markedly different nature or there is a high level of contamination. Development proposed for sites which have not previously been intensively developed are more likely to require EIA if: • the site area of the scheme is more than 5 hectares; or • it would provide a total of more than 10 000 square metres of new commercial floorspace; or • the development would have significant urbanising effects in a previously non-urbanised area (e.g. a new development of more than 1000 dwellings).
(b) Urban development projects, including the construction of shopping centres and car parks, sports stadiums, leisure centres and multiplex cinemas;	The area of the development exceeds 0.5 hectare.	In addition to the physical scale of the development, particular impacts for consideration are increased traffic, noise, emissions to air and water. Developments of more than 5 hectares are more likely to require EIA.

Table (continued)

Column 1 Description of development	Column 2 Applicable thresholds and criteria	Column 3 Indicative thresholds and criteria
10. Infrastructure projects (continued)		
(c) Construction of intermodal transshipment facilities and of intermodal terminals (unless included in Schedule 1); (d) Construction of railways (unless included in Schedule 1);	The area of the works exceeds 1 hectare.	For linear transport schemes, the likelihood of significant effects will generally depend on the estimated emissions, traffic, noise and vibration and degree of visual intrusion and impact on the surrounding ecology. EIA is more likely to be required for new development over 2 kilometres in length.
(e) Construction of airfields (unless included in Schedule 1);	(i) The development involves an extension to a runway; or (ii) the area of the works exceeds 1 hectare.	The main impacts to be considered in judging significance are noise, traffic generation and emissions. New permanent airfields will normally require EIA, as will major works (such as new runways or terminals with a site area of more than 10 hectares) at existing airports. Smaller scale development at existing airports is unlikely to require EIA unless it would lead to significant increases in air or road traffic.
(f) Construction of roads (unless included in Schedule 1);	The area of the works exceeds 1 hectare.	As for paragraph 10(d).
(g) Construction of harbours and port installations including fishing harbours (unless included in Schedule 1);	The area of the works exceeds 1 hectare.	Primary impacts for consideration are those on hydrology, ecology, noise and increased traffic. EIA is more likely to be required if the development is on a major scale (e.g. would cover a site of more than 10 hectares). Smaller developments may also have significant effects where they include a quay or pier which would extend beyond the high water mark or would affect wider coastal processes.
(h) Inland-waterway construction not included in Schedule 1, canalisation and flood-relief works;	The area of the works exceeds 1 hectare.	The likelihood of significant impacts is likely to depend primarily on the potential wider impacts on the surrounding hydrology and ecology. EIA is more likely to be required for development of over 2 kilometres of canal. The impact of flood relief works is especially dependent on the nature of the location and the potential effects on the surrounding ecology and hydrology. Schemes for which the area of the works would exceed 5 hectares or which are more than 2 kilometres in length would normally require EIA.
(i) Dams and other installations designed to hold water or store it on a long-term basis (unless included in Schedule 1);	The area of the works exceeds 1 hectare.	In considering such developments, particular regard should be had to the potential wider impacts on the hydrology and ecology, as well as to the physical scale of the development. EIA is likely to be required for any major new dam (e.g. where the construction site exceeds 20 hectares).
(j) Tramways, elevated and underground railways, suspended lines or similar lines of a particular type, used exclusively or mainly for passenger transport;	The area of the works exceeds 1 hectare.	As for paragraph 10(d).

Table (continued)

Column 1 Description of development	Column 2 Applicable thresholds and criteria	Column 3 Indicative thresholds and criteria
10. Infrastructure projects (continued)		
(k) Oil and gas pipe-line installations (unless included in Schedule 1); (l) Installations of long-distance aqueducts;	(i) The area of the works exceeds 1 hectare; or, (ii) In the case of a gas pipe-line, the installation has a design operating pressure exceeding 7 bar gauge.	For underground pipe-lines, the major impact to be considered will generally be the disruption to the surrounding ecosystems during construction, while for overground pipe-lines visual impact will be a key consideration. EIA is more likely to be required for any pipe-line over 5 kilometres long. EIA is unlikely to be required for pipe-lines laid underneath a road, or for those installed entirely by means of tunnelling.
(m) Coastal work to combat erosion and maritime works capable of altering the coast through the construction, for example, of dykes, moles, jetties and other sea defence works, excluding the maintenance and reconstruction of such works;	All development.	The impact of such works will depend largely on the nature of the particular site and the likely wider impacts on natural coastal processes outside the site. EIA will be more likely where the area of the works would exceed 1 hectare.
(n) Groundwater abstraction and artificial groundwater recharge schemes not included in Schedule 1; (o) Works for the transfer of water resources between river basins not included in Schedule 1;	The area of the works exceeds 1 hectare.	Impacts likely to be significant are those on hydrology and ecology. Developments of this sort can have significant effects on environments some kilometres distant. This is particularly important for wetland and other sites where the habitat and species are particularly dependent on an aquatic environment. EIA is likely to be required for developments where the area of the works exceeds 1 hectare.
(p) Motorway service areas.	The area of the development exceeds 0.5 hectare.	Impacts likely to be significant for traffic, noise, air quality, ecology and visual impact. EIA is more likely to be required for new motorway service areas which are proposed for previously undeveloped sites and if the proposed development would cover an area of more than 5 hectares.
11. Other projects		
(a) Permanent racing and test tracks for motorised vehicles;	The area of the development exceeds 1 hectare.	Particular consideration should be given to the size, noise impacts, emissions and the potential traffic generation. EIA is more likely to be required for developments with a site area of 20 hectares or more.
(b) Installations for the disposal of waste (unless included in Schedule 1);	(i) The disposal is by incineration; or (ii) the area of the development exceeds 0.5 hectare; or (iii) the installation is to be sited within 100 metres of any controlled waters.	The likelihood of significant effects will generally depend on the scale of the development and the nature of the potential impact in terms of discharge, emissions or odour. For installations (including landfill sites) for the deposit, recovery and/or disposal of household, industrial and/or commercial wastes (as defined by the Controlled Waste Regulations 1992) EIA is more likely to be required where new capacity is created to hold more than 50 000 tonnes per year, or to hold waste on a site of 10 hectares or more. Sites taking smaller quantities of these wastes, sites seeking only to accept inert wastes (demolition rubble, etc.) or civic amenity sites, are unlikely to require EIA.

Table (continued)

Column 1 Description of development	Column 2 Applicable thresholds and criteria	Column 3 Indicative thresholds and criteria
11. Other projects (continued)		
(c) Waste water treatment plants (unless included in Schedule 1);	The area of the development exceeds 1000 square metres.	Particular consideration should be given to the size, treatment process, pollution and nuisance potential, topography, proximity of dwellings and the potential impact of traffic movements. EIA is more likely to be required if the development would be on a substantial scale (e.g. site area of more than 10 hectares) or if it would lead to significant discharges (e.g. capacity exceeding 100 000 population equivalent). EIA should not be required simply because a plant is on a scale which required compliance with the Urban Waste Water Treatment Directive (91/271/EEC).
(d) Sludge-deposition site; (e) Storage of scrap iron, including scrap vehicles;	(i) The area of deposit or storage exceeds 0.5 hectare; or (ii) a deposit is to be made or scrap stored within 100 metres of any controlled waters.	Similar considerations will apply for sewage sludge lagoons as for waste disposal installations. EIA is more likely to be required where the site is intended to hold more than 5000 cubic metres of sewage sludge. Major impacts from storage of scrap iron are likely to be discharges to soil, site noise and traffic generation. EIA is more likely to be required where it is proposed to store scrap on an area of 10 hectares or more.
(f) Test benches for engines, turbines or reactors; (g) Installations for the manufacture of artificial mineral fibres; (h) Installations for the recovery or destruction of explosive substances; (i) Knackers' yards.	The area of new floorspace exceeds 1000 square metres.	As for paragraph 4.
12. Tourism and leisure		
(a) Ski-runs, ski-lifts and cable-cars and associated developments;	(i) The area of the works exceeds 1 hectare; or (ii) the height of any building or other structure exceeds 15 metres.	EIA is more likely to be required if the development is over 500 metres in length or if it requires a site of more than 5 hectares. In addition to any visual or ecological impacts, particular regard should also be had to the potential traffic generation.
(b) Marinas;	The area of the enclosed water surface exceeds 1000 square metres.	In assessing whether significant effects are likely, particular regard should be had to any wider impacts on natural coastal processes outside the site, as well as the potential noise and traffic generation. EIA is more likely to be required for large new marinas, for example where the proposal is for more than 300 berths (seawater site) or 100 berths (freshwater site). EIA is unlikely to be required where the development is located solely within an existing dock or basin.

Table (continued)

Column 1 Description of development	Column 2 Applicable thresholds and criteria	Column 3 Indicative thresholds and criteria
12. Tourism and leisure (continued)		
(c) Holiday villages and hotel complexes outside urban areas and associated developments; (d) Theme parks; (e) Permanent camp sites and caravan sites;	The area of the development exceeds 0.5 hectare. The area of the development exceeds 1 hectare.	In assessing the significance of tourism development, visual impacts, impacts on ecosystems and traffic generation will be key considerations. The effects of new theme parks are more likely to be significant if it is expected that they will generate more than 250 000 visitors per year. EIA is likely to be required for major new tourism and leisure developments which require a site of more than 10 hectares. In particular, EIA is more likely to be required for holiday villages or hotel complexes with more than 300 bed spaces, or for permanent camp sites or caravan sites with more than 200 pitches.
(f) Golf courses and associated developments.	The area of the development exceeds 1 hectare.	New 18-hole golf courses are likely to require EIA. The main impacts are likely to be those on the surrounding hydrology, ecosystems and landscape, as well as those from traffic generation. Developments at existing golf courses are unlikely to require EIA.
13.		
(a) Any change to or extension of development of a description listed in Schedule 1 or in paragraphs 1 to 12 of Column 1 of this table, where that development is already authorised, executed or in the process of being executed, and the change or extension may have significant adverse effects on the environment;	(i) In relation to development of a description mentioned in Column 1 of this table, the thresholds and criteria in the corresponding part of Column 2 of this table applied to the change or extension (and not to the development as changed or extended). (ii) In relation to development of a description mentioned in a paragraph in Schedule 1 (see Appendix 1) indicated below, the thresholds and criteria in Column 2 of the paragraph of this table indicated below applied to the change or extension (and not to the development as changed or extended):	Development which comprises a change or extension requires EIA only if the change or extension is likely to have significant environmental effects. This should be considered in the light of the general guidance in DETR Circular 2/99 (Welsh Office Circular 11/99) and the indicative thresholds shown above in Column 3. However, the significance of any effects must be considered in the context of the existing development. In some cases, repeated small extensions may be made to development. Quantified thresholds cannot easily deal with this kind of 'incremental' development. In such instances, it should be borne in mind that the Column 3 thresholds are indicative only. An expansion of the same size as a previous expansion will not automatically lead to the same determination on the need for EIA because the environment may have altered since the question was last addressed.

Paragraph in Schedule 1	Paragraph of this table
1	6(a)
2(a)	3(a)
2(b)	3(g)
3	3(g)
4	4
5	5
6	6(a)
7(a)	10(d) (in relation to railways) or 10(e) (in relation to airports)

Table (continued)

Column 1 Description of development	Column 2 Applicable thresholds and criteria	Column 3 Indicative thresholds and criteria
13. (continued)		
	7(b) and (c) 10(f)	
	8(a) 10(h)	
	8(b) 10(g)	
	9 11(b)	
	10 11(b)	
	11 10(n)	
	12 10(o)	
	13 11(c)	
	14 2(e)	
	15 10(i)	
	16 10(k)	
	17 1(c)	
	18 8(a)	
	19 2(a)	
	20 6(c).	
(b) Development of a description mentioned in Schedule 1 undertaken exclusively or mainly for the development and testing of new methods or products and not used for more than two years.	All development.	

Appendix 3

Schedule 3: Selection Criteria for Screening Schedule 2 Development (Annex III of the EU Directive 97/11/EC)

1. Characteristics of projects

The characteristics of projects must be considered having regard, in particular, to:

– the size of the project;
– the cumulation with other projects;
– the use of natural resources;
– the production of waste;
– pollution and nuisances;
– the risk of accidents, having regard in particular to substances or technologies used.

2. Location of projects

The environmental sensitivity of geographical areas likely to be affected by projects must be considered, having regard, in particular, to:

– the existing land use;
– the relative abundance, quality and regenerative capacity of natural resources in the area; the absorption capacity of the natural environment, paying particular attention to the following areas:
  (a) wetlands;
  (b) coastal zones;
  (c) mountain and forest areas;
  (d) nature reserves and parks;
  (e) areas classified or protected under Member States' legislation; special protection areas designated by Member States pursuant to Directive 79/409/EEC and 92/43/EEC;
  (f) areas in which the environmental quality standards laid down in Community legislation have already been exceeded;
  (g) densely populated areas;
  (h) landscapes of historical, cultural or archaeological significance.

3. Characteristics of the potential impact

The potential significant effects of projects must be considered in relation to criteria set out under 1 and 2 above, and having regard in particular to:

– the extent of the impact (geographical area and size of the affected population);
– the transfrontier nature of the impact;
– the magnitude and complexity of the impact;
– the probability of the impact;
– the duration, frequency and reversibility of the impact.

Reproduced from Statutory Instrument 1999 No. 293, HMSO

Appendix 4

Schedule 4: Requirements of the Regulations as to the Content of Environmental Statements

Below are the statutory provisions with respect to the content of environmental statements, as set out in Parts I and II of Schedule 4 to the Town and Country Planning (Environmental Impact Assessment) (England and Wales) Regulations 1999.

Under the definition in Regulation 2(1), 'environmental statement' means a statement:

(a) that includes such of the information referred to in Part I of Schedule 4 as is reasonably required to assess the environmental effects of the development and which the applicant can, having regard in particular to current knowledge and methods of assessment, reasonably be required to compile, but

(b) that includes at least the information referred to in Part II of Schedule 4.

Part I

1. Description of the development, including in particular:

   (a) a description of the physical characteristics of the whole development and the land-use requirements during the construction and operational phases;

   (b) a description of the main characteristics of the production process, for instance, nature and quantity of the materials used;

   (c) an estimate, by type and quantity, of expected residues and emissions (water, air and soil pollution, noise, vibration, light, heat, radiation, etc.) resulting from the operation of the proposed development.

2. An outline of the main alternatives studied by the applicant or appellant and an indication of the main reasons for his choice, taking into account the environmental effects.

3. A description of the aspects of the environment likely to be significantly affected by the development, including, in particular, population, fauna, flora, soil, water, air, climatic factors, material assets, including the architectural and archaeological heritage, landscape and the inter-relationship between the above factors.

4. A description of the likely significant effects of the development on the environment, which should cover the direct effects and any indirect, secondary, cumulative, short, medium and long-term, permanent and temporary, positive and negative effects of the development, resulting from:

   (a) the existence of the development;

   (b) the use of natural resources;

   (c) the emission of pollutants, the creation of nuisances and the elimination of waste, and the description by the applicant of the forecasting methods used to assess the effects on the environment.

5. A description of the measures envisaged to prevent, reduce and where possible offset any significant adverse effects on the environment.

6. A non-technical summary of the information provided under paragraphs 1 to 5 of this Part.

7. An indication of any difficulties (technical deficiencies or lack of know-how) encountered by the applicant in compiling the required information.

Part II

1. A description of the development comprising information on the site, design and size of the development.

2. A description of the measures envisaged in order to avoid, reduce and, if possible, remedy significant adverse effects.

3. The data required to identify and assess the main effects which the development is likely to have on the environment.

4. An outline of the main alternatives studied by the applicant or appellant and an indication of the main reasons for his choice, taking into account the environmental effects.

5. A non-technical summary of the information provided under paragraphs 1 to 4 of this Part.

Appendix 5

Review Criteria

The following identifies those criteria commonly used by reviewers of the content and quality of Environmental Statements (ESs).

General

Scoping

- Description of the scoping process.
- Consultation record – consultees and responses.
- Reasons for the exclusion of issues.

Alternatives

- Locations, construction and operational processes, and site layouts.
- Analysis of the advantages and disadvantages of each option.
- Description of the reasons for selection.
- Description of other factors influencing the final choice.

Description of the Proposed Development

- Purpose and objectives.
- Programme for construction, operation, decommissioning and restoration.
- Methods of construction.
- Physical characteristics – location, design, size, area of land take.
- Nature and quantity of materials.
- Type and quantity of traffic.
- Type and quantity of emissions and residues.

Site Description

- Existing land use of site and surrounding area.
- Description of plans, policies and designations of the site and surroundings.

Topic Specific

These criteria are tested for each topic, e.g. noise or water. Where appropriate, impacts evaluated should include direct, indirect, cumulative, short, medium and long term, permanent and temporary, positive and negative, and reversible and irreversible.

Baseline Conditions

- Description of the current condition.
- Source of the data.

- Evaluation of the sensitivity and importance.
- Limitations of surveys.

Prediction of Impact Magnitude

- Predictions of the magnitude of likely significant effects.
- Predictions for each phase of development.
- Methods of prediction should be described.
- Levels of confidence should be described.

Impact Significance

- Description of standards, thresholds and limits.
- Identify the significance of impacts after mitigation.

Mitigation

- Measures to avoid, reduce or remedy adverse impacts.
- Statement of effectiveness of mitigation.
- Commitment to mitigation.

Post-development

- Management plans.
- Monitoring.

Presentation of Results

Presentation

- Clear and logical.
- Avoid technical terms; use of glossary.
- Provision of references.
- Provision of plans, figures and illustrations.

Objectivity

- Balanced and unbiased.
- Summary of issues raised by consultees.
- Identification of difficulties in assessment.

Non-technical Summary

- Information for the non-specialist to understand environmental effects of development.
- Summary of the description of the development, alternatives, aspects of environment likely to be significantly affected, significant impacts, and mitigation measures.
- Provision as a standalone document with appropriate maps and illustrations.
- Accurate reflection of ES findings.

Review Grades

A   Excellent – no tasks left incomplete.

B   Good – only minor omissions and inadequacies.

C   Satisfactory – despite omissions and inadequacies.

D   Parts well attempted – but must as a whole be considered unsatisfactory because of omissions and/or inadequacies.

E   Poor – significant omissions or inadequacies.

F   Very poor – most tasks left incomplete.

N/A Not applicable – the review topic is not applicable or relevant in the context of this statement.

Adapted from *IEMA, ES Review Criteria* 1999 and Lee, N. and Colley, R. *Reviewing the Quality of ESs*

Appendix 6

Bibliography

These are some of the main texts giving guidance on various techniques and methods of EIA. Attention is drawn to more specific sources of information in the relevant sections of the book.

Becker, H. and Vanclay, F. 2003. *The International Handbook of Social Impact Assessment*. Edward Elgar, Cheltenham.

British Medical Association 1999. *Health and Environmental Impact Assessment – An Integrated Approach*. Earthscan, London.

Byron, H. 2000. *Biodiversity and EIA: A Good Practice Guide for Road Schemes*. RSPB WWF-UK, London.

Construction Industry Research and Information Association 2000. *Sustainable Urban Drainage Systems*, C522. CIRIA, London.

Dalal-Clayton, B. and Sadler, B. 2005. *Strategic Environmental Assessment: A Source Book and Reference Guide to International Experience*. Earthscan, London.

Department of Environment 1995. *Preparation of Environmental Statements for Planning Projects that Require Environmental Assessment – A Good Practice Guide*. HMSO, London.

Department of Environment, Transport and the Regions 1997. *Mitigation Measures Used in Environmental Statements*. HMSO, London.

Department of Environment, Transport and the Regions 2000. *Environmental Impact Assessment: A Guide to Procedures*. Thomas Telford, London.

Environment Agency 2002. *Environmental Assessment: Scoping Handbook for Projects*. Environment Agency, Bristol.

European Commission 2001. *Guidance on Screening and Scoping*. EC, Brussels.

Fischer, T. 2007. *The Theory and Practice of Strategic Environmental Assessment*. Earthscan, London.

Glasson, J., Therivel, R. and Chadwick, A. 2005. *Introduction to Environmental Impact Assessment*. UCL Press, London.

Harrop, O. and Nixon, A. 1999. *Environmental Assessment in Practice*. Routledge, London.

Institute of Ecology and Environmental Management 2006. *Guidelines for Ecological Impact Assessment in the United Kingdom*. IEEM, Winchester.

Institute of Environmental Assessment 1993. *Guidelines for the Environmental Assessment of Road Traffic*. IEA, Lincoln.

Institute of Environmental Assessment 1995. *Guidelines for Baseline Ecological Assessment*. E & FN Spon, London.

Institute of Environmental Management and Assessment 2004. *Guidelines for Environmental Impact Assessment*. IEMA, Lincoln.

Institute of Environmental Management and Assessment 2008. *Environmental Management Plans*. IEMA, Lincoln.

Institution of Highways and Transportation 1994. *Guidelines for Traffic Impact Assessment*. IHT, London.

International Association for Impact Assessment 2006. *Health Impact Assessment: International Best Practice Principles*. IAIA, Fargo, ND.

Joint Nature Conservation Committee 1990. *Handbook for Phase I Habitat Survey – A Technique for Environmental Audit.* JNCC, London.

Kent County Council (Planning Department) 1991. *Environmental Assessment Hand Book.* Kent County Council, Maidstone.

Landscape Institute, Wilson, S. and Institute of Environmental Management and Assessment 2002. *Guidelines for Landscape and Visual Impact Assessment.* Taylor and Francis, London.

Morris, P. and Therivel, R. 2001. *Methods of Environmental Impact Assessment.* E & FN Spon, London.

Morrison-Saunders, A. and Arts, J. 2006. *Assessing Impact: Handbook of EIA and SEA Follow-up.* Earthscan, London.

Organisation for Economic Co-operation and Development 1992. *Guidelines on Aid and Environment*, No. 1. *Good Practices for Environmental Impact Assessment of Development Projects.* OECD, Paris.

Organisation for Economic Co-operation and Development 2006. *Applying Strategic Environmental Assessment. Good Practice for Development Cooperation.* OECD, Paris.

Petts, J. 1999. *Handbook of Environmental Impact Assessment*, Vols 1 and 2. Blackwell Science, Oxford.

Therivel, R. 2004. *Strategic Environmental Assessment in Action.* Earthscan, London.

Treweek, J. 1999. *Ecological Impact Assessment.* Blackwell Science, Oxford.

United Nations Environment Programme 2002. *Environmental Training Resource Manual.* Earthprint, Stevanage.

Wathern, P. (ed.) 1992. *Environmental Impact Assessment: Theory and Practice.* Routledge, London.

Weston, J. 1997. *Planning and Environmental Impact Assessment in Practice.* Longman, Harlow.

Wood, C. 2002. *Environmental Impact Assessment – A Comparative Review.* Longman, Harlow.

World Bank 1996. *Environmental Assessment Source Book.* World Bank, Washington, DC.

Appendix 7

Organisations

Key Professional Organisations

Name:	Chartered Institute of Environmental Health (CIEH)
Tel.:	020 7928 6006
Address:	Chadwick Court, 15 Hatfields, London SE1 8DJ
Website:	www.cieh.org

Name:	Chartered Institute of Wastes Management (IWM)
Tel.:	01604 620426
Address:	9 Saxon Court, St Peter's Gardens, Northampton NN1 1SX
Website:	www.ciwm.co.uk

Name:	Chartered Institution of Water and Environmental Management (CIWEM)
Tel.:	020 7831 3110
Address:	15 John Street, London WC1N 2EB
Website:	www.ciwem.org

Name:	Landscape Institute
Tel.:	020 7299 4500
Address:	Landscape Institute, 33 Great Portland Street, London W1W 8QG
Website:	www.landscapeinstitute.org

Name:	Institution of Civil Engineers
Tel.:	020 7222 7722
Address:	1 Great George Street, Westminster, London SW1P 3AA
Website:	www.ice.org.uk

Name:	Institution of Environmental Sciences
Tel.:	020 7730 5516
Address:	Suite 7, 38 Ebury Street, London SW1W 0LU
Website:	www.ies-uk.org.uk

Name:	Institute of Ecology and Environmental Management (IEEM)
Tel.:	01962 868626
Address:	43 Southgate Street, Winchester, Hampshire SO23 9EH
Website:	www.ieem.org.uk

Name:	Institute of Environmental Management and Assessment (IEMA)
Tel.:	01522 540069
Address:	St Nicholas House, 70 Newport, Lincoln LN1 3DP
Website:	www.iema.net

Name:	Institute of Field Archaeologists (IFA)
Tel.:	0118 378 6446
Address:	SHES, Whiteknights, University of Reading, PO Box 227, Reading, Berkshire RG6 6AB

Website: www.archaeologists.net

Name: Institute of Sport, Parks and Leisure Professionals (ISPAL)
Tel.:   0844 418 0077
Address: Abbey Business Centre, 1650 Arlington Business Park, Theale, Reading, Berkshire RG7 4SA
Website: www.ispal.org.uk

Name: International Association for Impact Assessment (IAIA)
Tel.:   +1 701 297 7908
Address: 1330 23rd Street South, Suite C, Fargo, ND 58103, USA
Website: www.iaia.org

Name: Environmental Protection UK
Tel.:   01273 878770
Address: 44 Grand Parade, Brighton, East Sussex BN2 9QA
Website: www.environmental-protection.org.uk

Name: Royal Town Planning Institute (RTPI)
Tel.:   020 7929 9494
Address: 41 Botolph Lane, London EC3R 8DL
Website: www.rtpi.org.uk

Name: Society for the Environment
Tel.:   0845 337 2951
Address: The Old School House, 212 Long Street, Atherstone, Warwickshire CV9 1AH
Website: www.socenv.org.uk

Name: Town and Country Planning Association
Address: 17 Carlton House Terrace, London SW1Y 5AS
Tel.:   020 7930 8903
Website: www.tcpa.org.uk

Appendix 8

Training Courses

The courses listed here focus on Environmental Impact Assessment (EIA) or include a significant EIA component. Short courses are also available at a number of universities and institutions. Advice on the suitability of courses can be sought from the Institute of Environmental Management and Assessment (IEMA).

University of Aberdeen
MSc Rural Planning and Environmental Management
www.abdn.ac.uk

University of Aberystwyth
LLM/Diploma Environmental Law and Management
www.aber.ac.uk

University of Bath
MSc/PGDip Integrated Environmental Management
www.bath.ac.uk/iem

London School of Economics
MSc Environmental Policy and Regulation
www.lse.ac.uk

Oxford Brookes University
MSc/Diploma in Environmental Assessment and Management; MSc/Diploma in Environmental Management and Technology
www.brookes.ac.uk

University of Manchester
MA Environmental Impact Assessment and Management; MSc Environmental Management and Technology
www.sed.Manchester.ac.uk

University of Brighton
MSc/PDip/PGCert Environmental Assessment and Management
www.brighton.ac.uk

University of East Anglia
MSc Environmental Assessment and Management
www.uea.ac.uk

Index

Page numbers in *italic* type indicate figures; page numbers in **bold** indicate case examples.